Vocabulary Workshop

New Edition

With Online Audio Program 🎧

Level A

Jerome Shostak

Series Consultants

Sylvia A. Rendón, Ph.D.
Coord., Secondary Reading
Cypress-Fairbanks I.S.D.
Houston, Texas

John Heath, Ph.D.
Department of Classics
Santa Clara University
Santa Clara, California

Mel H. Farberman
Director of English
    Language Arts, K–12
Bay Shore U.F.S.D.
Bay Shore, New York

Sadlier-Oxford
A Division of William H. Sadlier, Inc.

Reviewers

The publisher wishes to thank for their comments and suggestions the following teachers and administrators, who read portions of the series prior to publication.

Anne S. Crane
Clinician, English Education
Georgia State University
Atlanta, GA

Arlene A. Oraby
Dept. Chair (Ret.), English 6–12
Briarcliff Public Schools
Briarcliff Manor, NY

Patricia M. Stack
English Teacher
South Park School District
South Park, PA

Susan W. Keogh
Curriculum Coordinator
Lake Highland Preparatory
Orlando, FL

Susan Cotter McDonough
English Department Chair
Wakefield High School
Wakefield, MA

Joy Vander Vliet
English Teacher
Council Rock High School
Newtown, PA

Mary Louise Ellena-Wygonik
English Teacher
Hampton High School
Allison Park, PA

Sr. M. Francis Regis Trojano
Sisters of St. Joseph (CSJ)
Educational Consultant
Boston, MA

Karen Christine Solheim
English Teacher
Jefferson High School
Jefferson, GA

Lisa Anne Pomi
Language Arts Chairperson
Woodside High School
Woodside, CA

Keith Yost
Director of Humanities
Tomball Ind. School District
Tomball, TX

Photo Credits

Corbis/Hulton-Deutsch Collection: 27; 34; Bettmann: 90, 149; 137; Philadelphia Museum of Art: 156; Philip Gould: 163. *Neal Farris*: 97. *Getty Images*/The Image Bank/Joseph McNally: 41; Stone/David Frazier: 57; Hulton Archive/Stringer: 64; The Image Bank/Deborah Gilbert: 71; Stone/Alan Bedding: 83; Stone/A&L Sinibaldi: 104; The Image Bank/Michael Melford: 170; Digital Vision: 182. *Image State*/Adventure Photo and Film/Thomas Ulrich: 123. *Index Stock Imagery*/Sandra Baker: 116. *The Natural History Museum, London*: 130.

Printed in the United States of America.
ISBN: 0-8215-7106-0
12/10 09

PREFACE

For more than five decades, VOCABULARY WORKSHOP has proven a highly successful tool for guiding systematic vocabulary growth and developing vocabulary skills. It has also been shown to be a valuable help to students preparing for standardized tests. This New Edition of VOCABULARY WORKSHOP has been prepared in recognition of important changes to these tests, with the introduction of two features designed to address the new emphasis on writing skills, including grammar, and reading skills on those tests.

A new **Vocabulary for Comprehension** section appears in each of the five Reviews. This two-page feature is modeled on the reading sections of standardized tests, and as in those tests, presents reading comprehension questions, including specific vocabulary-related ones, based on a reading passage. (For more on Vocabulary for Comprehension, see page 13.)

Following Vocabulary for Comprehension in each of the Reviews is another new feature called **Grammar in Context**. This one-page exercise is linked to the reading passage that precedes it, referring to a grammar or usage topic illustrated in the passage and then reviewing that topic with a brief explanation and practice questions. (For more on Grammar in Context, see page 16.)

The 15 Units that form the core of VOCABULARY WORKSHOP remain unchanged. Each of the Units comprises a five-part lesson consisting of **Definitions**, **Completing the Sentence**, **Synonyms and Antonyms**, **Choosing the Right Word**, and **Vocabulary in Context**. Together, these exercises provide multiple and varied exposures to the taught words, an approach that has been shown to be consistent with and supportive of research-based findings in vocabulary instruction.

Enrichment and vocabulary-building exercises also remain in the form of **Building with Classical Roots**, **Word Associations**, and **Word Families** in the Reviews, and **Analogies** and **Enriching Your Vocabulary** in the Cumulative Reviews.

In this Level of Vocabulary Workshop you will study 300 key words. The words in this Level, as well as all of the other Levels of this series, have been selected on the following bases: currency and general usefulness; frequency of appearance on recognized vocabulary lists; applicability to, and appearance on, standardized tests; and current grade-level research.

ONLINE COMPONENTS
www.vocabularyworkshop.com

At **www. vocabularyworkshop.com** you will find an **Online Audio Program** that provides pronunciations, definitions, and examples of usage for all of the key words presented in this level of VOCABULARY WORKSHOP. You can listen to one word at a time or, if you wish, download to an MP3 player all of the words of any given Unit. You will then be able to listen to the audio program for that Unit at your convenience.

At the **www.vocabularyworkshop.com** Web site you will also find **interactive vocabulary games and puzzles** that will help reinforce and enrich your understanding of the key words in this level of VOCABULARY WORKSHOP.

CONTENTS

🎧 **Online Audio Program available at www.vocabularyworkshop.com.**

🎧 Online Audio Program available at **www.vocabularyworkshop.com.**

PRONUNCIATION KEY

The pronunciation is indicated for every basic word introduced in this book. The symbols used for this purpose, as listed below, are similar to those appearing in most standard dictionaries of recent vintage. (Pronunciation keys and given pronunciations sometimes differ from dictionary to dictionary.) The author has consulted a large number of dictionaries for this purpose but has relied primarily on *Webster's Third New International Dictionary* and *The Random House Dictionary of the English Language (Unabridged)*.

There are, of course, many English words for which two (or more) pronunciations are commonly accepted. In virtually all cases where such words occur in this book, the author has sought to make things easier for the student by giving just one pronunciation. The only significant exception occurs when the pronunciation changes in accordance with a shift in the part of speech. Thus we would indicate that *project* in the verb form is pronounced prə jekt', and in the noun form, präj' ekt.

Vowels	ā	lake	e	stress	ü	loot, new
	a	mat	ī	knife	ủ	foot, pull
	â	care	i	sit	ə	jumping, broken
	ä	bark, bottle	ō	flow	ər	bird, better
	aủ	doubt	ô	all, cord		
	ē	beat, wordy	oi	oil		

Consonants	ch	child, lecture	s	cellar	wh	what
	g	give	sh	shun	y	yearn
	j	gentle, bridge	th	thank	z	is
	ŋ	sing	<u>th</u>	those	zh	measure

All other consonants are sounded as in the alphabet.

Stress	The accent mark *follows* the syllable receiving the major stress: en rich'

Abbreviations	*adj.* adjective	*n.* noun	*prep.* preposition
	adv. adverb	*part.* participle	*v.* verb
	int. interjection	*pl.* plural	

ONLINE COMPONENTS
www.vocabularyworkshop.com

Note: A spoken pronunciation of each key word may be heard by going to **www.vocabularyworkshop.com**. The **Online Audio Program** permits you to hear not only the pronunciation of each word, but also its definition and an example of its usage in a sentence. You can listen to one word at a time, or, if you wish, download all of the words of a Unit to an MP3 player, and listen to the audio program for that Unit at your convenience.

THE VOCABULARY OF VOCABULARY

There are some interesting and useful words that we use to describe and identify words. The exercises that follow will help you to check and strengthen your knowledge of this "vocabulary of vocabulary."

Denotation and Connotation

The **denotation** of a word is its specific dictionary meaning. Here are a few examples:

Word	Denotation
peerless	without equal
lethal	deadly
specimen	sample

The **connotation** of a word is its **tone**—that is, the emotions or associations it normally arouses in people using, hearing, or reading it. Depending on what these feelings are, the connotation of a word may be *favorable* (*positive*) or *unfavorable* (*negative, pejorative*). A word that does not normally arouse strong feelings of any kind has a *neutral* connotation. Here are some examples of words with different connotations:

Word	Connotation
peerless	favorable
lethal	unfavorable
specimen	neutral

Exercises In the space provided, label the connotation of each of the following words **F** for "favorable," **U** for "unfavorable," or **N** for "neutral."

_____ **1.** fork   _____ **3.** quote   _____ **5.** gallant

_____ **2.** snobbish   _____ **4.** ruthless   _____ **6.** gracious

Literal and Figurative Usage

When a word is used in a **literal** sense, it is being employed in its strict (or primary) dictionary meaning in a situation (or context) that "makes sense" from a purely logical or realistic point of view. For example:

When we *cross that bridge*, we will be in New York.

In this sentence, *crossing that bridge* is employed literally. We will cross over that roadway to get into New York.

Sometimes words are used in a symbolic or nonliteral way in situations that do not "make sense" from a purely logical or realistic point of view. We call this nonliteral application of a word a **figurative** or **metaphorical** usage. For example:

"I realize that this decision may mean trouble for us down the road," said the senator, "but we'll *cross that bridge* when we come to it."

In this sentence, *crossing that bridge* is not being used in a literal sense. That is, the senator did not suggest crossing an actual bridge. Rather, the expression is intended to convey dealing with a particular obstacle.

Exercises *In the space provided, write **L** for "literal" or **F** for "figurative" next to each of the following sentences to show how the italicized expression is being used.*

_____ **1.** The new press secretary *fielded* the reporters' questions like a seasoned pro.

_____ **2.** When I was a boy, one of my favorite dishes was the savory hunter's *stew* that Grandmother used to make.

_____ **3.** When our luggage failed to appear at the airport baggage terminal, we really began to *stew*.

Synonyms

A **synonym** is a word that has *the same* or *almost the same* meaning as another word. Here are some examples:

under—beneath   rough—coarse
entire—whole   final—last
silent—quiet   pile—heap

Exercises *In each of the following groups, circle the word that is most nearly the **synonym** of the word in **boldface** type.*

1. rule	**2. spring**	**3. tidy**	**4. craving**
a. cover	a. walk	a. neat	a. feast
b. leave	b. ride	b. sloppy	b. hunger
c. change	c. jump	c. poor	c. fullness
d. govern	d. drive	d. helpful	d. anger

Antonyms

An **antonym** is a word that means *the opposite* of or *almost the opposite* of another word. Here are some examples:

fail—succeed   crowded—empty
hire—fire   grief—joy
bend—straighten   beneath—above

Exercises *In each of the following groups, circle the word that is most nearly the **antonym** of the word in **boldface** type.*

1. guilt	**2. definite**	**3. healthy**	**4. create**
a. innocence	a. tardy	a. sturdy	a. make
b. sentence	b. unusual	b. messy	b. suggest
c. freedom	c. vague	c. bossy	c. destroy
d. judgment	d. certain	d. sickly	d. reveal

VOCABULARY STRATEGY:
USING CONTEXT

How do you go about finding the meaning of an unknown or unfamiliar word that you come across in your reading? You might look the word up in a dictionary, of course, provided one is at hand. But there are two other useful strategies that you might employ to find the meaning of a word that you do not know at all or that is used in a way that you do not recognize. One strategy is to analyze the **structure** or parts of the word. (See pages 11 and 12 for more on this strategy.) The other strategy is to try to figure out the meaning of the word by reference to context.

When we speak of the **context** of a word, we mean the words that are near to or modify that word. By studying the context, we may find **clues** that lead us to its meaning. We might find a clue in the immediate sentence or phrase in which the word appears (and sometimes in adjoining sentences or phrases, too); or we might find a clue in the topic or subject matter of the passage in which the word appears; or we might even find a clue in the physical features of a page itself. (Photographs, illustrations, charts, graphs, captions, and headings are some examples of such features.)

One way to use context as a strategy is to ask yourself what you know already about the topic or subject matter in question. By applying what you have learned before about deserts, for example, you would probably be able to figure out that the word *arid* in the phrase "the arid climate of the desert" means "dry."

The **Vocabulary in Context** exercises that appear in the Units and the **Vocabulary for Comprehension** and the **Choosing the Right Meaning** exercises that appear in the Reviews and Cumulative Reviews both provide practice in using subject matter or topic to determine the meaning of given words.

When you do the various word-omission exercises in this book, look for **context clues** built into the sentence or passage to guide you to the correct answer. Three types of context clues appear in the exercises in this book.

A **restatement clue** consists of a *synonym* for, or a *definition* of, the missing word. For example:

> The noise and commotion in the crowded gymnasium were so great that we could barely make ourselves heard above the
>
> _____.
>
> a. score   b. referees   (c. din)   d. bleachers

In this sentence *noise and commotion* are synonyms of the missing word, *din*, and act as a restatement clue for it.

A **contrast clue** consists of an *antonym* for, or a phrase that means the *opposite* of, the missing word. For example:

> When bad weather prevented the bomber from striking the ((**primary,** secret) target, the pilot guided the plane to the secondary objective.

In this sentence, *secondary* is an antonym of the missing word, *primary.* Since bad weather prevented the bomber from accomplishing his main objective, he had to resort to his second choice.

An **inference clue** implies but does not directly state the meaning of the missing word or words. For example:

> Those in the audience who <u>agreed</u> with the speaker _____
> their _____ by cheering, while those who
> <u>disagreed booed.</u>
> a. registered . . . boredom   c. indicated . . . horror
> (b. expressed . . . approval)   d. showed . . . dislike

In this sentence, there are several inference clues: (a) The word *cheering* has a favorable connotation. *Approval* is the only word in any of the answer choices that also has a favorable connotation; (b) Just as booing is an *expression* of disagreement, cheering is an *expression* of approval. Accordingly, these words are inference clues because they suggest or imply, but do not directly state, the missing word or words.

Exercises *Use context clues to choose the word or words that complete each of the following sentences or sets of sentences.*

1. The climbers inched their way to the top of the peak until at last they stood upon the very _____ of the mountain.
a. bottom   b. slope   c. range   d. summit

2. There were a few moments of excitement in the first set, but on the whole it was an extremely (**thrilling, monotonous**) tennis match.

3. After we measured out the _____ that the recipe called for, we used a mixer to _____ them in a bowl.
a. amounts . . . separate   c. ingredients . . . combine
b. directions . . . shred   d. temperature . . . bake

VOCABULARY STRATEGY: WORD STRUCTURE

One important way to build your vocabulary is to learn the meaning of word parts that make up many English words. These word parts consist of **prefixes**, **suffixes**, and **roots**, or **bases**. A useful strategy for determining the meaning of an unknown word is to "take apart" the word and think about the parts. For example, when you look at the word parts in the word *invisible,* you find the prefix *in-* ("not") + the root *-vis-* ("see") + the suffix *-ible* ("capable of"). From knowing the meanings of the parts of this word, you can figure out that *invisible* means "not capable of being seen."

Following is a list of common prefixes. Knowing the meaning of a prefix can help you determine the meaning of a word in which the prefix appears.

Prefix	Meaning	Sample Words
bi-	two	bicycle
com-, con-	together, with	compatriot, contact
de-, dis-	lower, opposite	devalue, disloyal
fore-, pre-	before, ahead of time	forewarn, preplan
il-, im-, in-, ir, non-, un-	not	illegal, impossible, inactive, irregular, nonsense, unable
in-, im-	in, into	inhale, import
mid-	middle	midway
mis-	wrongly, badly	mistake, misbehave
re-	again, back	redo, repay
sub-	under, less than	submarine, subzero
super-	above, greater than	superimpose, superstar
tri-	three	triangle

Following is a list of common suffixes. Knowing the meaning and grammatical function of a suffix can help you determine the meaning of a word.

Noun Suffix	Meaning	Sample Nouns
-acy, -ance, -ence, -hood, -ity, -ment, -ness, -ship	state, quality, or condition of, act or process of	adequacy, attendance, persistence, neighborhood, activity, judgment, brightness, friendship
-ant, -eer, -ent, -er, -ian, -ier, -ist, -or	one who does or makes something	contestant, auctioneer, resident, banker, comedian, financier, dentist, doctor
-ation, -ition, -ion	act or result of	organization, imposition, election

Verb Suffix	Meaning	Sample Verbs
-ate	to become, produce, or treat	validate, salivate, chlorinate
-en	to make, cause to be	weaken
-fy, -ify, -ize	to cause, make	liquefy, glorify, legalize

Adjective Suffix	Meaning	Sample Adjectives
-able, -ible	able, capable of	believable, incredible
-al, -ic	relating to, characteristic of	natural, romantic
-ful, -ive, -ous	full of, given to, marked by	beautiful, protective, poisonous
-ish, -like	like, resembling	foolish, childlike
-less	lacking, without	careless

A **base** or **root** is the main part of a word to which prefixes and suffixes may be added. Many roots come to English from Latin, such as *-socio-,* meaning "society," or from Greek, such as *-logy-,* meaning "the study of." Knowing Greek and Latin roots can help you determine the meaning of a word such as *sociology,* which means "the study of society."

In the **Building with Classical Roots** sections of this book you will learn more about some of these Latin and Greek roots and about English words that derive from them. The lists that follow may help you figure out the meaning of new or unfamiliar words that you encounter in your reading.

Greek Root	Meaning	Sample Word
-astr-, -aster-, -astro-	star	astral, asteroid, astronaut
-auto-	self	autograph
-bio-	life	biography
-chron-, chrono-	time	chronic, chronological
-cosm-, -cosmo-	universe, order	microcosm, cosmopolitan
-cryph-, -crypt-	hidden, secret	apocryphal, cryptographer
-dem-, -demo-	people	epidemic, democracy
-dia-	through, across, between	diameter
-dog-, -dox-	opinion, teaching	dogmatic, orthodox
-gen-	race, kind, origin, birth	generation
-gnos-	know	diagnostic
-graph-, -graphy-, -gram-	write	graphite, autobiography, telegram
-log-, -logue-	speech, word, reasoning	logic, dialogue
-lys-	break down	analysis
-metr-, -meter-	measure	metric, kilometer
-micro-	small	microchip
-morph-	form, shape	amorphous
-naut-	sailor	cosmonaut
-phon-, -phone-, -phono-	sound, voice	phonics, telephone, phonograph
-pol-, -polis-	city, state	police, metropolis
-scop-, -scope-	watch, look at	telescopic, microscope
-tele-	far off, distant	television
-the-	put or place	parentheses

Latin Root	Meaning	Sample Word
-cap-, -capt-, -cept-, -cip-	take	capitulate, captive, concept, recipient
-cede-, -ceed-, -ceas-, -cess-	happen, yield, go	precede, proceed, decease, cessation
-cred-	believe	incredible
-dic-, -dict-	speak, say, tell	indicate, diction
-duc-, -duct-, -duit-	lead, conduct, draw	educate, conduct, conduit
-fac-, -fact-, -fect-, -fic-, -fy-	make	faculty, artifact, defect, beneficial, clarify
-ject-	throw	eject
-mis-, -miss-, -mit-, -mitt-	send	promise, missile, transmit, intermittent
-note-, -not-	know, recognize	denote, notion
-pel-, -puls-	drive	expel, compulsive
-pend-, -pens-	hang, weight, set aside	pendulum, pension
-pon-, -pos-	put, place	component, position
-port-	carry	portable
-rupt-	break	bankrupt
-scrib-, -scribe-, -script-	write	scribble, describe, inscription
-spec-, -spic-	look, see	spectator, conspicuous
-tac-, -tag-, -tang-, -teg-	touch	contact, contagious, tangible, integral
-tain-, -ten-, -tin-	hold, keep	contain, tenure, retinue
-temp-	time	tempo
-ven-, -vent-	come	intervene, convention
-vers-, -vert-	turn	reverse, invert
-voc-, -vok-	call	vocal, invoke

VOCABULARY AND READING

Word knowledge is essential to reading comprehension. Quite simply, the more words you know, the easier it is to make sense of what you read. Your growing knowledge of word meanings combined with an ability to read carefully and think about what you read will help you succeed in school and do well on standardized tests, including the new SAT, the ACT, and the PSAT.

The **Vocabulary for Comprehension** exercises in this book will give you the opportunity to put your vocabulary knowledge and critical reading skills to use. Each exercise consists of a nonfiction reading passage followed by comprehension questions. The passages and questions are similar to those that you are likely to find on standardized tests.

Kinds of Questions

The questions on the reading sections of standardized tests are formulated in many different ways, but they are usually only of a small number of kinds, or types— the same ones that appear most frequently in the Vocabulary for Comprehension exercises in this book.

Main Idea Questions generally ask what the passage as a whole is about. Questions about the main idea may begin like this:

- The primary or main purpose of the passage is
- The primary focus of the passage is on
- The passage is best described as
- The passage is primarily concerned with
- The title that best describes the content of the passage is

Often the main idea is stated in the first paragraph of the passage. Sometimes, however, the first paragraph serves as an introduction and the main idea is included later on. When you answer questions about the main idea, you should make sure that the answers you choose reflect the focus of the entire passage and not just part of it. You may also be asked the main idea of a specific paragraph.

Detail Questions focus on important information that is explicitly stated in the passage. Often, however, the correct answer choices do not use the exact language of the passage. They are instead restatements, or paraphrases, of the text. So, for example, the answer to a question about "trash production and disposal" might use the term "waste management."

Vocabulary-in-Context Questions check your ability to use context to identify a word's meaning. All vocabulary-in-context questions include line references so that you can refer back to the passage to see how and in what context the word is used.

Here are some examples:

- **Condone** (line 6) most nearly means
- **Eminent** (line 8) is best defined as
- The meaning of **diffuse** (line 30) is

It is important to use context to check your answer choices, particularly when the vocabulary word has more than one meaning. Among the choices may be two (or more) correct meanings of the word in question. Your task is to choose the meaning that best fits the context.

Inference Questions ask you to make inferences or draw conclusions from the passage. These questions often begin like this:

- It can be inferred from the passage that
- The author implies that
- The passage suggests that
- Evidently the author feels that

The inferences you make and the conclusions you draw must be based on the information in the passage. Your own knowledge and reasoning come into play in understanding what is implied and in reaching conclusions that are logical.

Questions about Tone show your understanding of the author's attitude toward the subject of the passage. Words that describe tone, or attitude, are "feeling" words, for example, *indifferent, ambivalent, scornful, astonished, respectful*. These are typical questions:

- The author's attitude toward . . . is best described as
- The author's perspective is that of . . .
- Which word best describes the author's tone . . .

To determine the tone, it's important to pay attention to the author's choice of words and note your personal reaction. The author's attitude may be positive *(respectful, astonished)*, negative *(scornful)*, or neutral *(indifferent, ambivalent)*.

Questions about Author's Technique focus on the way a text is organized and the language the author uses. These questions ask you to think about structure and function. For example:

- The final paragraph serves to
- What is the function of the phrase . . . ?
- What does the author mean by . . . ?
- The author cites . . . in order to . . . .

To answer the questions, you must demonstrate an understanding of the way the author presents information and develops ideas.

Strategies

Here are some general strategies to help you in reading each passage and answering the questions.

- Read the introduction first. The introduction will provide a focus for the selection.

- Be an active reader. As you read, ask yourself questions about the passage, for example: What is this paragraph about? What does the writer mean here? Why does the writer include this information?

- Refer back to the passage when you answer the questions. In general, the order of the questions mirrors the organization of the passage, and many of the questions include paragraph or line references. It is often helpful to go back and reread before choosing an answer.

- Read carefully, and be sure to base your answer choices on the passage. There are answer choices that make sense, but are not based on the information in the passage. These may be true statements, but incorrect answers. The correct answers are either restatements of ideas in the text or inferences that can be made from the text.

- Consider each exercise a learning experience. Keep in mind that your ability to answer the questions correctly shows as much about your understanding of the questions as about your understanding of the passage.

GRAMMAR AND WRITING

In order to write well, so that your meaning and your purpose are clearly understood, you must use words correctly; but, more than that, you must also make sure that what you write is grammatically correct. Knowing the rules of grammar, usage, and mechanics—the conventions of standard English—make your writing not just correct but more powerful and persuasive, too.

As a student you are regularly challenged to write effectively and correctly not only in your English classes but in your social studies, science, and history classes, too. Furthermore, high schools and colleges have raised their expectations for graduates. If you have taken a standardized test recently or are preparing to take one, you know this only too well. The writing and grammar sections of these tests have grown more demanding than ever.

On these grammar sections, questions usually appear in one or two multiple-choice formats. In one, you must decide if a mistake has been made in a sentence and, if one has been made, identify it. In another format, you must decide if an identified word or phrase is incorrect and, if it is incorrect, choose from several options the best way to correct it.

The **Grammar in Context** exercise that appears in each of the five Reviews in this book will provide you with opportunity to review and apply grammar and usage rules that are critical to good writing and that are frequently tested on the multiple-choice parts of standardized tests. In Level A, these topics are:

- Run-on sentences, sentence fragments
- Subject-verb agreement
- Adjectives, adverbs
- Pronoun-antecedent agreement
- Misplaced modifiers

(For the sake of convenience, we sometimes use the term *grammar* to embrace all of the "rules" of English; but it's important to note that grammar, usage, and mechanics represent different aspects of writing. Grammar deals mostly with parts of speech and with parts of sentences and their relations. Usage, as the name suggests, concerns the way that words and phrases are used; usage topics would include, for example, irregular verbs, active and passive voice, subject-verb agreement, and double negatives. Mechanics deals with punctuation, capitalization, and spelling.)

There are many reasons to write and speak correctly other than to score well on standardized tests. You are judged by the way you write and speak. Your use of English is evaluated in the writing you do in school, on college applications, and in many different kinds of careers. You should be able to write and speak correctly when the situation calls for it—in a formal writing assignment, on a test, or in an interview. The more you practice standard English, the more comfortable and confident you will become when you write and speak.

WORKING WITH ANALOGIES

A verbal analogy expresses a relationship or comparison between sets of words. Normally, an analogy contains two pairs of words linked by a word or symbol that stands for an equals (=) sign. A complete analogy compares the two pairs of words and makes a statement about them. It asserts that the relationship between the first pair of words is the same as the relationship between the second pair.

In the **Analogies** exercises that appear in the Cumulative Reviews, you will be asked to complete analogies, that is, to choose the pair of words that best matches or parallels the relationship of the key, or given, pair of words. Here are two examples:

1. **maple** is to **tree** as
   a. acorn is to oak
   b. hen is to rooster
   c. rose is to flower
   d. shrub is to lilac

2. **joyful** is to **gloomy** as
   a. cheerful is to happy
   b. strong is to weak
   c. quick is to famous
   d. hungry is to starving

In order to find the correct answer to exercise 1, you must first determine the relationship between the two key words, **maple** and **tree**. In this case, that relationship might be expressed as "a maple is a kind (or type) of tree." The next step is to select from choices a, b, c, and d the pair of words that best reflects the same relationship. Clearly, the correct answer is (c); it is the only choice that parallels the relationship of the key words: a rose is a kind (or type) of flower, just as a maple is a kind (or type) of tree. The other choices do not express the same relationship.

In exercise 2, the relationship between the key words can be expressed as "joyful means the opposite of gloomy." Which of the choices best represents the same relationship? The answer, of course, is (b): "strong" means the opposite of "weak."

Here are examples of some other common analogy relationships:

Analogy	Key Relationship
big is to **large** as **little** is to **small**	**Big** means the same thing as **large**, just as **little** means the same thing as **small**.
brave is to **favorable** as **cowardly** is to **unfavorable**	The tone of **brave** is **favorable**, just as the tone of **cowardly** is **unfavorable**.
busybody is to **nosy** as **klutz** is to **clumsy**	A **busybody** is by definition someone who is **nosy**, just as a **klutz** is by definition someone who is **clumsy**.
cowardly is to **courage** as **awkward** is to **grace**	Someone who is **cowardly** lacks **courage**, just as someone who is **awkward** lacks **grace**.
visible is to **see** as **audible** is to **hear**	If something is **visible**, you can by definition **see** it, just as if something is **audible**, you can by definition **hear** it.
liar is to **truthful** as **bigot** is to **fair-minded**	A **liar** is by definition not likely to be **truthful**, just as a **bigot** is by definition not likely to be **fair-minded**.
eyes are to **see** as **ears** are to **hear**	You use your **eyes** to **see** with, just as you use your **ears** to **hear** with.

There are many different kinds of relationships represented in the analogy questions you will find in this book, but the key to solving any analogy is to find and express the relationship between the two key words.

This test contains a sampling of the words that are to be found in the exercises in this Level of VOCABULARY WORKSHOP. It will give you an idea of the types of words to be studied and their level of difficulty. When you have completed all the units, the Final Mastery Test at the end of this book will assess what you have learned. By comparing your results on the Final Mastery Test with your results on the Diagnostic Test below, you will be able to judge your progress.

Synonyms

*In each of the following groups, circle the word or phrase that **most nearly** expresses the meaning of the word in **boldface** type in the given phrase.*

1. a **synopsis** of the play
   a. performance b. review c. summary d. defense

2. the **plight** of the homeless
   a. misfortune b. plans c. hopes d. hunger

3. **mimic** my way of speaking
   a. notice b. study c. improve d. imitate

4. an **ingenious** scheme
   a. clever b. wicked c. clumsy d. childish

5. plan to **rendezvous** at a certain place
   a. eat b. meet c. dance d. sleep

6. **relish** the idea
   a. hate b. ignore c. delight in d. examine

7. an **inflammatory** speech
   a. fiery b. boring c. long-winded d. informal

8. the **indisputable** leader
   a. unquestioned b. powerful c. experienced d. cruel

9. a **strapping** fellow
   a. timid b. husky c. hardworking d. dependable

10. a **gory** horror movie
    a. successful b. bloody c. new d. long

11. **designate** her successor
    a. dislike b. name c. criticize d. fire

12. **rummaged** in the attic
    a. hid b. cleaned up c. searched d. played

13. **pacify** the angry customers
    a. arrest b. calm c. scold d. ignore

14. **dissect** the report
    a. accept b. reject c. make fun of d. analyze

15. **foil** the plot
    a. cover up b. defeat c. join d. help

16. an **acute** attack
a. unpleasant   b. fatal   c. severe   d. mild

17. adhere to his promise
a. break   b. explain   c. stick to   d. listen to

18. vie for the championship
a. compete   b. travel   c. rehearse   d. cheat

19. abduct the official
a. introduce   b. kidnap   c. fire   d. elect

20. as his troubles **receded**
a. grew worse   b. remained   c. retreated   d. grew larger

21. made **rigorous** demands
a. expected   b. tough   c. fair   d. easy

22. stored the **data** in the computer
a. surplus   b. information   c. supplies   d. equipment

23. forsake their comrades
a. call together   b. desert   c. protect   d. arm

24. topple the government
a. join   b. strengthen   c. threaten   d. overthrow

25. confiscated the weapon
a. sold   b. seized   c. hid   d. displayed

26. quash a rebellion
a. lead   b. crush   c. explain   d. start

27. sage advice
a. wise   b. odd   c. old-fashioned   d. foolish

28. a **pathetic** sight
a. vivid   b. humorous   c. moving   d. unexplained

29. enumerate the rules
a. list   b. enforce   c. break   d. change

30. an **unerring** aim
a. noble   b. uncertain   c. unfailing   d. hurried

31. an **extinct** animal
a. vanished   b. tame   c. common   d. local

32. traffic **fatalities**
a. lights   b. expenditures   c. regulations   d. deaths

33. show **scant** concern
a. great   b. false   c. very little   d. sincere

34. verging on insanity
a. curing   b. approaching   c. preventing   d. discussing

35. taut nerves
a. strong   b. tense   c. weak   d. damaged

36. a useful **implement**
a. suggestion   b. idea   c. move   d. tool

37. built a **replica** of the ship
a. side   b. copy   c. deck   d. mast

38. with a **serene** expression on her face
a. worried   b. cruel   c. peaceful   d. surprised

39. share our **reveries**
a. profits   b. dreams   c. troubles   d. possessions

40. a **wholesome** development
a. bad   b. popular   c. healthy   d. strange

41. show remarkable **discretion**
a. judgment   b. courage   c. pride   d. carelessness

42. a **far-fetched** excuse
a. convincing   b. unlikely   c. written   d. overused

43. a **sluggish** economy
a. competitive   b. slow-moving   c. free   d. growing

44. a **self-seeking** attitude
a. selfish   b. noble   c. intelligent   d. effective

45. disquieting news
a. upsetting   b. sensational   c. funny   d. encouraging

46. blighted the neighborhood
a. beautified   b. rebuilt   c. lived in   d. ruined

47. broke his **vow**
a. sword   b. arm   c. habit   d. promise

48. amalgamated their forces
a. disbanded   b. weakened   c. led   d. combined

49. took **optional** courses
a. easy   b. advanced   c. not required   d. time-consuming

50. having **global** significance
a. little   b. unexpected   c. worldwide   d. personal

Hear the words for this Unit pronounced, defined, and used in sentences at **www.vocabularyworkshop.com**.

UNIT I

Definitions

Note carefully the spelling, pronunciation, part(s) of speech, and definition(s) of each of the following words. Then write the word in the blank space(s) in the illustrative sentence(s) following. Finally, study the lists of synonyms and antonyms given at the end of each entry.

1. apparel
(ə par′ əl)

(*n.*) clothing, that which serves as dress or decoration; (*v.*) to put clothes on, dress up

Winter _____ should be warm and cozy.

Let's _____ our cats for the party.

SYNONYMS: (*n.*) attire, garments; (*v.*) deck out
ANTONYMS: (*v.*) undress, unclothe, strip, denude

2. besiege
(bi sēj′)

(*v.*) to attack by surrounding with military forces; to cause worry or trouble

If troops _____ their stronghold, the rebel forces may be forced to surrender.

SYNONYMS: blockade, encircle, pressure, hound

3. compress
(*v.*, kəm pres′,
n., käm′ pres)

(*v.*) to press together; to reduce in size or volume; (*n.*) a folded cloth or pad applied to an injury

The editor helped to _____ my rambling 25-page mystery into an 8-page thriller.

A cold _____ may soothe headache pain.

SYNONYMS: (*v.*) condense, shrink, shorten
ANTONYMS: (*v.*) expand, enlarge

4. denounce
(di naùns′)

(*v.*) to condemn openly; to accuse formally

The United Nations decided to publicly _____ the tyrant's crimes against his people.

SYNONYMS: criticize, censure
ANTONYMS: hail, acclaim

5. dispatch
(dis pach′)

(*v.*) to send off or out for a purpose; to kill; (*n.*) an official message; promptness, speed; the act of killing

We'll _____ a repair crew right away.

He approved the request with _____.

SYNONYMS: (*v.*) slay; (*n.*) report, communication
ANTONYMS: (*v.*) recall, withhold

6. douse
(daùs)

(*v.*) to plunge into a liquid, drench; to put out quickly, extinguish

I'll _____ the flames with the hose.

SYNONYMS: submerge, soak, dunk, immerse
ANTONYMS: dry out, dehydrate, kindle, ignite

Hear the words for this Unit pronounced, defined, and
used in sentences at **www.vocabularyworkshop.com**.

7. expressly
(ek spres' lē)

(*adv.*) plainly, in so many words; for a particular purpose

At the meeting, parents _____
stated their approval of students wearing school uniforms.

SYNONYMS: clearly, pointedly, explicitly
ANTONYMS: implicitly, accidentally

8. famished
(fam' isht)

(*adj., part.*) suffering severely from hunger or from lack of
something

The Vietnamese immigrants, new to a strange American city,
were _____ for news of home.

SYNONYMS: hungry, starving, ravenous
ANTONYMS: well fed, full, satisfied, satiated

9. forsake
(fôr sāk')

(*v.*) to give up, renounce; to leave, abandon

I will never _____ my children, no
matter what they do or say.

SYNONYMS: desert, disown
ANTONYMS: keep, hold on to, stand by

10. gainful
(gān' fəl)

(*adj.*) profitable; bringing in money or some special advantage

I hope to find _____ employment
that is pleasing to me.

SYNONYMS: moneymaking, paying
ANTONYMS: unprofitable, unrewarding, nonpaying

11. immense
(i mens')

(*adj.*) very large or great; beyond ordinary means of
measurement

Alaska enjoys _____ natural
resources, but its severe climate makes those resources
difficult to use.

SYNONYMS: vast, enormous, immeasurable, gigantic
ANTONYMS: small, tiny, minute, infinitesimal

12. inept
(in ept')

(*adj.*) totally without skill or appropriateness

The scientist is brilliant in the research laboratory but is
_____ at dealing with people.

SYNONYMS: clumsy, unskilled, bungling, incompetent
ANTONYMS: skillful, accomplished, adroit

13. ingenious
(in jēn yəs)

(*adj.*) showing remarkable originality, inventiveness, or
resourcefulness; clever

The students found an _____
solution to the math problem.

SYNONYMS: imaginative, inventive, resourceful
ANTONYMS: unimaginative, unoriginal, uninventive

22 ■ Unit 1

Hear the words for this Unit pronounced, defined, and used in sentences at **www.vocabularyworkshop.com**.

I

4. instantaneous
(in stən tā′ nē əs)

(*adj.*) done in an instant; immediate

Most computer software is designed so that users can obtain nearly _____ responses.

SYNONYMS: prompt, quick, speedy
ANTONYMS: delayed, slow, gradual

5. irk
(ərk)

(*v.*) to annoy, trouble, make weary

Questions that show a student's lack of attention _____ the teacher.

SYNONYMS: bother, irritate, vex
ANTONYMS: please, delight, cheer, gladden

6. libel
(lī′ bəl)

(*n.*) a written statement that unfairly or falsely harms the reputation of the person about whom it is made; (*v.*) to write or publish such a statement

The celebrity accused her biographer of _____.

It is a crime to _____ others, no matter how you feel about them.

SYNONYMS: (*n.*) slur; (*v.*) smear, defame

7. misgiving
(mis giv′ iŋ)

(*n.*) a feeling of fear, doubt, or uncertainty

They had _____ about joining the chorus because of its demanding schedule.

SYNONYMS: worry, qualm, hesitation
ANTONYMS: feeling of confidence, assurance

8. oaf
(ōf)

(*n.*) a stupid person; a big, clumsy, slow individual

He generally moved like an _____, so I was surprised to see how graceful he was on the dance floor.

SYNONYMS: bonehead, dunce, clod, lout

9. recede
(ri sēd′)

(*v.*) to go or move backward; to become more distant

The town residents must wait for the flood waters to _____ before they can deal with the terrible mess left behind.

SYNONYMS: retreat, go back, back up, ebb
ANTONYMS: advance, come closer

0. repast
(ri past′)

(*n.*) a meal, food

Let's get together after the show at Callie's Café for a late-night _____.

SYNONYM: victuals

Completing the Sentence

From the words for this unit, choose the one that best completes each of the following sentences. Write the word in the space provided.

1. Some people hailed the man as a genius; others _____ him as a quack.

2. While all true vegetarians _____ animal meats, some do eat dairy products.

3. Your _____ can be neat and attractive without being expensive.

4. The terms of our agreement _____ forbade us to take any of the goods for our own use.

5. When you are really hungry, even the simplest foods will be a delicious _____

6. Since it was well past their lunchtime by the time we arrived home, the children were _____ .

7. You had no right to call me a clumsy _____ just because I spilled some water on you.

8. The laws of this land do not shield public figures from just criticism, but they do protect them against _____ .

9. Far away on the horizon, we saw the tiny figures of a lonely traveler and his mule _____ into the sunset.

10. On my first baby-sitting job, I found that one must have _____ patience to take care of young children.

11. Let's make certain to _____ the fire before leaving camp.

12. When you play tennis for the first time, you are going to find that your attempts to hit the ball are very _____ .

13. If you _____ all the items as much as possible, you will be able to get everything into a single suitcase.

14. As an inexperienced sailor, I had more than a few _____ about taking out the small boat in such rough weather.

15. Don't allow yourself to be _____ by every small trouble that may arise during the day.

16. Because I have reached an age at which I am unwilling to depend on my parents, I am out to find a _____ occupation.

17. None of us could figure out how the _____ magician had managed to escape from the trunk submerged in the tank of water.

8. How can we hope to _____ a city that is surrounded by such strong walls and has ample supplies of everything it needs?

9. A(n) _____ will be sent to all our representatives in Latin America advising them how to handle the problem.

0. Some of life's rewards are _____; others are a long time in coming.

Synonyms

*Choose the word from this unit that is **the same** or **most nearly the same** in meaning as the **boldface** word or expression in the given phrase. Write the word on the line provided.*

1. enjoyed the **meal** served to them

2. had to fire the **bungling** carpenter

3. thought the article **smeared** her reputation

4. **resourceful** use for lumber scraps

5. refused to invite the **lout**

6. fashionable hand-me-down **garments**

7. waiting until the crowds **ebb**

8. **qualms** about the leading candidate

9. is **clearly** forbidden for use by minors

0. sent them a top-secret **communication**

1. compelled to **desert** the leaky boat

2. were far too **hungry** to wait politely

3. can provide **speedy** results at home

4. chose a **profitable** career in advertising

5. **pressure** us with repeated phone calls

Antonyms

*Choose the word from this unit that is **most nearly opposite** in meaning to the **boldface** word or expression in the given phrase. Write the word on the line provided.*

6. sailing across the **tiny** ocean

7. knew when to **kindle** the torch

8. **expand** the bundle to fit

9. was certain to **gladden** the passengers

0. reasons to **acclaim** the winner

Choosing the Right Word

*Circle the **boldface** word that more satisfactorily completes each of the following sentences.*

1. Which job would you take—one that is more (**ingenious, gainful**) right now or one that pays a small salary but offers a chance for valuable training?

2. We were pleasantly surprised to see that she completed the difficult task we had given her with neatness and (**irk, dispatch**).

3. As soon as she took over the office of Mayor, she was (**besieged, dispatched**) by dozens of people eager to get city jobs.

4. I will never (**recede, forsake**) the people who helped me in my hour of need!

5. (**Famished, Compressed**) for a chance to see her work in print, the young writer begged the magazine editor to publish her story.

6. After all the bad things he has done, I feel no (**dispatches, misgivings**) about telling him that I don't want him to be my "friend" anymore.

7. As soon as he began his long, boring speech, our excitement died down, as though we had been (**denounced, doused**) with cold water.

8. Each day, after she finishes her homework, she enjoys a light (**repast, misgiving**) of the detective stories she loves so well.

9. Her conscience forced her to (**denounce, libel**) the conspirators to the authorities.

10. His notebooks show that Leonardo da Vinci was not only a masterful artist but an (**inept, ingenious**) inventor as well.

11. Tom may not be as polished and clever as some of the other boys, but I think it is unfair of you to call him an (**apparel, oaf**).

12. We can (**compress, besiege**) the message of the sermon into one short sentence: "Do unto others as you would have others do unto you."

13. His conceit is so (**immense, gainful**) that he cannot imagine anyone voting against him in the election for class president.

14. Instead of feeling (**forsaken, irked**) because you did poorly on the exam, why don't you make up your mind to study harder in the future?

15. We are working hard to improve conditions in our community, but we cannot expect (**famished, instantaneous**) results.

16. He may claim that we have (**libeled, doused**) him, but we have facts to back up every statement made in the column about him.

17. You may criticize the roads and the lights, but the fact is that most car accidents are caused by (**inept, immense**) drivers.

18. When I realized that I was thoroughly prepared for the final exams, my fears quickly (**receded, irked**).

19. Where did he ever get the curious idea that we set up this volleyball court (**expressly, instantaneously**) for him and his friends?

20. I always feel sad at the end of the autumn, when the trees lose their beautiful (**repast, apparel**) of leaves.

receive

pg 26

① gainful
② dispatch
③ besieged
④ forsake
⑤ Famished
⑥ misgivings
⑦ doused
⑧ repast
⑨ denounce
⓪ ingenious

13 immener
(14) irked
(15) instantaneous
(16) libeled
(17) inept
(18) receded
(19) expressly
(20) apparel

Vocabulary in Context

*Read the following passage, in which some of the words you have studied in this unit appear in **boldface** type. Then complete each statement given below the passage by circling the letter of the item that is **the same** or **almost the same** in meaning as the highlighted word.*

Clothing Fads of the 1960s

(Line)

The 1960s left a definite mark on American **apparel**. This influence began when First Lady Jacqueline Kennedy moved into the White House in 1961 with her husband, President John Kennedy. Her sophisticated sense of style appealed to many. Fashion designers, department stores, and boutiques could barely satisfy the
(5) **immense** demand for pillbox hats, two-piece suits, A-line skirts, wraparound sunglasses, and low-heeled pumps.

After the tragic Kennedy assassination in 1963, fashion looked elsewhere for inspiration. The Nehru jacket, named for
(10) India's first Prime Minister, had no lapels and a small stand-up collar. The Beatles promoted this style, which became an **instantaneous** hit.

What about everyday attire? Enter bell-
(15) bottoms. These wide-legged pants, which flared out at the bottom, were modeled after traditional sailor pants. In an effort to distance bell-bottoms from their military origins, **ingenious** designers widened the
(20) bells and added broad belts, a hip-hugging line, fancy cuffs or pleats, and outrageous patterns and fabrics.

Even accessories had a distinctly sixties air. Opticians were **besieged** by people

Raffia pillbox hat with attached pigtails, wraparound sunglasses, matching bag

(25) begging for Ben Franklins—delicate, wire-rimmed glasses whose lenses came in many colors. Long hair parted down the middle completed the look.

Don't forget mini-skirts. These super-short skirts were **denounced** as being shameless, unhealthy, and totally ridiculous. But negative opinion didn't stop fad-conscious teens.
(30) Do these styles seem to be more than just a part of history? That is because some of them have made a comeback and are very much a part of today's fashions.

---

1. The meaning of **apparel** (line 1) is
a. promptness   c. clothing
b. victuals   d. slander

Immense (line 5) most nearly means
a. enormous   c. accidental
b. clumsy   d. gradual

Instantaneous (line 13) is best defined as
a. particular   c. profitable
b. gradual   d. immediate

4. The meaning of **ingenious** (line 19) is
a. unskilled   c. starving
b. clever   d. explicit

5. **Besieged** (line 24) most nearly means
a. criticized   c. hounded
b. soaked   d. abandoned

6. **Denounced** (line 27) is best defined as
a. acclaimed   c. shortened
b. recalled   d. condemned

Definitions

Note carefully the spelling, pronunciation, part(s) of speech, and definition(s) of each of the following words. Then write the word in the blank space(s) in the illustrative sentence(s) following. Finally, study the lists of synonyms and antonyms given at the end of each entry.

1. adverse
(ad vərs′)

(*adj.*) unfavorable, negative; working against, hostile

Some people suffer an _____ reaction if they eat peanut butter or anything with peanuts.

SYNONYMS: difficult, trying
ANTONYMS: favorable, positive, helpful, beneficial

2. arid
(ar′ id)

(*adj.*) extremely dry; uninteresting, dull

Although California leads the nation in farming, crops won't grow in its most _____ regions.

SYNONYMS: waterless, parched, boring, unimaginative
ANTONYMS: waterlogged, soggy, fertile, lush

3. assailant
(ə sa′ lənt)

(*n.*) a person who attacks violently (with blows or words)

The jogger was injured by an unknown _____ who left him immobile at the side of the road.

SYNONYMS: assaulter, attacker, mugger
ANTONYMS: victim, prey, injured party

4. billow
(bil′ o)

(*n.*) a large wave; (*v.*) to rise or swell like a wave

The ocean _____ rose and fell, attracting the most daring surfers.

Fans cheered enthusiastically when they saw their team's flags _____ over the stadium.

SYNONYMS: (*n.*) breaker; (*v.*) surge, bulge, balloon
ANTONYMS: (*n.*) trough; (*v.*) deflate, collapse

5. confront
(kən frənt′)

(*v.*) to meet face-to-face, especially as a challenge; come to grips with

In court, defendants can _____ their accusers in a controlled setting.

SYNONYMS: face, encounter
ANTONYMS: avoid, evade, sidestep

6. constrain
(kən strān′)

(*v.*) to force, compel; to restrain, hold back

You can't _____ me against my will

SYNONYMS: pressure, restrict, confine, limit
ANTONYMS: loosen, liberate, unfetter, relax

7. contemporary
(kən tem′ pə rer ē)

(*adj.*) belonging to the same period of time as oneself; (*n.*) a person of the same time

Hear the words for this Unit pronounced, defined, and used in sentences at **www.vocabularyworkshop.com**.

2

His novel used a _____ style but had a historical setting.

Rather than ask parents for help, teens often turn to a _____ for advice.

SYNONYMS: (*adj.*) present-day, modern, current; (*n.*) peer
ANTONYMS: (*adj.*) ancient, prehistoric, antique, antiquated

8. depict
(di pikt′)

(*v.*) to portray; to represent or show in the form of a picture

The painter chose to _____ a plain prairie landscape using bold colors and shadows.

SYNONYMS: sketch, draw, picture, illustrate

9. disinterested
(dis in′ trəst id)

(*adj.*) fair-minded, free from selfish motives; indifferent

A judge must remain _____ in order to render an evenhanded and logical decision.

SYNONYMS: neutral, impartial, unbiased, apathetic
ANTONYMS: partial, biased, prejudiced

0. encompass
(en kəm′ pəs)

(*v.*) to encircle, go or reach around; to enclose; to include with a certain group or class

Oceans _____ about three-fourths of the surface of our planet.

SYNONYMS: surround, envelop, comprise
ANTONYMS: leave out, omit, exclude

1. groundless
(graùnd′ ləs)

(*adj.*) without any good reason or cause, unjustified

Kate's _____ fear of hurting herself during exercise has left her weak and out of shape.

SYNONYMS: baseless, unsupported
ANTONYMS: well-founded, reasonable, justified

2. hypocrite
(hip′ ə krit)

(*n.*) a person who pretends to be what he or she is not or better than he or she really is; a two-faced person

The speaker who said one thing but did something else entirely was regarded as a _____.

SYNONYMS: phony, charlatan, fraud

3. incomprehensible
(in käm pri hen′ sə bəl)

(*adj.*) impossible to understand

Our school's intercom system is so old that this morning's announcements were almost _____.

SYNONYMS: baffling, confusing, bewildering
ANTONYMS: understandable, clear, plain, intelligible

4. manipulate
(mə nip′ yə lāt)

(*v.*) to handle or use skillfully; to manage or control for personal gain or advantage

Scientists should not _____ data.

SYNONYMS: work, maneuver, exploit, influence

15. maximum
(mak′ sə məm)

(n.) the greatest possible amount or degree; (adj.) reaching the greatest possible amount or degree

This postage scale can weigh a _____ of only five pounds.

To ease the patient's suffering, the doctor prescribed the _____ dosage of painkillers.

SYNONYMS: largest, highest, utmost
ANTONYMS: least, lowest, minimum, smallest

16. mimic
(mim′ ik)

(n.) a person who does imitations; (v.) to imitate; to make fun of

The comedy troupe has many talented members, but it still needs to hire a good _____.

Troy continually entertains his friends because he can _____ any accent he hears.

SYNONYMS: (n.) copycat, impersonator; (v.) parrot, impersonate

17. ruffle
(rəf′ əl)

(v.) to wrinkle, make uneven; to annoy, upset; to flip through; (n.) a gathered strip of material used for trimming edges; a ripple; a low drumbeat

Try not to let wisecracks _____ your feelings.

My favorite pillow is soft and fluffy to the touch and has a velvet _____.

SYNONYMS: (v.) disturb; (n.) frill
ANTONYMS: (v.) smooth out, soothe

18. serene
(sə rēn′)

(adj.) peaceful, calm; free of emotional upset; clear and free of storm; majestic, grand

How does she manage to stay so _____ in the face of such chaos?

SYNONYMS: tranquil, composed, fair, august
ANTONYMS: agitated, troubled, stormy, inclement

19. sheepish
(shēp′ ish)

(adj.) embarrassed; resembling a sheep in meekness, timid

His _____ grin made the crowds cheer all the more for his unlikely victory.

SYNONYMS: shamefaced, meek
ANTONYMS: bold, saucy, brazen, confident

20. stamina
(stam′ ə nə)

(n.) the strength needed to keep going or overcome physical or mental strain; staying power

Marathon runners need a great deal of _____

SYNONYM: endurance

 **Completing the Sentence**

From the words for this unit, choose the one that best completes each of the following sentences. Write the word in the space provided.

1. The brisk breeze caused the sheets on the line to _____ like the sails on a yacht that is running with the wind.

2. The hot, _____ climate of Arizona is favorable for many people suffering from various diseases, such as arthritis.

3. The skyscraper is one of the best-known forms of _____ architecture.

4. Although I may hurt your feelings, my conscience _____ me to tell you exactly what is on my mind.

5. Since Tom is both smart and _____, I think he is just the person to decide which of us is right in this long and bitter quarrel.

6. Fortunately, I was able to fight off my _____, even though his attack took me by complete surprise.

7. You talk so fast and in such a low tone of voice that you are going to be completely _____ to most people.

8. Held back by _____ winds, the plane arrived at the airport two hours late.

9. Parrots and a few other kinds of birds can _____ sounds, particularly human speech.

10. Under the law, the _____ number of people who may ride in this bus is seventy-five.

11. For a long time, I thought that he was a good and sincere person, but I finally saw that he was no more than a(n) _____.

12. The _____ expression on her face showed that she was totally undisturbed by the confusion and turmoil around her.

13. This basic textbook _____ all the information you will have to master for the entrance examination.

14. Using the entire east wall of the new Post Office building, the painter tried to _____ the founding of our city.

15. The jury found the defendant "not guilty" because they were convinced that the charges against her were _____.

16. I was so embarrassed by my blunder that I could do nothing but grin in a(n) _____ and self-conscious way.

17. You and Lucy will never settle your quarrel unless you _____ each other directly and listen to what the other person has to say.

18. Very few starting pitchers have the _____ to pitch well for nine innings.

19. A breeze sprang up and began to _____ the smooth and tranquil surface of the water.

20. As you become a more skillful driver, you will be able to _____ all the controls of the car while keeping your eyes on the road.

Synonyms

*Choose the word from this unit that is **the same** or **most nearly the same** in meaning as the **boldface** word or expression in the given phrase. Write the word on the line provided.*

1. enough **endurance** for the walk-a-thon _____

2. the **largest** quantity available _____

3. **maneuver** the dial to the exact position _____

4. that she can **parrot** my every action _____

5. could not mask that **shamefaced** look _____

6. confused by the child's **bewildering** behavior _____

7. mistrustful of that **phony** _____

8. a **tranquil** expanse of clear blue sky _____

9. tried to **restrict** the patient _____

10. to serve as a **neutral** witness _____

11. as colorful parachutes **surge** open _____

12. difficult to iron those lace **frills** _____

13. will never forget the **attacker's** voice _____

14. used pastels to **illustrate** the scene _____

15. a fence to **surround** the whole backyard _____

Antonyms

*Choose the word from this unit that is **most nearly opposite** in meaning to the **boldface** word or expression in the given phrase. Write the word on the line provided.*

16. has a very **fertile** imagination _____

17. with a collection of **antique** chairs _____

18. **reasonable** concerns about our safety _____

19. due to **favorable** experiences in the past _____

20. to continually **evade** problems _____

Choosing the Right Word

*Circle the **boldface** word that more satisfactorily completes each of the following sentences.*

1. If you (**billow, confront**) your problems honestly and openly, instead of trying to hide them, you will have a better chance of solving them.

2. The big-league shortstop (**manipulates, constrains**) his glove like a magician, snaring every ball hit within reach.

3. A good scientist must have a keen mind, an unquenchable curiosity, and a (**groundless, disinterested**) desire to discover the truth.

4. She has many interesting ideas, but she seems to lack the physical and mental (**stamina, assailant**) to make good use of them.

5. The (**adverse, sheepish**) publicity that he received during the investigation was probably the cause of his defeat in the next election.

6. Do you think it would be a good idea to set a (**maximum, contemporary**) figure for the amount of homework any teacher is allowed to assign?

7. After giving a few (**sheepish, serene**) excuses, the swimmers packed up and left the private beach.

8. Anyone who has ever sailed a small boat knows how thrilling it is to feel the spray in your face while the sails (**billow, encompass**) overhead.

9. After many stormy years in the service of his country, George Washington retired to the (**serene, adverse**) life of his beloved Mount Vernon.

10. After living for many years in that roomy old farmhouse, I felt awfully (**arid, constrained**) in that small apartment.

11. My idea of a(n) (**assailant, hypocrite**) is a person who gives advice that he or she is not willing to follow.

12. His decision not to accept our sincere offer of assistance is completely (**disinterested, incomprehensible**) to me.

13. I didn't want to (**ruffle, manipulate**) the feelings of the hotel manager, but I felt that I had to complain about the miserable service.

14. Martin Luther King, Jr. and Robert F. Kennedy were (**contemporaries, mimics**), born within a few years of each other.

15. We expected the lecture on the energy crisis to be exciting, but it turned out to be a(n) (**ruffled, arid**) rundown of well-known facts and figures.

16. Despite the fact that she was in shock, the victim gave a clear description of her (**hypocrite, assailant**).

17. The science program in our school (**depicts, encompasses**) biology, chemistry, physics, earth science, and other related courses.

18. What a relief to learn that my parents had been delayed by a storm, and that all my fears about an accident were (**groundless, maximum**)!

19. She has gained success as a writer who knows how to (**confront, depict**) in a lifelike way the hopes, fears, and problems of young people today.

20. Instead of working so hard to (**mimic, ruffle**) popular TV stars, why don't you try to develop an acting style of your own?

Vocabulary in Context

Read the following passage, in which some of the words you have studied in this unit appear in **boldface** type. Then complete each statement given below the passage by circling the letter of the item that is **the same** or **almost the same** in meaning as the highlighted word.

"A Pageant of Fatigue"

(Line)

One of the most **incomprehensible** public competitions ever conceived was the dance marathon. The object of this crazy contest, first held in 1923, was to see which couple could dance for longer than any other. Grace and style didn't matter. **Stamina** was the only thing that counted.

Dance marathons were wildly popular in the 1920s and 1930s. Young couples (5) staggered around dance floors, moving to the **contemporary** tunes of the day. The music was played by live bands or on records. The last couple to remain standing won. Winners might be rewarded up to a **maximum** of $1000, which was a vast sum at that time. But they faced (10) highly **adverse** conditions in their efforts to win.

Rules varied slightly from contest to contest, but the main idea was always the same. Dancers could never leave the dance floor, except to use the rest room. They were (15) **constrained** to eat, drink, and sleep on their feet. They always had to move, at least a little. Partners took turns supporting each other as best they could.

Critics claimed that the dance marathons (20) were simply physical cruelty. Lawmakers tried to get the contests banned. However, curious onlookers packed the dance halls. To them, it was entertaining to watch weary dancers.

A woman struggles to hold up her fast-fading dance partner.

Why did people put themselves through this? (25) Of course, there was prize money at stake. But the major reason seemed to be the power of the fad itself. Marathon dancers became overnight celebrities. Morning papers ran ongoing stories on them. People couldn't resist tales of wacky, risk-taking heroism, and juicy gossip about the dancers, whose relationships suffered as much as their bodies did during those grueling hours. (30)

---

1. The meaning of **incomprehensible** (line 1) is
   a. understandable
   b. famous
   c. baffling
   d. tiring

2. The meaning of **stamina** (line 4) is
   a. endurance
   b. weakness
   c. rhythm
   d. intelligence

3. Contemporary (line 6) most nearly means
   a. ancient
   b. jazzy
   c. popular
   d. current

4. Maximum (line 9) is best defined as
   a. money reward
   b. special prize
   c. lowest amount
   d. greatest amount

5. Adverse (line 11) most nearly means
   a. helpful
   b. difficult
   c. musical
   d. competitive

6. Constrained (line 16) is best defined as
   a. liberated
   b. compelled
   c. portrayed
   d. exploited

Hear the words for this Unit pronounced, defined, and used in sentences at **www.vocabularyworkshop.com**.

UNIT 3

Definitions

Note carefully the spelling, pronunciation, part(s) of speech, and definition(s) of each of the following words. Then write the word in the blank space(s) in the illustrative sentence(s) following. Finally, study the lists of synonyms and antonyms given at the end of each entry.

1. barrage
(bə räzh′)

(*n.*) a rapid, large-scale outpouring of something

The governor faced a _____ of questions about possible budget cuts.

SYNONYMS: bombardment, shelling, volley, blast

2. bigot
(big′ ət)

(*n.*) an intolerant, prejudiced, or biased person

When you speak in that narrow-minded way, you sound like a _____.

SYNONYM: racist

3. designate
(dez′ ig nāt)

(*v.*) to indicate, point out; to appoint; (*adj.*) selected but not yet installed

Will you please tell me when the coach will _____ a team leader?

The new student council _____ is looking forward to making many changes to the student government.

SYNONYMS: (*v.*) name, signify, denote, nominate, choose

4. diversity
(di vər′ sə tē)

(*n.*) difference, variety; a condition of having many different types or forms

Our science teacher has a _____ of interests, including an appreciation of Russian literature.

SYNONYM: dissimilarity
ANTONYMS: similarity, sameness, uniformity

5. enigma
(i nig′ mə)

(*n.*) someone or something that is extremely puzzling; that which cannot be understood or explained

Critics complained that the plot twists in the new mystery movie make it an _____.

SYNONYMS: riddle, mystery, puzzle, conundrum

6. gloat
(glōt)

(*v.*) to look at or think about with great intensity and satisfaction; to take great personal joy in

I will try not to _____ about winning a scholarship to music camp.

SYNONYMS: relish, revel in, crow over
ANTONYMS: regret, bemoan, mourn, feel chagrined

7. global
(glō′ bəl)

(*adj.*) of, relating to, or involving the entire world; comprehensive

E-mail and the Internet have linked the entire world into a _____ village.

SYNONYMS: worldwide, universal, widespread
ANTONYMS: local, regional, provincial

8. illusion
(i lü′ zhən)

(*n.*) a false idea; something that one seems to see or to be aware of that really does not exist

Artist M. C. Escher often used optical _____

SYNONYMS: delusion, fantasy, deception
ANTONYMS: reality, truth, actuality

9. infuriate
(in fyúr′ ē āt)

(*v.*) to make very angry, enrage

It _____ most parents when their children refuse to listen to them and treat them with disrespect.

SYNONYMS: provoke, incense, madden
ANTONYMS: calm, soothe, pacify, please

10. motivate
(mō′ tə vāt)

(*v.*) to provide with a reason for doing; to push on to some goal or course of action

What is the best way to _____ students to undertake challenging work?

SYNONYMS: spur on, encourage, prompt, goad
ANTONYMS: discourage, dissuade, disincline

11. pacifist
(pas′ ə fist)

(*n.*) one who is against war or the use of violence; (*adj.*) opposing war or violence

Martin Luther King, Jr. was a famous _____ who had a very strong influence on the civil rights movement.

_____ students protested the war.

SYNONYMS:(*n.*) peacemaker, dove
ANTONYM: (*n.*) warmonger

12. queue
(kyü)

(*n.*) a line of people waiting for something (such as a bus or the opening of a store); (*v.*) to form such a line

The long _____ at the bus stop indicated that a bus had not come for a while.

Eager fans _____ up hours before the box office opens, hoping to get the best tickets.

SYNONYMS: (*n.*) column, file, row, line
ANTONYM: (*n.*) disorganized crowd

13. restrict
(ri strikt′)

(*v.*) to keep within set limits; to confine

Doctors often advise patients to _____ their intake of fatty or salty foods.

SYNONYMS: hold back, limit
ANTONYMS: open up, enlarge, expand

 Hear the words for this Unit pronounced, defined, and used in sentences at **www.vocabularyworkshop.com**.

3

14. sage
(sāj)

(*adj.*) wise; (*n.*) a very wise person

My aunt always gives me _____ advice when I'm struggling with a decision.

Let's ask the _____ for his opinion on how to handle this problem.

SYNONYMS: (*adj.*) sagacious; (*n.*) philosopher, Solomon
ANTONYMS: (*adj.*) foolish, unwise; (*n.*) fool, dunce

15. slake
(slāk)

(*v.*) to satisfy, relieve, or bring to an end

Nothing can _____ my thirst better than a tall glass of ice water.

SYNONYMS: quench, gratify, sate, ease, assuage
ANTONYMS: increase, intensify, aggravate

16. terrain
(tə rān')

(*n.*) the landscape, especially considered with regard to its physical features or fitness for some use; a field of knowledge

Mountain bikes are designed to stand up to even the most rugged _____.

SYNONYMS: ground, topography, territory

17. vocation
(vō kā' shən)

(*n.*) any trade, profession, or occupation; a sense of fitness or special calling for one's work

After many years of searching, she found her true _____ as a horse trainer.

SYNONYMS: career, pursuit
ANTONYMS: hobby, pastime, avocation

18. vow
(vaů)

(*n.*) a solemn or sacred promise or pledge; (*v.*) to declare or promise in a solemn way

Prince Hamlet made a solemn _____ to avenge his father's murder.

A bride and groom _____ to love, honor, and respect each other throughout their marriage.

SYNONYMS: (*n.*) word of honor; (*v.*) pledge

19. waylay
(wā' lā)

(*v.*) to lie in wait for and attack, ambush

Thugs often choose to _____ travelers as they wearily make their way back home.

SYNONYMS: entrap, ensnare

20. wither
(with' ər)

(*v.*) to dry up, wilt, sag; to cause someone to feel ashamed, humiliated, or very small

Despite people's best efforts to remain young looking, skin will eventually _____ with age.

SYNONYMS: shrivel, droop, shame, abash
ANTONYMS: bloom, flower, flourish, burgeon

Completing the Sentence

From the words for this unit, choose the one that best completes each of the following sentences. Write the word in the space provided.

1. Since he greatly enjoys woodworking and also makes a living from it, his hobby and his _____ are one and the same.

2. I came to regard my grandmother as a(n) _____ whose wisdom helped to solve many family problems.

3. Even before the new president took office, he _____ the men and women who were to serve in his cabinet.

4. No decent person will _____ over someone else's failures or misfortunes.

5. How sad it is to see such beautiful flowers _____ and die!

6. Is it possible to be a(n) _____ in a world where so many people are using force to take unfair advantage of others?

7. The animals in the drought area traveled for many miles to reach a body of water where they could _____ their thirst.

8. A person can usually tell how popular a new movie is by the length of the _____ in front of the box office.

9. The desire to be the world's top tennis player _____ the young woman to spend hours every day improving her game.

10. Our hike was not very long, but the _____ was so rocky and hilly that we were exhausted by the time we reached our goal.

11. The rich _____ of plant and animal life in a tropical rain forest never ceases to amaze me.

12. I don't understand what he is aiming at or why he behaves as he does; in fact, his whole personality is a(n) _____ to me.

13. Because the show is scheduled to end after midnight, the management will _____ admission to people over sixteen.

14. As she was sworn in, she made a(n) _____ that she would never use the powers of her office for selfish or unworthy purposes.

15. Like a typical _____, he believes that any customs different from his own are "wrong" and "uncivilized."

16. For better or for worse, as you become older and more experienced, you will lose many of the comforting _____ of youth.

17. The deadly _____ of shells from our guns pinned down the enemy troops on the narrow beach where they had landed.

18. The pollution problem, far from being limited to the United States, is truly
_____ in scope.

19. Nothing _____ my boss more than an employee who is late for
work and then offers a foolish excuse for not arriving on time.

20. The police now believe that the mugger _____ the elderly woman
as she entered the elevator of her apartment house.

Synonyms

Choose the word from this unit that is **the same** or **most nearly the same** in meaning as the **boldface** word or expression in the given phrase. Write the word on the line provided.

1. a dirty look that made me **droop** _____

2. **quench** their cravings for a refreshing drink _____

3. a plot to **ensnare** unsuspecting victims _____

4. the most respected **philosopher** of them all _____

5. must **pledge** to tell the truth _____

6. ignored the ravings of that **biased person** _____

7. the magician's most unique **deception** _____

8. to **revel in** our team's victory _____

9. trying to **incense** the manager _____

0. the rewarding **career** of being a chef _____

1. ending with a **volley** of fireworks _____

2. close-ups of the **topography** of Mars _____

3. **choose** it as the team's new logo _____

4. **mystery** to anyone who stumbled upon it _____

5. the last in the **row** of guests _____

Antonyms

Choose the word from this unit that is **most nearly opposite** in meaning to the **boldface** word or expression in the given phrase. Write the word on the line provided.

6. appreciated the **uniformity** of the activities _____

7. to **expand** their options _____

8. might **discourage** people who aren't sure _____

9. in speeches given by a notable **warmonger** _____

0. part of a **local** manufacturing company _____

*Circle the **boldface** word that more satisfactorily completes each of the following sentences.*

1. The United States has laws that (**restrict, waylay**) the numbers and kinds of immigrants allowed to enter this country.

2. By the time you are old enough to enter the workforce, many (**vocations, sages**) that are important today may not even exist anymore.

3. As the defense attorney left the courtroom, he was (**waylaid, designated**) by a group of eager reporters trying to get a statement from him.

4. With the other team ten points ahead and only a few minutes left to play, our hopes o victory began to (**wither, gloat**).

5. Since I am convinced that violence always creates more problems than it solves, I have become a (**pacifist, bigot**).

6. The children who are admitted free to the ball game will be allowed to sit only in certain (**designated, motivated**) parts of the stands.

7. To (**slake, restrict**) our curiosity, you will have to tell us everything that happened during that strange trip.

8. No matter what it may cost me to carry out, I will never break my sacred (**vow, illusion**).

9. Before we begin our backpacking trip, we should have a good idea of the (**terrain, vocation**) we are going to cover.

10. Has it ever occurred to you that your belief that you are a superior person and a natural leader may be no more than a(n) (**illusion, barrage**)?

11. Just how and why two people fall in love is a(n) (**queue, enigma**) that no scientist has ever been able to explain.

12. A good loser doesn't sulk over defeat; a good winner doesn't (**gloat, vow**) after victory.

13. Since you have so many prejudices of your own, you should think twice before you accuse other people of being (**enigmas, bigots**).

14. A great teacher not only makes the material of the course understandable but also (**infuriates, motivates**) the students to want to learn more.

15. World War II was a truly (**global, pacifist**) struggle, fought in all parts of the world by people of every race and background.

16. She is never bored because she has a great (**enigma, diversity**) of interests, ranging from folk dancing to mathematics.

17. The applicants for the job will have to (**queue, slake**) up in an orderly way and wait their turns to be interviewed.

18. Entangled in the trapper's net, the (**infuriated, withered**) lion roared in helpless anger.

19. When the speaker asked for opinions from the audience, he was greeted with a (**barrage, terrain**) of critical remarks and angry questions.

20. Her analysis of what is wrong with our city government seems to me remarkably (**sage, global**) and helpful.

Read the following passage, in which some of the words you have studied in this unit appear in **boldface** type. Then complete each statement given below the passage by circling the letter of the item that is **the same** or **almost the same** in meaning as the highlighted word.

Welcome to Ellis Island

(Line)

A range of factors **motivated** immigrants to leave their homelands to come to America. Many sought to escape poverty or prejudice. Some wanted to follow dreams, such as promises of jobs, safe homes, or their own farms. Others clung to exciting **illusions** about how grand life in America would be. Whatever the
(5) reasons, between 1892 and 1954, more than twelve million immigrants passed through the Federal Immigration Center on Ellis Island in New York Harbor. There, beneath the welcoming arms of the Statue of Liberty, a
(10) **diversity** of hopeful newcomers took their first steps on American soil.

Many immigrants had spent as long as two miserable, seasick weeks on the harsh ocean crossing. What a joy it must have been for
(15) these weary newcomers to step onto land. At Ellis Island, they were greeted by a **barrage** of languages, sights, and smells.

Not all immigrants arriving in New York entered through Ellis Island. Those rich enough
(20) to travel as first- or second-class passengers did not have to wait and worry on the endless **queues** of the inspection process. These lucky ones had brief shipboard inspections and could exit right into the hustle and bustle of New York City.

The third-class passengers had to endure many medical and legal inspections. Lucky ones might complete the Ellis Island process in about five hours. Inspectors
(25) checked legal papers and asked questions about the immigrant's family and **vocation**. The process was nerve-racking, but nearly 98% of new arrivals were let into the United States when it was over.

Visitors to the Ellis Island Immigration Museum today can retrace the footsteps of those immigrants. They can pass through the original Great Hall, which was restored in
(30) the 1980s. They can see photographs, documents, and precious possessions and hear recordings of immigrants sharing their experiences.

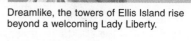

Dreamlike, the towers of Ellis Island rise beyond a welcoming Lady Liberty.

. The meaning of **motivated** (line 1) is
a. prompted   c. angered
b. dissuaded   d. confined

. **Illusions** (line 4) is best defined as
a. realities   c. stories
b. fantasies   d. notes

. **Diversity** (line 10) most nearly means
a. college   c. uniformity
b. swarm   d. variety

4. The meaning of **barrage** (line16) is
a. landscape   c. bombardment
b. scarcity   d. scene

5. **Queues** (line 21) most nearly means
a. crowds   c. questions
b. lines   d. process

6. **Vocation** (line 26) is best defined as
a. friends   c. background
b. hobbies   d. occupation

Vocabulary for Comprehension

*Read the following passage, in which some of the words you have studied in Units 1–3 appear in **boldface** type. Then answer questions 1–12 on page 43 on the basis of what is <u>stated</u> or <u>implied</u> in the passage and in the introductory statement.*

From its humble beginnings, the annual winter festival in Sapporo, Japan, has become a world-class event, as this passage shows.

(Line)

Picture a vast castle, or imagine an oversized cartoon figure. Now try to imagine each of them made of snow and ice. This is what you might see if
(5) you attend the Sapporo Snow Festival, a weeklong event held each year in northern Japan, on the island of Hokkaido.

Unlike other cities in Japan,
(10) Sapporo is fairly young. It has no ancient temples. Its streets are unusually wide and straight. The city is a popular destination for those who enjoy winter sports. In fact, the 1972
(15) Winter Olympic Games were held in Sapporo.

The Sapporo Snow Festival draws both young and old into its wintry wonderland fantasies. Most people
(20) familiar with winter festivals **designate** the Sapporo Snow Festival as the most famous of its kind. The city plans ahead for months. It is impossible for visitors to
(25) get hotel rooms without **expressly** reserving them far in advance.

The Sapporo Snow Festival had modest beginnings. In 1950, high school students made six snow
(30) sculptures in a **serene** park in the center of town. What began as fun for creative teenagers has grown into an event that has **global** appeal. Odori

Park, the location of those first snow
(35) sculptures, continues to be one of the three main festival sites.

Since the early days, much of the work to mount the festival has been done by the Self-Defense Forces.
(40) This branch of the Japanese military **dispatches** hundreds of soldiers in army trucks to haul snow from nearb mountains into the city. This peacetime work serves the public
(45) and keeps festival costs down.

Visitors to the Snow Festival toda might see gigantic sculptures that **depict** prehistoric animals, Viking warriors, famous people, and even
(50) cartoon characters! Bands play music from atop huge sound stage built of snow. Daredevils can zoom down elaborate ice slides. Nightly fireworks, colored lights, and other
(55) special sound and lighting effects add extra excitement.

Make your reservations now!

1. The primary purpose of the passage is to
   a. describe traditional Japanese customs
   b. praise the Japanese Self-Defense Forces
   c. entertain the reader with amusing anecdotes
   d. inform the reader about the Sapporo Snow Festival
   e. persuade other cities to hold winter snow festivals

2. The meaning of **designate** (line 21) is
   a. avoid
   b. name
   c. deny
   d. attend
   e. photograph

3. **Expressly** (line 25) most nearly means
   a. quickly
   b. efficiently
   c. explicitly
   d. tentatively
   e. accidentally

4. Paragraph 3 (lines 17–26) focuses on the festival's
   a. history
   b. main events
   c. attendance
   d. artists
   e. rules

5. **Serene** (line 30) is best defined as
   a. enormous
   b. municipal
   c. popular
   d. tranquil
   e. pretty

6. The meaning of **global** (line 33) is
   a. festive
   b. limited
   c. regional
   d. mysterious
   e. widespread

7. How did the Sapporo Snow Festival get started in the 1950s?
   a. A great blizzard dumped three feet of snow on Sapporo.
   b. High school students built six snow sculptures in a park.
   c. The city held a competition for best snow sculptures.
   d. The Winter Olympic Games were held in Sapporo.
   e. A winter wedding was held outdoors in Odori Park.

8. **Dispatches** (line 41) most nearly means
   a. sends out
   b. trains
   c. rewards
   d. joins with
   e. recruits

9. **Depict** (line 48) is best defined as
   a. replace
   b. analyze
   c. surround
   d. represent
   e. restore

10. Which of the following best describes the author's tone, or attitude, toward the subject?
    a. formal
    b. skeptical
    c. critical
    d. solemn
    e. enthusiastic

11. You can infer from the passage that the author is trying to
    a. suggest improvements in the festival
    b. caution visitors about the dangers and the crowds
    c. promote attendance at the festival
    d. encourage other Japanese cities to hold festivals
    e. analyze athletic events in Japanese cities

12. In paragraph 6 (lines 46–56), the author makes the festival come alive by using many
    a. sensory details
    b. generalizations
    c. statistics
    d. exaggerations
    e. exclamation points

Grammar in Context

There is nothing wrong with the sentence "This is what you might see if you attend the Sapporo Snow Festival, a weeklong event held every year in northern Japan, on the island of Hokkaido" (lines 4–8 on page 42). But suppose that the author had written it this way: "This is what you might see if you attend the Sapporo Snow Festival. A weeklong event held each year in northern Japan, on the island of Hokkaido." It would not work because the second group of words is missing a subject and is therefore not a sentence. If a group of words lacks a subject, a verb, or both, it is called a **sentence fragment**.

A **sentence** is a group of words that expresses a complete thought. It has two main parts: a complete subject (a noun or pronoun plus any modifiers) and a complete predicate (a verb or verb phrase plus any modifiers). When you write, be sure to write complete sentences.

A **run-on sentence** is really two or more sentences masquerading as a single sentence because of incorrect punctuation. To avoid run-ons, there are four things you can do: (1) Use capitalization and punctuation to separate the sentence into two short sentences. (2) Use a conjunction preceded by a comma. (3) Insert a semicolon or a semicolon with a transitional word or phrase followed by a comma. (4) Use a subordinating conjunction to make one of the two sentences a subordinate clause.

On the lines provided, rewrite each of the groups of words to eliminate the run-ons and fragments. Write "correct" if the sentence is correct.

1. Visitors to the Sapporo Snow Festival each year.

_____

_____

2. Visitors to the festival agree, they all would go again.

_____

_____

3. If you wish to create snow sculptures, you had better have lots of snow.

_____

_____

4. Traveling to Japan is quite an undertaking, for one thing, it is a very long flight.

_____

_____

5. Have you ever seen sand sculptures, many people are fond of building them.

_____

_____

6. Where I live, there is plenty of snow and ice, however there aren't many sculptors.

_____

_____

Two-Word Completions

Circle the pair of words that best complete the meaning of each of the following passages.

1. As the travelers crossed the hot and _____ wasteland known as the Sahara Desert, their eyes were deceived more than once by mirages and other optical _____.

a. adverse . . . mimics
b. immense . . . vocations
c. groundless . . . enigmas
d. arid . . . illusions

2. It took a great deal of _____ to keep up with the rest of the pack as they sped across the broken and hilly _____ that separated them from the finish line in the cross-country race.

a. dispatch . . . apparel
b. misgiving . . . repast
c. stamina . . . terrain
d. diversity . . . barrage

3. Two ruffians _____ the weary traveler on a lonely stretch of road, but the man was able to beat off his _____ with the help of his stout staff.

a. waylaid . . . assailants
b. dispatched . . . oafs
c. confronted . . . hypocrites
d. constrained . . . pacifists

4. The demand for tickets to the play-offs was so heavy that for days the box office was _____ like some embattled fortress by mobs of people waiting more or less impatiently in long _____ that snaked endlessly around the whole block.

a. denounced . . . enigmas
b. besieged . . . queues
c. confronted . . . ruffles
d. encompassed . . . billows

5. Though other people have been moved to action by high ideals, Thomas Alva Edison, one of the most _____ inventors ever to be produced by this country, seems in part to have been _____ simply by the love of a challenge.

a. disinterested . . . manipulated
b. ingenious . . . motivated
c. inept . . . infuriated
d. immense . . . dispatched

6. Despite the _____ of vigorous insults coming from the other gubernatorial candidate, she refused to retaliate and _____ her competition.

a. illusion . . . libel
b. billow . . . infuriate
c. apparel . . . besiege
d. barrage . . . denounce

Choosing the Right Meaning

Read each sentence carefully. Then circle the item that best completes the statement below the sentence.

In keeping with his strong pacifist beliefs, the poet Robert Lowell served a prison term for refusing to bear arms during World War II. (2

1. In line 1 the word **pacifist** most nearly means

a. militant   b. criminal   c. old-fashioned   d. antiwar

When compresses failed to slow the bleeding, medics applied a tourniquet above the soldier's wound. (2

2. The word **compresses** in line 1 is used to mean

a. bandage pads   b. medicines   c. condensations   d. reductions

In computer terminology a global command is one that applies to an entire file, document, or program. (2

3. The word **global** in line 1 is best defined as

a. worldwide   b. widespread   c. random   d. comprehensive

Before they are confirmed by the Senate, those whom the president selects for cabinet posts are termed "secretaries designate." (2

4. The word **designate** in line 2 is used to mean

a. veteran   b. resigned   c. nominated   d. experienced

The well-dressed gentleman of the late eighteenth century wore ruffles of sheer linen or lace at his throat and wrists. (2

5. In line 1 the word **ruffles** most nearly means

a. wrinkles   c. ripples
b. gathered trimmings   d. irritations

Antonyms

*In each of the following groups, circle the word or expression that is most nearly the **opposite** of the word in **boldface** type.*

1. immense
a. illegal
b. vast
c. useless
d. small

2. adverse
a. fatal
b. harmful
c. positive
d. puzzling

3. maximum
a. lowest
b. highest
c. biggest
d. average

4. sheepish
a. unfriendly
b. bold
c. timid
d. silly

5. sage
a. foolish
b. wise
c. strange
d. unexpected

6. expressly
a. purposely
b. accidentally
c. quickly
d. cleverly

7. infuriate
a. anger
b. cheat
c. please
d. ignore

8. wither
a. flourish
b. ensnare
c. discourage
d. pressure

9. famished
a. frozen
b. confident
c. satiated
d. hungry

11. global
a. local
b. worldwide
c. vast
d. unmeasured

13. contemporary
a. intelligent
b. puzzling
c. ancient
d. famous

15. forsake
a. stall
b. stand by
c. hire
d. leave

10. disinterested
a. wise
b. prejudiced
c. bored
d. foreign

12. vocation
a. job
b. house
c. family
d. hobby

14. irk
a. smear
b. delight
c. punish
d. hurt

16. incomprehensible
a. puzzling
b. understandable
c. interesting
d. boring

Word Families

A. On the line provided, write the word you have learned in Units 1–3 that is related to each of the following nouns.
EXAMPLE: compression—**compress**

1. manipulator, manipulation
2. restriction
3. motivation, motivator
4. confrontation, confrontationist
5. designation, designator
6. denouncement, denunciation
7. adversity, adverseness
8. recession
9. ingeniousness
10. depicter, depiction
11. immenseness, immensity
12. ineptitude
13. encompassment
14. aridity, aridness
15. fury
16 instant

B. On the line provided, write the word you have learned in Units 1–3 that is related to each of the following verbs.
EXAMPLE: pacify—**pacifist**

17. maximize
18. divert
19. assail
20. comprehend

In each of the following groups, circle the word that is best defined or suggested by the given phrase.

1. living at the same time
   a. gainful   b. maximum   c. global   d. contemporary

2. to hold someone back
   a. constrain   b. vow   c. wither   d. slake

3. totally lacking skill or appropriateness
   a. instantaneous   b. inept   c. immense   d. arid

4. something that is deeply puzzling
   a. dispatch   b. illusion   c. bigot   d. enigma

5. to enrage
   a. billow   b. infuriate   c. recede   d. ruffle

6. to provide a reason or purpose for doing something
   a. motivate   b. restrict   c. forsake   d. designate

7. a feeling of doubt or uneasiness
   a. libel   b. diversity   c. misgiving   d. stamina

8. having no substance or foundation
   a. ingenious   b. disinterested   c. groundless   d. sheepish

9. a heavy outpouring (as of questions)
   a. barrage   b. queue   c. compress   d. terrain

10. one who pretends to be better than he or she really is
   a. hypocrite   b. assailant   c. contemporary   d. pacifist

11. to quench
   a. slake   b. constrain   c. gloat   d. dispatch

12. an idea not based on reality
   a. billow   b. hypocrite   c. illusion   d. sage

13. calm and composed
   a. sheepish   b. gainful   c. instantaneous   d. serene

14. a person's lifework or career
   a. terrain   b. libel   c. stamina   d. vocation

15. a solemn promise
   a. vow   b. repast   c. apparel   d. misgiving

16. to include or enclose within certain boundaries
   a. depict   b. encompass   c. manipulate   d. denounce

17. a person whose prejudices are always showing
   a. pacifist   b. oaf   c. bigot   d. mimic

18. the swelling waters
   a. dispatching   b. dousing   c. billowing   d. receding

19. to brag about their victory
   a. encompass   b. gloat   c. confront   d. motivate

20. writing that can harm someone's reputation
   a. dispatch   b. libel   c. ruffle   d. diversity

de—down; away from; completely; not

Building with Classical Roots

Many words in English are made up of a root and/or a prefix and suffix. In order to determine the meanings of many words, you have to know the meaning of the root, prefix, and/or suffix. The prefix *de*, for example, appears in **denounce** (page 21), **depict** (page 29), and **designate** (page 35). Some other words in which this prefix appears are listed below.

debunk	**default**	**demerit**	**desperate**
decapitate	**defraud**	**depression**	**devolve**

From the list of words above, choose the one that corresponds to each of the brief definitions below. Write the word in the blank space in the illustrative sentence below the definition.

1. a mark against, usually involving the loss of some privilege or right; a fault, defect

Unacceptable behavior earned him so many _____ that he was not allowed to go on the class trip.

2. to fail to perform a task or fulfill an obligation; the failure to do something required by law or duty

Because the challenger failed to show up, the defender won the match by _____ .

3. to cut off the head, behead

Experienced chefs know how to gut, scale, and _____ a fish before cooking it.

4. driven to take any risk; hopeless; extreme

Lack of water led homesteaders to take _____ measures to save their families.

5. an area that is sunk below its surroundings; a period of severe economic decline; a mood of dejection or sadness.

Slapstick comedy films were popular during the Great _____ of the 1930s.

6. to pass on (a duty, task, or the like) to someone else; to be passed on to; to be conferred on

Little will change when the mayor's powers _____ upon her successor.

7. to cheat, take away from, or deprive of by deceit or trickery

The corrupt attorney tried to _____ her of her rightful inheritance.

8. to expose the falseness of unsound or exaggerated claims

New evidence has emerged that allows us to _____ a time-honored legend.

From the list of words on page 49, choose the one that best completes each of the following sentences. Write the word in the space provided.

1. The rescue team made one last, _____ attempt to save the people still trapped in the sinking ship.

2. On the whole, I'd say that the new program's good points far outweigh its _____.

3. When my boss became ill, many of the duties and responsibilities of his job suddenly _____ upon me.

4. When the debtor failed to repay the loan in a timely manner, the bank was forced to declare him in _____.

5. Scores of those condemned to death by the French revolutionary tribunals were _____ by the guillotine.

6. Over the years, historians have _____ many of the famous stories associated with George Washington because they have no basis in fact.

7. After we had lost the championship game by one point, we returned to the locker room in a state of profound _____.

8. Posing as investment counselors, the wily swindlers managed to _____ the elderly couple of most of their savings.

---

*Circle the **boldface** word that more satisfactorily completes each of the following sentences.*

1. Most working parents who would share their personal stories could easily (**debunk, devolve**) the myth that it's easy to have it all.

2. After spending hours customizing my computer display to fit my exacting standards, I accidentally engaged the (**desperate, default**) settings and wound up back where I started.

3. Although the brilliant student was full of potential, the major (**depression, demerit**) for failing to complete her senior project blocked her graduation.

4. After all conventional approaches to curing her illness failed, she felt (**desperate, defrauded**) and decided to take part in experimental clinical trials of new medications.

5. In 1536, King Henry VIII ordered his wife Anne Boleyn to be (**decapitated, defaulted**) as the ultimate punishment for treason.

6. The corrupt official attempted to (**defraud, debunk**) the city when she claimed certain personal expenses were business expenses.

7. Meteor Crater is a deep (**demerit, depression**) in northern Arizona formed about 50,000 years ago when a meteorite crashed into the earth's surface.

8. During flu season, the job of music teacher (**devolved, decapitated**) to the janitor, who was able to reveal his rich talent for singing.

Hear the words for this Unit pronounced, defined, and used in sentences at **www.vocabularyworkshop.com**.

UNIT 4

 **Definitions**

Note carefully the spelling, pronunciation, part(s) of speech, and definition(s) of each of the following words. Then write the word in the blank space(s) in the illustrative sentence(s) following. Finally, study the lists of synonyms and antonyms given at the end of each entry.

1. acquit
(ə kwit′)

(*v.*) to declare not guilty, free from blame, discharge completely; to conduct or behave oneself

Now that we have proof of their innocence, we can _____ them of all charges.

SYNONYMS: exonerate, dismiss
ANTONYMS: convict, declare guilty

2. deem
(dēm)

(*v.*) to think, believe; to consider, have an opinion

Most people _____ it a wise plan to set aside savings for the future.

SYNONYMS: judge, regard

3. devastate
(dev′ ə stāt)

(*v.*) to destroy, lay waste, leave in ruins

Failure or harsh criticism can _____ a person who has shaky self-esteem.

SYNONYMS: wreck, desolate
ANTONYMS: develop, improve

4. discredit
(dis kred′ it)

(*v.*) to throw doubt upon, cause to be distrusted; to damage in reputation; (*n.*) a loss or lack of belief, confidence, or reputation

We have gathered a considerable amount of evidence to

_____ her story.

Both parents and students felt strongly that the cheating scandal was a _____ to the school.

SYNONYM: (*v.*) disparage
ANTONYMS: (*v.*) confirm, corroborate, bolster

5. elusive
(ē lü′ siv)

(*adj.*) difficult to catch or to hold; hard to explain or understand

According to legend, Zorro, the heroic Mexican character, was too _____ for local police to capture.

SYNONYMS: slippery, wily, fleeting, puzzling, baffling

6. generate
(jen′ ə rāt)

(*v.*) to bring into existence; to be the cause of

Solar power uses the energy of the sun to _____ electricity.

SYNONYMS: create, produce, beget, cause
ANTONYMS: end, terminate, extinguish, stifle

7. idolize
(ī′ dəl īz)

(*v.*) to worship as an idol, make an idol of; to love very much

Teens who _____ a movie star may repeatedly see the same movie featuring that actor or actress.

SYNONYMS: adore, revere
ANTONYMS: despise, scorn, disdain, detest

8. ingratitude
(in grat′ ə tüd)

(*n.*) a lack of thankfulness

Hosts who make every effort to please their guests are apt to be hurt by _____.

SYNONYMS: thanklessness, ungratefulness
ANTONYMS: thankfulness, gratefulness, recognition

9. keepsake
(kēp′ sāk)

(*n.*) something kept in memory of the giver; a souvenir

Before my grandmother died, she made me a special quilt as a _____ of her love.

SYNONYMS: reminder, memento

10. mortal
(môr′ təl)

(*n.*) a being that must eventually die; (*adj.*) of or relating to such a being; causing death, fatal; possible, conceivable

In the mythology of many cultures, a heavenly god can come down to Earth and act as a _____.

The soldier was the only one in her battalion to suffer a _____ injury.

SYNONYMS: (*n.*) human; (*adj.*) fleeting, extreme
ANTONYMS: (*n.*) a god; (*adj.*) undying, everlasting, eternal, divine

11. ovation
(ō vā′ shən)

(*n.*) an enthusiastic public welcome, an outburst of applause

The audience gave the dancer a standing _____ after his impressive performance.

SYNONYMS: cheers, bravos, hurrahs
ANTONYMS: boos, jeers

12. petty
(pet′ ē)

(*adj.*) unimportant, trivial; narrow-minded; secondary in rank, minor

You say my complaint is _____, but to me it is an issue of great importance.

SYNONYMS: insignificant, piddling
ANTONYMS: important, major, significant, weighty

13. plight
(plīt)

(*n.*) a sorry condition or state; (*v.*) to pledge, promise solemnly

The _____ of the homeless upsets many concerned citizens.

Wedding guests watched the bride and groom _____ their undying love.

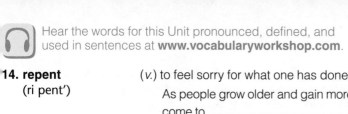
Hear the words for this Unit pronounced, defined, and used in sentences at **www.vocabularyworkshop.com**.

4

14. repent
(ri pent′)

(*v.*) to feel sorry for what one has done or has failed to do

As people grow older and gain more maturity, some of them come to _____ their youthful mistakes.

SYNONYM: regret
ANTONYMS: rejoice over

15. reverie
(rev′ ə rē)

(*n.*) a daydream; the condition of being lost in thought

My boss interrupted my deep and pleasant _____ by reminding me about our deadline.

SYNONYMS: fantasy, meditation

16. revocation
(rev ə kā′ shən)

(*n.*) an act or instance of calling back, an annulment, cancellation

His failure to complete the job according to schedule led to a _____ of his contract.

SYNONYMS: repeal, withdrawal
ANTONYMS: ratification, confirmation

17. scan
(skan)

(*v.*) to examine closely; to look over quickly but thoroughly; to analyze the rhythm of a poem; (*n.*) an examination

Let's _____ the list to see the finishing times of each marathon runner.

The doctor did a bone _____ to discover the location of each fracture.

SYNONYMS: (*v.*) study, glance at, skim; *(v., n.)* survey

18. strand
(strand)

(*n.*) a beach or shore; a string of wire, hair, etc.; (*v.*) to drive or run aground; to leave in a hopeless position

We asked the waiter to take back the soup when we discovered a _____ of hair in it.

I don't want to be the third out in the inning and _____ the two base runners.

SYNONYMS: (*n.*) fiber, thread; (*v.*) abandon, maroon
ANTONYMS: (*v.*) rescue, save

19. strife
(strīf)

(*n.*) bitter disagreement; fighting, struggle

The experienced senator from South Carolina was a veteran of political _____.

SYNONYMS: conflict, discord, turmoil
ANTONYMS: peace, calm, harmony, agreement

20. topple
(täp′ əl)

(v.) to fall forward; to overturn, bring about the downfall of

The trains that rumble past our apartment often cause books to _____ from the shelves.

SYNONYMS: unseat, upset, tumble
ANTONYMS: remain upright, establish, set up

Completing the Sentence

From the words for this unit, choose the one that best completes each of the following sentences. Write the word in the space provided.

1. Though that actress's name and face are all but forgotten today, she used to be _____ by adoring fans all over the world.

2. The hurricane so _____ a large section of the coast that the president declared it a disaster area.

3. I plan to save this old notebook as a(n) _____ of one of the best and most enjoyable classes I have ever had.

4. Since I sincerely appreciate all my parents have done for me, how can you accuse me of _____?

5. Because the members of my family disagree on so many matters, the dinner table is often the scene of much verbal _____.

6. The evidence against the accused man proved to be so weak that the jury had no choice but to _____ him.

7. I don't have the time to read every word of that long newspaper article, but I'll _____ it quickly to get the main idea.

8. Since it is clear that his only interest is to make money for himself, his plan for building a new highway has been completely _____.

9. The wound at first did not appear to be too serious, but to our great grief it proved to be _____.

10. Instead of telling us how much you _____ your outrageous conduct, why don't you sincerely try to reform?

11. Regardless of what you may think proper, I do not _____ it necessary for someone of your age to wear an evening gown to the dance.

12. The TV program made us keenly aware of the _____ of elderly people trying to live on Social Security payments.

13. Tom is not a very fast runner, but he is so _____ that he is extremely hard to tackle on the football field.

14. Why argue about such _____ matters when there are so many important problems to deal with?

15. The rope is made of many _____ of fiber woven together.

16. We learned that even unfavorable reviews of a new book may help to _____ a certain amount of public interest in it.

17. The defendant was warned that another speeding ticket would result in the _____ of her driver's license.

18. The sudden racket produced by a noisy car radio jolted me out of my peaceful

_____ .

19. The famous Leaning Tower of Pisa looks as though it were going to _____ over any minute.

20. She richly deserved the audience's _____ for her brilliant performance.

Synonyms

Choose the word from this unit that is **the same** or **most nearly the same** in meaning as the **boldface** word or expression in the given phrase. Write the word on the line provided.

1. argued for a **repeal** of the law

2. **pledge** to leave them all my worldly goods

3. too much **discord** to remain partners

4. to **maroon** them on a deserted island

5. may never **regret** his evil deeds

6. power to **wreck** an entire community

7. waved his cap to acknowledge the **cheers**

8. **study** the night sky for shooting stars

9. dim lights and soft music during my **meditation**

10. expect **thanklessness** from so selfish a person

11. for the computer to **produce** a list of dates

12. so **baffling** an idea to explain to children

13. to **regard** this as my best work so far

14. a **memento** of our trip to Canada

15. **damage** his standing within the group

Antonyms

Choose the word from this unit that is **most nearly opposite** in meaning to the **boldface** word or expression in the given phrase. Write the word on the line provided.

16. no choice but to **convict** the defendant

17. accused of a **major** offense

18. how they **disdain** their coach

19. **divine** beings, according to the legend

20. may **establish** the championship team

Choosing the Right Word

Circle the **boldface** word that more satisfactorily completes each of the following sentences.

1. Imagine his (**plight, ingratitude**)—penniless, unemployed, and with a large family to support!

2. After so many years of (**strife, strand**)—in business, politics, and the family—he wants only to retire to the peace and quiet of his ranch.

3. I knew that she was wrapped up in herself, but I never dreamed that even she could be guilty of such (**revocation, ingratitude**).

4. We should respect our national leaders, but we should not (**idolize, discredit**) them and assume that they can do no wrong.

5. A special edition of poems by the noted writer was presented as a (**keepsake, strife**) to all who attended her 80th birthday party.

6. What an (**ovation, reverie**) he received when he trotted back to the bench after scoring the winning touchdown!

7. In my composition, I tried to give a definition of "humor," but I found the idea too (**petty, elusive**) to pin down.

8. In Shakespeare's *A Midsummer Night's Dream*, which character speaks the line, "Lord, what fools these (**mortals, keepsakes**) be"?

9. Many diseases that have disappeared in the United States continue to (**devastate, idolize**) countries in other parts of the world.

10. Since you are the only one of us who has had experience with this kind of problem, we shall do whatever you (**deem, scan**) necessary.

11. Our business is barely managing to pay its bills; one bad break will be enough to (**acquit, topple**) it into bankruptcy.

12. Are we going to allow (**elusive, petty**) quarrels to destroy a friendship that has been built up for so many years?

13. We will never allow vicious rumors to (**deem, generate**) racial hatred in our school!

14. At times we all enjoy a(n) (**ovation, reverie**) about "what might have been," but before long we must return to "the way things are."

15. Once order had been restored, the leaders of the opposition called for the (**revocation, keepsake**) of martial law.

16. At times it is quite natural to feel afraid, and it is certainly no (**discredit, mortal**) to anyone to admit it.

17. While the actors were busy rehearsing, the manager ran away with all the money and left them (**stranded, plighted**) in a strange town.

18. By reelecting him to Congress, the court of public opinion has forever (**generated, acquitted**) him of the charges of neglecting his duties.

19. Father often says that he has never stopped (**repenting, devastating**) the decision he made many years ago to give up the study of medicine.

20. Our supervisor (**topples, scans**) the newspaper each morning for items that may serve as leads for the sales force.

Read the following passage, in which some of the words you have studied in this unit appear in **boldface** type. Then complete each statement given below the passage by circling the letter of the item that is **the same** or **almost the same** in meaning as the highlighted word.

Quimby's Quest

(Line)

In May of 1911, a young pilot from Long Island's Moisant Avenue Aviation School was practicing flying. When a gust of wind blew back the person's veil, onlookers realized that the pilot was *not* a man! It was journalist Harriet Quimby. How did this plucky reporter **acquit herself** so successfully in such a dangerous new field?

(5)   Flying was risky for anyone at that time. Just eight years earlier, the success of the Wright Brothers' flight at Kitty Hawk, North Carolina, **generated** new goals for adventurers. Pioneering pilots **deemed** flying as the greatest challenge of the day. Determined not to let her gender hold her back, Harriet

(10) Quimby started to take flying lessons.

Quimby earned her pilot's license on August 1, 1911, making her the world's second woman—and the first American woman—to do so. Dressed in a flight suit of

(15) purple satin, she gave flying demonstrations around the United States and Mexico.

Quimby was the first pilot ever to cross the English Channel. Nowadays, it may be easy to **discredit** this accomplishment since some

(20) people actually swim the 32 miles of water that separates England from France. Yet, in Quimby's time, people had little knowledge of

Today women pilot all types of aircraft.

flying or of predicting weather. She was lucky to get through the clouds that day to land safely, though way off course. Imagine

(25) the shock French fishermen must have felt when they **scanned** the horizon to see a flying machine headed for their beach!

Less than a year after Harriet Quimby became a pilot, she suffered **mortal** injuries when she and a passenger were suddenly thrown from their seats, falling nearly a mile to their deaths in the waters near Boston. The world lost a

(30) legendary pioneer.

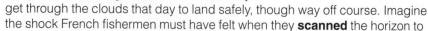

1. The meaning of **acquit herself** (line 4) is
  a. behave
  b. steer
  c. react
  d. gamble

2. The meaning of **generated** (line 6) is
  a. stifled
  b. described
  c. created
  d. promised

3. Deemed (line 7) most nearly means
  a. feared
  b. ignored
  c. chose
  d. considered

4. Discredit (line 19) most nearly means
  a. explain
  b. disparage
  c. ignore
  d. honor

5. Scanned (line 25) is best defined as
  a. raced
  b. ran from
  c. glanced at
  d. avoided

6. Mortal (line 27) is best defined as
  a. fatal
  b. minor
  c. divine
  d. major

UNIT 5

Hear the words for this Unit pronounced, defined, and used in sentences at **www.vocabularyworkshop.com**.

Definitions

Note carefully the spelling, pronunciation, part(s) of speech, and definition(s) of each of the following words. Then write the word in the blank space(s) in the illustrative sentence(s) following. Finally, study the lists of synonyms and antonyms given at the end of each entry.

1. acute
(ə kyüt′)

(*adj.*) with a sharp point; keen and alert; sharp and severe; rising quickly to a high point and lasting for a short time

One who is an _____ observer of human nature may notice subtle changes in people's behavior.

SYNONYMS: clever, penetrating
ANTONYMS: dull, blunted, mild, stupid, obtuse

2. bluster
(bləs′ tər)

(*v.*) to talk or act in a noisy and threatening way; to blow in stormy gusts; (*n.*) speech that is loud and threatening

When we saw harsh winds _____ around our tent, we decided to change our plans for the weekend.

Dad's manner is all _____, but beneath it all, he's really a kind-hearted man.

SYNONYMS: (*v.*) spout, rant, brag, swagger; (*n.*) bravado

3. bungle
(bəŋ′ gəl)

(*v.*) to act or work clumsily and awkwardly; to ruin something through clumsiness

If we _____ this project, we may never get another chance to prove ourselves as a worthy team.

SYNONYMS: blunder, botch, mess up

4. commentary
(käm′ ən ter ē)

(*n.*) a series of notes clarifying or explaining something; an expression of opinion

Our spiritual leader gave us a helpful _____ on the true meaning of the Ten Commandments.

SYNONYMS: explanation, remarks, narration, description, account, review, analysis

5. duration
(dù rā′ shən)

(*n.*) the length of time that something continues or lasts

Even though the story was hard to follow, my friends decided to stay for the _____ of the opera.

6. eerie
(ē′ rē)

(*adj.*) causing fear because of strangeness; weird, mysterious

It is a lot of fun to tell _____ ghost stories around a campfire.

SYNONYMS: frightening, spooky, creepy

Hear the words for this Unit pronounced, defined, and used in sentences at **www.vocabularyworkshop.com**.

5

7. facet
(fas′ ət)

(*n.*) one aspect or side of a subject or problem; one of the cut surfaces of a gem

One important _____ of problem solving is to recognize when a solution makes no sense.

SYNONYMS: angle, characteristic, factor, element, cut

8. fidelity
(fi del′ ə tē)

(*n.*) the state of being faithful; accuracy in details, exactness

The _____ of scratchy old records can't match the clarity of CDs or DVDs.

SYNONYMS: loyalty, faithfulness
ANTONYMS: disloyalty, treachery, inexactness

9. fray
(frā)

(*n.*) a brawl, a noisy quarrel; (*v.*) to wear away by rubbing; make ragged or worn; to strain, irritate

After the two loudest students began arguing, the whole class jumped into the _____.

A faucet that drips continuously can _____ anyone's nerves.

SYNONYMS: (*n.*) scuffle; (*v.*) unravel

10. headstrong
(hed′ strôŋ)

(*adj.*) willful, stubborn

Even the most patient caregiver may feel challenged when faced with a _____ child.

SYNONYMS: obstinate, mulish, unruly
ANTONYMS: obedient, docile, submissive

11. inhabitant
(in hab′ ə tənt)

(*n.*) one living permanently in a given place

Although she enjoys traveling to exotic places, she's a lifelong _____ of this small town.

SYNONYMS: resident, native, occupant, tenant
ANTONYMS: stranger, outsider, visitor, foreigner

12. numb
(nəm)

(*adj.*) having lost the power of feeling or movement; (*v.*) to dull the feelings of; to cause to lose feeling

Bitter cold may leave your toes _____, so try to wear woolen socks.

This injection will _____ the area so that the doctor can stitch the cut painlessly.

SYNONYMS: (*adj.*) unfeeling, insensible, dazed; (*v.*) deaden
ANTONYMS: (*adj.*) sensitive, alert

13. pacify
(pas′ ə fī)

(*v.*) to make peaceful or calm; to soothe

The factory owners hope to _____ the angry protesters with promises of higher wages and shorter working hours.

SYNONYMS: mollify, placate
ANTONYMS: anger, arouse, stir up, foment, ignite

14. ravenous
(rav′ ə nəs)

(*adj.*) greedy; very hungry; eager for satisfaction

Exercising vigorously for several hours gives me a
_____ appetite.

SYNONYMS: starved, famished, voracious, wolfish
ANTONYMS: not hungry, well-fed, satisfied, satiated

15. refute
(ri fyüt′)

(*v.*) to prove incorrect

After analyzing the situation, I now know a foolproof way to
_____ the original claim.

SYNONYMS: disprove, rebut
ANTONYMS: prove, support, confirm, corroborate

16. remorse
(ri mors′)

(*n.*) deep and painful regret for one's past misdeeds; pangs of conscience

When the driver realized what a terrible accident he had
caused, he was overcome with _____.

SYNONYM: guilt
ANTONYMS: clear conscience, guiltlessness

17. setback
(set′ bak)

(*n.*) something that interferes with progress; a disappointment, unexpected loss or defeat; a steplike recession in a wall

A broken toe can be a major _____
for a skater who hopes to qualify for the Olympics.

SYNONYMS: failure, reversal
ANTONYMS: advance, gain, progress, triumph

18. smug
(sməg)

(*adj.*) overly self-satisfied, self-righteous

Just because he got the lead in the school play doesn't
justify his irritating air of _____
superiority.

SYNONYMS: conceited, complacent
ANTONYMS: discontented, disgruntled

19. synopsis
(si näp′ sis)

(*n.*) a brief statement giving a general view of some subject, book, etc.; a summary

The teacher's guide gives a _____
of the plot of each story in the collection.

SYNONYMS: outline, digest, abstract

20. tarry
(tar′ ē)

(*v.*) to delay leaving; to linger, wait; to remain or stay for a while

He will be tempted to _____
longer if he thinks that this might be their last visit together.

SYNONYMS: dawdle, dally
ANTONYMS: rush, hasten, leave, depart

Completing the Sentence

From the words for this unit, choose the one that best completes each of the following sentences. Write the word in the space provided.

1. By _____ in a loud, confident voice, he tried to convince us that he had nothing to do with the accident.

2. The program contained a(n) _____ of the opera, so that we were able to follow the action even though the singing was in Italian.

3. No one can question her complete _____ to basic American ideas and ideals.

4. His _____ expression showed how highly he valued his own opinions and scorned the views of others.

5. Some children are as docile as sheep; others are as _____ as mules.

6. Our team suffered a tough _____ when our best player was hurt in the first few minutes of play.

7. Because of our inexperience and haste, we _____ the little repair job so badly that it became necessary to replace the entire motor.

8. Is it true that the _____ of Maine are sometimes called "Mainiacs"?

9. We had eaten only a light breakfast before hiking for hours in the crisp mountain air, so you can imagine how _____ we were by lunchtime.

10. Since the convicted felon had shown no _____ for his crimes, the judge sentenced him to the maximum prison term allowed.

11. Anyone who has never had a sprained ankle will find it hard to imagine how _____ the pain is.

12. After the dentist gave me an injection of novocaine, the whole side of my jaw turned _____.

13. I had a(n) _____ feeling that we were being followed and that something bad might happen.

14. The accused person must be given every chance to _____ the charges against him or her.

15. Because I _____ at the book fair, I was ten minutes late for my piano lesson.

16. When my two sisters began their bitter quarrel, only Mother had enough nerve to enter the _____ and tell them to stop.

17. Although the rain was heavy, it was of such short _____ that it didn't interfere with our plans.

18. Do you think it is a good idea to try to _____ the weeping child by giving her a lollipop?

19. Warmth and understanding are two outstanding _____ of her personality.

20. The newscaster on my favorite TV program not only tells the facts of the news but offers a(n) _____ that helps us to understand it.

Synonyms

*Choose the word from this unit that is **the same** or **most nearly the same** in meaning as the **boldface** word or expression in the given phrase. Write the word on the line provided.*

1. reflected off the **cuts** of the diamond _____

2. shock that left them **dazed** and speechless _____

3. lip-smacking sounds of the **voracious** eaters _____

4. to endure yet another **reversal** _____

5. always **dawdle** over juice and doughnuts _____

6. after they **botched** the paint job _____

7. offer a brief **outline** of the plan _____

8. flashing that **conceited** grin of hers _____

9. gave some **remarks** after the speech _____

10. no sense of **guilt** for what happened _____

11. began to **unravel** at the cuffs _____

12. the cause of such **bravado** _____

13. what it's like to be **occupants** of a houseboat _____

14. decided to stay for the **length** of the party _____

15. at the **frightening** howl of a lone wolf _____

Antonyms

*Choose the word from this unit that is **most nearly opposite** in meaning to the **boldface** word or expression in the given phrase. Write the word on the line provided.*

16. discussions with the **submissive** guide _____

17. could never **support** their opinion _____

18. the perfect medication for my **mild** headache _____

19. tried to **arouse** the crowd _____

20. the reasons for their **disloyalty** _____

Choosing the Right Word

*Circle the **boldface** word that more satisfactorily completes each of the following sentences.*

1. With a winter storm (**blustering, bungling**) outside, what could be more welcome than a warm room, a good meal, and my favorite TV program?

2. The idea that most people usually behave in a calm and reasonable way is (**refuted, numbed**) by all the facts of history.

3. We cannot assume that all the people that one sees on the streets of a large city are actually (**facets, inhabitants**) of the place.

4. There is so much wear and tear on the ropes in this pulley system that they become (**frayed, refuted**) in only a few days.

5. On the camping trip out West some of the children were frightened when they first heard the (**smug, eerie**) howls of coyotes at night.

6. "It's your job to help (**pacify, fray**) the conquered area," the general said, "not to add fuel to an already explosive situation."

7. The victims of the disaster were so (**numbed, tarried**) by the scope of the tragedy that they scarcely showed any emotion at all.

8. When I realized how deeply I had hurt my friend with my careless insult, I suffered a pang of (**remorse, duration**).

9. I keep telling you things for your own good, but you're just too (**eerie, headstrong**) to listen.

10. We know that we are going through a period of economic instability, but there is no way of telling what its (**duration, remorse**) will be.

11. If you read no more than a(n) (**inhabitant, synopsis**) of the plot of any one of Shakespeare's plays, you will get very little idea of what it is all about.

12. Each time she answered a question correctly, she rewarded herself with a (**smug, ravenous**) little smile of self-congratulation.

13. After the way you (**bungled, blustered**) the job of arranging the class trip, I can never again trust you with anything important.

14. The strength of this book lies in the author's ability to describe and explain different (**setbacks, facets**) of human experience.

15. Since it had seemed that winter would (**tarry, pacify**) forever, we were all heartily glad when it finally quit dragging its heels and departed.

16. Florence's illness, after she had been chosen for the leading role in the class show, was a serious (**setback, commentary**) to our plans.

17. The character Scrooge in Charles Dickens's *A Christmas Carol* starts out as a(n) (**acute, ravenous**) miser, but he undergoes a great change.

18. Although I don't agree with all her ideas, I must admire her unshakable (**fidelity, synopsis**) to them.

19. His (**headstrong, acute**) analysis of the housing problem in our town gave us a clear idea of what we would have to overcome.

20. The fact that so many people are still living in poverty is indeed a sad (**fidelity, commentary**) on our civilization.

*Read the following passage, in which some of the words you have studied in this unit appear in **boldface** type. Then complete each statement given below the passage by circling the letter of the item that is **the same** or **almost the same** in meaning as the highlighted word.*

An Olympic Star

(Line)

James Cleveland Owens had always been called J. C. In 1922, his family left their farm in Alabama to become **inhabitants** of Ohio. His **acute** Southern accent must have confused his new teacher, who thought that his name was "Jesse." The new name stuck. And by 1936, everyone knew Jesse Owens, who had become a real-life legend. (5)

Owens was a sickly child, but poor health during his early years proved not to be a **setback**. As he grew, so did his speed and strength. Owens developed a

talent for running and jumping. Record-breaking successes in high school and college track and field prepared him for the (10) 1936 Olympic Games, which were held in Berlin, Germany, where Adolf Hitler's Nazi Party was in control. Owens won four gold medals for the U.S.—the most won by any single Olympic athlete at that time. (15)

To this day, many consider Owens' performance at the 1936 Olympics to be the greatest moment in all Olympic history. He was never **smug** about his successes and continued to inspire others for the **duration** (20) of his life. There were many **facets** to Owens' accomplishments. After the Olympics he traveled the world to promote the importance of sports for young people. He started the Jesse Owens Games, a playground sports (25) event for children through age 15. The Jesse

Jesse Owens, on his way to winning four Olympic gold medals in Berlin, 1936

Owens Foundation continues to grant scholarships to young people who can't afford college. Since Jesse Owens' impact endures even today, it is fitting that in 1990, he posthumously received a fifth gold medal—the Congressional Gold Medal—to honor his humanitarian contributions. (30)

1. Inhabitants (line 2) is best defined as
a. farmers
b. teachers
c. residents
d. workers

2. The meaning of **acute** (line 2) is
a. cute
b. mild
c. sharp
d. annoying

3. Setback (line 7) most nearly means
a. illness
b. medicine
c. impediment
d. sport

4. The meaning of **smug** (line 19) is
a. happy
b. satisfied
c. discontented
d. conceited

5. Duration (line 20) most nearly means
a. beginning
b. end
c. length
d. story

6. Facets (line 21) is best defined as
a. aspects
b. demands
c. locations
d. obstacles

64 ■ Unit 5

Hear the words for this Unit pronounced, defined, and used in sentences at **www.vocabularyworkshop.com**.

UNIT 6

Definitions

Note carefully the spelling, pronunciation, part(s) of speech, and definition(s) of each of the following words. Then write the word in the blank space(s) in the illustrative sentence(s) following. Finally, study the lists of synonyms and antonyms given at the end of each entry.

1. agenda
(ə jen′ də)

(*n.*) the program for a meeting; a list, outline, or plan of things to be considered or done

The _____ for today's assembly includes a plan for recycling in the classroom.

SYNONYMS: schedule, docket

2. amiable
(ā′ mē ə bəl)

(*adj.*) friendly, good-natured

Marty, whose sense of humor and good spirits never fail, is an _____ companion.

SYNONYMS: pleasant, agreeable
ANTONYMS: unfriendly, ill-humored, gruff, hostile

3. befuddle
(bi fəd′ əl)

(*v.*) to confuse, make stupid

A difficult scientific experiment with many steps is likely to _____ most beginners.

SYNONYMS: bewilder, boggle, stupefy
ANTONYMS: enlighten, set straight

4. blight
(blīt)

(*n.*) a disease that causes plants to wither and die; a condition of disease or ruin; (*v.*) to destroy, ruin

Dutch elm disease was a _____ that forever changed the look of my neighborhood.

Though she received several letters of rejection, she determined not to let them _____ her hopes of going to college.

SYNONYMS: (*n.*) eyesore; (*v.*) spoil, nip
ANTONYMS: (*v.*) foster, promote, nourish, encourage

5. boisterous
(boi′ strəs)

(*adj.*) rough and noisy in a cheerful way; high-spirited

The _____ schoolchildren made it clear to their teacher how much they enjoyed the class trip.

SYNONYMS: loud, unruly, disorderly
ANTONYMS: quiet, calm, peaceful, well-behaved, sedate

6. clarity
(klar′ ə tē)

(*n.*) clearness, accuracy

The vet explained with great _____ how best to housebreak our new puppy.

SYNONYMS: lucidity, precision
ANTONYMS: confusion, murkiness, ambiguity

7. compliant
(kəm plī' ənt)

(*adj.*) willing to do what someone else wants; obedient

A _____ child is easy to discipline, even when in an unfamiliar environment.

SYNONYMS: meek, docile, submissive
ANTONYMS: disobedient, obstinate, rebellious, perverse

8. conserve
(kən sərv')

(*v.*) to preserve; to keep from being damaged, lost, or wasted; to save

Responsible citizens try to _____ our precious natural resources.

SYNONYMS: guard, care for
ANTONYMS: waste, squander, dissipate

9. debut
(dā' byü)

(*n.*) a first public appearance; a formal entrance into society; (*v.*) to make a first appearance

The talented flute player in the marching band finally made her _____ as a soloist today.

Many theaters will _____ the film tonight.

SYNONYM: (*n.*) coming-out
ANTONYMS: (*n.*) retirement, departure

10. gory
(gôr' ē)

(*adj.*) marked by bloodshed, slaughter, or violence

The Civil War battle of Antietam is, to this day, the most _____ one-day fight in our history.

SYNONYMS: bloody, gruesome
ANTONYM: bloodless

11. gross
(grōs)

(*adj.*) overweight; coarse, vulgar; very noticeable; total; (*n.*) an overall total (without deductions); twelve dozen; (*v.*) to earn

They responded to the _____ injustice in an unsatisfactory manner.

A _____ of pencils lasts all year.

She expects to _____ $3000 in tips.

SYNONYMS: (*adj.*) fat, sheer, utter, flagrant
ANTONYMS: (*adj.*) slender, thin, delicate, fine, partial; (*n., v.*) net

12. induce
(in düs')

(*v.*) to cause, bring about; to persuade

Can drinking warm milk _____ sleep?

SYNONYMS: prevail upon, influence
ANTONYMS: prevent, deter, hinder

13. leeway
(lē' wā)

(*n.*) extra space for moving along a certain route; allowance for mistakes or inaccuracies; margin of error

Experienced planners allow _____ of a week or so in case a project runs into snags or delays.

SYNONYMS: latitude, elbow room

Hear the words for this Unit pronounced, defined, and used in sentences at **www.vocabularyworkshop.com**.

6

4. limber
(lim′ bər)

(*adj.*) flexible; (*v.*) to cause to become flexible

Dancers work hard to develop _____ bodies.

Runners _____ up before a race.

SYNONYMS: (*adj.*) supple, pliable; (*v.*) stretch
ANTONYMS: (*adj.*) stiff, rigid, wooden; (*v.*) stiffen

5. maze
(māz)

(*n.*) a network of paths through which it is hard to find one's way; something very mixed-up and confusing

Ancient Rome was a _____ of narrow streets and winding alleys.

SYNONYMS: labyrinth, puzzle, tangle

6. oracle
(ôr′ ə kəl)

(*n.*) someone or something that can predict the future

According to Greek legend, people sought prophecy at the great _____ at Delphi.

SYNONYMS: prophet, seer, sibyl

7. partisan
(pärt′ ə zən)

(*n.*) a strong supporter of a person, party, or cause; one whose support is unreasoning; a resistance fighter, guerrilla; (*adj.*) strongly supporting one side only

That mayoral candidate is a strong _____ of term limits.

_____ hometown fans can be hostile to those from out of town.

SYNONYMS: (*n.*) fan, booster; (*adj.*) partial, biased
ANTONYMS: (*n.*) critic, foe; (*adj.*) impartial, neutral

8. reimburse
(rē im bərs′)

(*v.*) to pay back; to give payment for

When Mom goes on business trips, she records the cost of hotels and meals so her company will _____ her.

SYNONYMS: repay, refund, compensate

9. vacate
(vā′ kāt)

(*v.*) to go away from, leave empty; to make empty; to void, annul

We have a lot of cleaning up to do before we _____ the apartment at the end of the month.

SYNONYMS: depart, give up, abandon
ANTONYMS: occupy, keep, hold, hang on to

10. vagabond
(vag′ ə bänd)

(*n.*) an idle wanderer; a tramp; (*adj.*) wandering; irresponsible

The _____ carried his few belongings in a shabby cardboard suitcase.

The _____ life interests some people, but it doesn't appeal to me.

SYNONYMS: (*n.*) vagrant, hobo; (*adj.*) unsettled, footloose
ANTONYMS: (*n.*) homebody, resident; (*adj.*) settled

*From the words for this unit, choose the one that best
completes each of the following sentences. Write the
word in the space provided.*

1. Why do you always ask me what's going to happen? I'm no _____!

2. For years, his restless spirit led him to wander the highways and byways of this great
land like any other footloose _____.

3. If you would be kind enough to buy a loose-leaf notebook for me while you are in the
stationery store, I'll _____ you immediately.

4. The crowd is so _____ that the umpire is booed every time he
makes a decision against the home team.

5. Trying to untangle a badly snarled fishing line is like trying to find one's way through
a(n) _____.

6. Because our energy resources are limited, the American people must try to do
everything possible to _____ fuel.

7. Each of the items on the _____ for our meeting today will probably
require a good deal of discussion.

8. Ms. Fillmer explained with such _____ how to go about changing
a tire that I felt that even someone as clumsy as I could do it.

9. I was not prepared for the _____ sight that met my eyes at the
scene of that horrible massacre.

10. The high standard of excellence that the woman had set for herself left her no
_____ for mistakes.

11. None of us could possibly overlook the _____ error that the waiter
had made in adding up our check.

12. No matter what you may say, you cannot _____ me to do
something that I know is wrong.

13. The high point of the social season was the formal _____ of young
ladies at the annual Society Ball.

14. Before the game starts, the players _____ up by doing a few deep
knee bends, sit-ups, and other exercises.

15. If the Superintendent of Schools should _____ his position by
resigning, the Mayor has the right to name someone else to the job.

16. Because of her outgoing and _____ personality, she is liked by
everyone.

17. How can a mind _____ by alcohol make the type of snap
decisions needed to drive safely in heavy traffic?

18. You certainly have a right to cheer for your team, but try not to become too
_____ and unruly.

19. We cannot allow the lives of millions of people to be _____ by
poverty.

20. Because you are working with older and more experienced people, you should be
_____ with their requests and advice.

Synonyms

*Choose the word from this unit that is **the same** or **most nearly the same** in meaning as the **boldface** word or expression in the given phrase. Write the word on the line provided.*

1. offended by that **flagrant** insult _____

2. **persuade** them to speak softly _____

3. an **eyesore** hidden behind thick shrubs _____

4. when he saw the **gruesome** spectacle _____

5. can't rely on their **biased** viewpoint _____

6. had never consulted the **prophet** before _____

7. following a **tangle** of clues _____

8. enough **latitude** for a beginner to succeed _____

9. no choice but to **depart** the cabin _____

0. known for being a **docile** pet _____

1. **compensate** you for your time _____

2. directions written with **precision** _____

3. a **hobo** who hopped freight trains _____

4. publishes the **schedule** a week in advance _____

5. for her **coming-out** party at the country club _____

Antonyms

*Choose the word from this unit that is **most nearly opposite** in meaning to the **boldface** word or expression in the given phrase. Write the word on the line provided.*

6. a **sedate** group of bikers _____

7. to **squander** our limited food supplies _____

8. the guitar player's **rigid** fingers _____

9. **enlighten** us with new passwords and commands _____

0. socializing with our **gruff** neighbors _____

Choosing the Right Word

*Circle the **boldface** word that more satisfactorily completes each of the following sentences.*

1. Poland received top priority on Adolf Hitler's (**agenda, maze**) of military conquests in the fall of 1939.

2. Students must take many required courses, but they also have a little (**oracle, leeway**) to choose courses that they find especially interesting.

3. At the end of the long series of discussions and arguments, we felt that we were trapped in a (**blight, maze**) of conflicting ideas and plans.

4. This matter is so important to all the people of the community that we must forget (**partisan, boisterous**) politics and work together.

5. What I thought was going to be a(n) (**amiable, vagabond**) little chat with my boss soon turned into a real argument.

6. One of the biggest problems facing the United States today is how to stop the (**blight, agenda**) that is creeping over large parts of our great cities.

7. Since he is an expert gymnast and works out every day, his body has remained as (**limber, gory**) as that of a boy.

8. Because she is usually so (**compliant, partisan**), we were all surprised when she said that she didn't like our plans and wouldn't accept them.

9. Over the years, so many of the columnist's predictions have come true that he is now looked on as something of a(n) (**debut, oracle**).

10. As we moved higher up the mountain, I was overcome by dizziness and fatigue (**induced, grossed**) by the thin air.

11. In her graphic description of the most gruesome scenes in the horror film, Maria left out none of the (**amiable, gory**) details.

12. After all the deductions had been made from my (**gross, limber**) salary, the sum that remained seemed pitifully small.

13. Many a student dreams about spending a (**vagabond, partisan**) year idly hitchhiking through Europe.

14. The disc jockey promised to (**vacate, debut**) the band's long-awaited new CD as soon as it was released by the recording company.

15. An experienced backpacker can give you many useful suggestions for (**befuddling, conserving**) energy on a long, tough hike.

16. The landlord ordered all tenants to (**vacate, reimburse**) the premises by noon.

17. Don't let the (**clarity, leeway**) of the water fool you into supposing that it's safe for drinking.

18. Mr. Roth, the librarian, cracks down hard on (**compliant, boisterous**) students.

19. If you want to get a clear picture of just what went wrong, you must not (**induce, befuddle**) your mind with all kinds of wild rumors.

20. I will feel fully (**reimbursed, conserved**) for all that I have done for her if I can see her in good health again.

Vocabulary in Context

*Read the following passage, in which some of the words you have studied in this unit appear in **boldface** type. Then complete each statement given below the passage by circling the letter of the item that is **the same** or **almost the same** in meaning as the highlighted word.*

ine)

Send in the Clowns

Do you have a good sense of humor and enjoy working with people? Do you have an **amiable** disposition? Can your behavior be characterized as **boisterous**? Are you ready to learn to juggle, paint your
face, and sculpt balloons? If so, you might
5) have what it takes to become a clown.

The art of clowning has been around for
centuries. A clown performed as a jester in
Pharaoh's court during Egypt's Fifth Dynasty,
about 2500 B.C. Court jesters have performed
0) in China since 1818 B.C. Clowns who
performed as court jesters were often the only
ones allowed to speak against the ruler's
policies. The fools in Shakespeare's plays were
often the ones with the smartest things to say!

15) There are three basic types of clowns.
Whiteface clowns cover their face with white
makeup and then use different colors to
highlight their facial features. They try to look
like dolls who have come to life. *Auguste*
20) clowns are more human looking; their base
makeup is a fleshy tone, but they exaggerate
their facial features with additional makeup.

A full wig and sociable nature contribute to the appeal of this *Auguste* clown.

Their hair is often wild, and they wear brightly
colored, mismatched, and oversized clothes. The *character* clown is a third type.
25) This type is often a tramp or a hobo, a **vagabond** down on his or her luck. Makeup
is flesh-based with gray tones to simulate dirt and tears.

Clowns may seem clumsy and **befuddled**, but good clowning requires a **limber**
body and quick mind. Clown antics are like well-tuned gymnastics or dance routines,
which often don't allow **leeway** for mistakes. They demand strong muscles and great
30) timing. Without advanced preparation, clowns could get injured. Worse, they might
not be the least bit funny!

The meaning of **amiable** (line 2) is
a. strict   c. agreeable
b. peaceful   d. hostile

Boisterous (line 2) most nearly means
a. ridiculous   c. peaceful
b. nervous   d. high-spirited

Vagabond (line 25) is best defined as
a. person   c. employee
b. student   d. vagrant

4. The meaning of **befuddled** (line 27) is
a. confused   c. innocent
b. enlightened   d. silly

5. Limber (line 27) most nearly means
a. wooden   c. trained
b. flexible   d. quick

6. Leeway (line 29) is best defined as
a. excuse   c. rules
b. latitude   d. witness

Vocabulary for Comprehension

*Read the following passage, in which some of the words you have studied in Units 4–6 appear in **boldface** type. Then answer questions 1–12 on page 73 on the basis of what is stated or implied in the passage and in the introductory statement.*

Oseola McCarty, the subject of this passage, led a simple life but managed to amass a fortune and make an amazing contribution to others.

(Line)

Oseola McCarty left school after sixth grade to help care for ailing relatives. She was sorry not to be able to continue her education, but (5) her family needed her. Pursuing an education was an **elusive** dream to this lifelong **inhabitant** of Mississippi. She eked out a living washing and ironing other people's clothing. She (10) lived most of her life in a small house her uncle had once owned.

For seventy-five years, Oseola McCarty served her customers. She walked wherever she had to go. She (15) earned little money yet managed to put aside a small amount almost every week. She knew it was wise to plan for the future.

Oseola McCarty never felt right (20) about taking money out of her bank account. The money she put into the bank earned interest. What must have seemed like **petty** deposits of nickels and dimes eventually grew into a (25) fortune. By the time McCarty was 87, she had nearly $300,000! McCarty's dreams of education had never faded. She knew she was too old to attend college but felt no **remorse** (30) about her life. Instead she thought of an **agenda** to help others attend college. She gave $150,000 of her life's savings to the University of

Southern Mississippi. Suddenly, an (35) elderly laundry woman was a local hero! Oseola McCarty's generosity touched people. Many were moved to make their own contributions to increase the Oseola McCarty (40) Scholarship Fund.

Although she was finally rich, McCarty remained a straightforward, honest, and humble person. Her **commentaries** on life were right to (45) the point. "If you want to feel proud of yourself," she once said, "you've got to do things you can be proud of." When McCarty died at the age of 9, people throughout the United States (50) remembered her with pride and admiration.

. The author's primary purpose in the passage is to
a. persuade the reader to stay in school
b. persuade the reader to save money
c. persuade the reader to help others
d. tell an inspirational true story
e. tell an inspirational fictional story

. The meaning of **elusive** (line 6) is
a. passionate
b. steady
c. magical
d. cherished
e. fleeting

. **Inhabitant** (line 7) most nearly means
a. visitor
b. worker
c. student
d. resident
e. fan

. From paragraph 2 (lines 12–18), we can infer that Oseola McCarty was all of the following EXCEPT
a. frugal
b. hard-working
c. nervous
d. independent
e. humble

. **Petty** (line 23) is best defined as
a. insignificant
b. major
c. sensible
d. narrow-minded
e. regular

. The meaning of **remorse** (line 29) is
a. sympathy
b. failure
c. confusion
d. responsibility
e. regret

. **Agenda** (line 31) most nearly means
a. plan
b. dream
c. scheme
d. contest
e. way

8. Which of the following sayings best describes how McCarty amassed her wealth?
a. Slow and steady wins the race.
b. Here today, gone tomorrow.
c. Out of sight, out of mind.
d. Live only in the here and now.
e. Eat, drink, and be merry, for tomorrow we may die.

9. Who started the Oseola McCarty Scholarship Fund?
a. the University of Southern Mississippi
b. Oseola McCarty
c. Oseola's students
d. Oseola's relatives
e. Oseola's employers

10. Commentaries (line 44) is best defined as
a. writings
b. anecdotes
c. remarks
d. keepsakes
e. ideas

11. Which word best describes the author's attitude toward the subject of this passage?
a. disbelief
b. criticism
c. amusement
d. respect
e. pity

12. Which of the following is a generalization the author would most likely agree with?
a. The most important thing in life is a college education.
b. One person can make a big difference in the lives of others.
c. Without an education, a person is permanently handicapped.
d. You do not have to save money for a rainy day. Someone will always help you.
e. Live as if today is your last day on Earth.

Grammar in Context

In the sentence "Pursuing an education was an elusive dream to this lifelong inhabitant of Mississippi" (lines 5–7), the author of the passage on page 72 has made sure that the **singular subject** "Pursuing an education" has the **singular verb** "was." There are two basic rules of **subject-verb agreement**: A singular subject must have a singular verb. A **plural subject** must have a **plural verb**.

All verbs must agree with their subjects even when other words come between them. Verbs must agree with compound subjects (linked by *and*, *or*, or *nor*) and with subjects that are collective nouns (such as *team* and *class*). They must agree with indefinite pronouns (such as *each*, *anyone*, and *several*), with nouns that are singular in meaning although plural in form (such as *acoustics* and *politics*), and with measurements or amounts. Verbs also must agree with their subjects when those subjects are confusing, as is the case when the subject follows the verb in a sentence.

Choose the verb in parentheses that agrees with the subject of each sentence, and write it on the line provided.

1. Most would agree that getting a good education (**is, are**) very important.

_____

2. Three hundred thousand dollars (**was, were**) the amount of money she had saved.

_____

3. Neither my grandfather nor my grandmother (**has, have**) been to college.

_____

4. Many students at the university (**has, have**) Oseola McCarty to thank for their education.

_____

5. Many people (**gets, get**) pleasure and satisfaction from helping or caring for others.

_____

6. The charity I contribute to (**provides, provide**) money to soup kitchens and shelters for the homeless.

_____

7. A monument to the founder of the college (**stands, stand**) near the entrance to the campus.

_____

8. Her caring and her generosity (**reaches, reach**) the people who need help the most.

_____

Two-Word Completions

Circle the pair of words that best complete the meaning of each of the following passages.

1. In the third century, bands of savage barbarians repeatedly broke through the frontier defenses of the Roman province of Gaul, _____ the countryside with fire and sword, and either slew or carried off the _____.
a. scanned . . . partisans
b. pacified . . . vagabonds
c. devastated . . . inhabitants
d. blighted . . . oracles

2. The defense was able to _____ the prosecution's case so convincingly that the jury _____ the defendant after only five minutes of deliberation.
a. devastate . . . befuddled
b. refute . . . acquitted
c. topple . . . discredited
d. bungle . . . reimbursed

3. The TV special not only brought in huge sums of money to help relieve the _____ of millions of Africans suffering from the effects of a severe famine but also _____ a great deal of sympathy for them.
a. setback . . . induced
b. plight . . . generated
c. duration . . . deemed
d. strife . . . conserved

4. "The Scholar Gypsy" tells the tale of a poor student who left school to join a band of _____. He and his companions roamed the countryside endlessly, never _____ in one place for long.
a. inhabitants . . . deeming
b. debutantes . . . vacating
c. partisans . . . generating
d. vagabonds . . . tarrying

5. When the new government came to power, its first order of business was to _____ a country that had been torn by _____ and revolution for over ten years.
a. pacify . . . strife
b. topple . . . ingratitude
c. strand . . . fidelity
d. conserve . . . remorse

6. "I want to maintain _____ to the book in bringing this story to the screen," the director instructed the scriptwriter. "However, I recognize that one has to have a little _____ when translating print into film."
a. clarity . . . synopsis
b. fidelity . . . leeway
c. strife . . . facet
d. partisan . . . commentary

Choosing the Right Meaning

Read each sentence carefully. Then circle the item that best completes the statement below the sentence.

The fellow is so off-putting and mean that I am sure he must count his enemies by the gross. (2)

1. The word **gross** in line 2 is used to mean
a. total   b. twelve dozen   c. weight   d. score

On June 30, 1971, the Supreme Court vacated a lower court's restraining order, thus freeing newspapers to resume publication of the Pentagon Papers. (2)

2. The best definition for the word **vacated** in line 1 is
a. annulled/voided   b. deserted   c. emptied   d. gave up

At Dunkirk in the spring of 1940, an armada of warships and civilian craft evacuated hundreds of thousands of Allied soldiers from the northern French strand, where (2) they had been pinned by the German army.

3. In line 2 the word **strand** most nearly means
a. fiber   b. shore   c. abandonment   d. battle

The commentator's petty evaluation of the election results betrays a woeful ignorance of American political history. (2)

4. In line 1 the word **petty** most nearly means
a. unimportant   b. minor   c. narrow-minded   d. insignificant

Skyscrapers of the 1930s, such as the Empire State Building in New York, typically are crowned with setbacks that lead like steps to a spire at the summit. (2)

5. The word **setbacks** in line 2 is best defined as
a. defeats   b. reversals   c. disappointments   d. recesses

Antonyms

*In each of the following groups, circle the word or expression that is most nearly the **opposite** of the word in **boldface** type.*

1. limber
a. stiff
b. large
c. tiny
d. loose

2. headstrong
a. neat
b. intelligent
c. wealthy
d. docile

3. vacate
a. own
b. paint
c. clean
d. occupy

4. idolize
a. despise
b. bore
c. train
d. deceive

5. tarry
a. stay
b. leave
c. eat
d. loiter

6. setback
a. advance
b. defeat
c. problem
d. effort

7. strife
a. harmony
b. unemployment
c. plenty
d. trouble

8. partisan
a. separate
b. rare
c. biased
d. neutral

9. acute
a. strange
b. dull
c. new
d. sharp

11. blight
a. squander
b. bewilder
c. foster
d. starve

13. refute
a. disprove
b. lessen
c. confirm
d. change

15. ingratitude
a. wisdom
b. trust
c. thankfulness
d. money

10. conserve
a. store
b. waste
c. purchase
d. save

12. devastate
a. inhabit
b. liberate
c. develop
d. conquer

14. ovation
a. smiles
b. cheers
c. boos
d. cries

16. debut
a. employment
b. coming-out
c. retirement
d. investment

Word Families

A. *On the line provided, write the word you have learned in Units 4–6 that is related to each of the following nouns.*
EXAMPLE: pettiness—**petty**

1. bungler _____

2. reimbursement _____

3. eerieness _____

4. inducement, inducer, inducibility _____

5. conservation, conservationist, conservatory, conservative _____

6. befuddlement _____

7. devastation, devastator _____

8. repentance, repenter _____

9. gore, goriness _____

10. acquittal, acquittance, acquitter _____

11. smugness _____

12. pacifist, pacifier, pacification, pacifism _____

13. idolization, idolizer _____

14. blusterer _____

15. amiability, amiableness _____

B. *On the line provided, write the word you have learned in Units 4–6 that is related to each of the following verbs.*
EXAMPLE: inhabit—**inhabitant**

16. revoke _____

17. comply _____

18. comment _____

19. synopsize _____

20. elude _____

Word Associations

In each of the following groups, circle the word that is best defined or suggested by the given phrase.

1. state of being faithful
a. revocation   b. synopsis   c. maze   d. fidelity

2. to look over quickly
a. scan   b. generate   c. bungle   d. discredit

3. to throw doubt or uncertainty on
a. idolize   b. fray   c. conserve   d. discredit

4. to make a first appearance in public
a. strife   b. setback   c. debut   d. agenda

5. to find not guilty of a charge
a. induce   b. devastate   c. idolize   d. acquit

6. deep regret for some past misdeed
a. strand   b. ingratitude   c. bluster   d. remorse

7. one who speaks with wisdom and authority
a. inhabitant   b. partisan   c. oracle   d. mortal

8. to think or believe
a. deem   b. topple   c. vacate   d. pacify

9. friendly and pleasant
a. elusive   b. amiable   c. limber   d. gross

10. reminder of a special event
a. keepsake   b. ovation   c. reverie   d. synopsis

11. showing great insight or sharpness
a. acute   b. gory   c. numb   d. smug

12. to pay back
a. repent   b. reimburse   c. debut   d. refute

13. series of notes explaining a book
a. commentary   b. facet   c. plight   d. agenda

14. bringing about death
a. headstrong   b. acute   c. mortal   d. ravenous

15. to confuse or bewilder
a. tarry   b. befuddle   c. scan   d. fray

16. length of time that something lasts
a. leeway   b. duration   c. clarity   d. ovation

17. loud and noisy
a. boisterous   b. compliant   c. eerie   d. petty

18. one who lives in a particular place
a. vagabond   b. mortal   c. inhabitant   d. partisan

19. condition of being lost in thought
a. remorse   b. reverie   c. strand   d. maze

20. to show sorrow for bad conduct
a. repent   b. tarry   c. generate   d. bluster

re—back; again

This prefix appears in **repent** (page 53), **revocation** (page 53), **refute** (page 60), **remorse** (page 60), and **reimburse** (page 67). Some other words in which this prefix appears are listed below.

rebuke	refrain	renege	retract
redeem	relic	restraint	revive

From the list of words above, choose the one that corresponds to each of the brief definitions below. Write the word in the blank space in the illustrative sentence below the definition.

1. something that has survived the passage of time

We marveled at the delicate artistry in the Indian _____ we saw at the museum.

2. to give new life to; to restore

Lively cheers from a hopeful crowd may _____ a team's dampened spirits.

3. to take back something that has been said, offered, or published

The angry candidate demanded that the newspaper _____ the scandalous story.

4. to hold oneself back; a repeated verse, chorus

On Thanksgiving it is always hard for me to _____ from overeating.

5. to go back on a promise

They were surprised when the buyer suddenly decided to _____ on the deal.

6. a device that restricts or confines; control over the expression of one's feelings or behavior

The police officers placed _____ on the violent prisoner.

7. to scold, express sharp disapproval; a scolding

The babysitter had to _____ the children for misbehaving after dinner.

8. to buy back; to make up for; to fulfill a pledge

Consumers who _____ discount coupons they clip from magazines and newspapers can lower their weekly grocery bills.

From the list of words on page 79, choose the one that best completes each of the following sentences. Write the word in the blank space provided.

1. The recruit's failure to salute earned him a stern _____ from the sergeant.

2. When she _____ on her promise, we felt that we could no longer trust her to keep her word.

3. "If you do not immediately _____ those outrageous allegations," declared the lawyer, "my client will sue for libel."

4. The fans were asked to _____ from rushing onto the court until the basketball game was officially over.

5. The rookie's brilliant play in the final game of the series more than _____ the crucial error he had made in the opener.

6. The rescue squad worked resolutely to _____ the child who had been overcome by smoke.

7. Dressed in their old uniforms, the aging veterans looked like _____ of a bygone era.

8. It took incredible _____ on the part of the speaker not to respond to the taunts of the hecklers.

---

*Circle the **boldface** word that more satisfactorily completes each of the following sentences.*

1. The conductor's withering (**rebuke, refrain**) prompted the flutist to relinquish her solo to another player who was better rehearsed.

2. In less than a year, we will (**revive, redeem**) the mortgage, owning our house free and clear.

3. Archaeologists nearly missed the (**relic, restraint**) amid the stones and dust of the dig site.

4. As soon as they heard the familiar (**refrain, relic**) of the school song, the homecoming crowd stood to sing the anthem once again.

5. "If you (**retract, renege**) on your commitment to the team," the coach reasoned, "how can you expect me to rely on you in the future?"

6. The eager opening-night audience showed great (**restraint, rebuke**) as a technician repaired the broken projector.

7. The popularity of the show's theme song has served to (**renege, revive**) widespread interest in swing dancing.

8. Following the actor's dreadful performance in the screen test, the director had no choice but to (**retract, redeem**) the offer of the lead role.

Analogies — *In each of the following, circle the item that best completes the comparison.*

1. eerie is to **ghosts** as
a. frightening is to monsters
b. elusive is to cowboys
c. incomprehensible is to clowns
d. sage is to spies

2. elusive is to **grasp** as
a. hazy is to see
b. spicy is to taste
c. sharp is to smell
d. loud is to hear

3. irk is to **annoyance** as
a. befuddle is to understanding
b. ruffle is to joy
c. infuriate is to rage
d. pacify is to discontent

4. messenger is to **dispatch** as
a. partisan is to synopsis
b. oracle is to prophecy
c. bigot is to keepsake
d. oaf is to ovation

5. illusion is to **deceive** as
a. enigma is to mystify
b. vow is to devastate
c. repast is to disturb
d. leeway is to restrict

6. gloat is to **satisfaction** as
a. repent is to regret
b. forsake is to delight
c. confront is to fear
d. idolize is to amusement

7. famished is to **ravenous** as
a. contemporary is to prehistoric
b. global is to aquatic
c. dazed is to numb
d. stiff is to limber

8. hairline is to **recede** as
a. city is to besiege
b. tide is to ebb
c. building is to topple
d. task is to bungle

9. fray is to **boisterous** as
a. skyscraper is to petty
b. ocean is to arid
c. tempest is to sheepish
d. massacre is to gory

10. compress is to **swelling** as
a. splint is to snakebite
b. bandage is to broken leg
c. steak is to black eye
d. crutch is to bloody nose

Choosing the Right Meaning — *Read each sentence carefully. Then circle the item that best completes the statement below the sentence.*

Of Silvia, in *Two Gentlemen of Verona,* Shakespeare has the players sing, "She excels each mortal thing upon the dull earth dwelling." (2)

1. The word **mortal** in line 2 most nearly means
  a. often deadly   b. potentially fatal   c. usually lethal   d. certain to die

A truly gifted mimic can adopt not only another's voice but that person's expressions and mannerisms as well. (2)

2. The word **mimic** in line 1 is best defined as
  a. comedian   b. imitator   c. magician   d. ventriloquist

The naturalist and author John Burroughs (1837–1921) was one of the first to advocate the conservation of our country's natural resources. (2)

3. In line 2 the word **conservation** is best defined as

a. waste   b. study   c. supervision   d. preservation

Their disinterested expressions suggested that many of the soldiers returning from
the front were suffering the effects of battle fatigue.   (2)

4. In line 1 the word **disinterested** most nearly means

a. apathetic   b. impartial   c. unselfish   d. frightened

The new management introduced a number of cost-cutting measures designed to
wring a maximum of profit from the struggling business.   (2)

5. The word **maximum** in line 2 is best defined as

a. greatest possible amount   c. least possible amount
b. modest amount   d. record level

Two-Word Completions

Circle the pair of words that best complete the meaning of each of the following sentences.

1. On that cold and _____ November morning, the sails on our boat
_____ and flapped in the wind like so many sheets on a giant
clothesline.

a. serene . . . constrained   c. eerie . . . generated
b. blustery . . . billowed   d. adverse . . . tarried

2. During the ten years that he spent conquering Gaul, Julius Caesar wrote a series of
_____ on his campaigns. In these accounts, he not only tells the
story of the war but also _____ the daily life and customs of the
peoples he subdued.

a. reveries . . . conserves   c. commentaries . . . depicts
b. barrages . . . discredits   d. mazes . . . designates

3. "Though I didn't expect to be _____ in any monetary way for the
help I'd given them," I replied, "I was totally taken aback by their complete lack of
_____ for what I'd done."

a. irked . . . remorse   c. confronted . . . clarity
b. reimbursed . . . gratitude   d. befuddled . . . diversity

4. When a series of natural disasters turned their once fertile valley into a "dust bowl,"
the _____ of the area _____ their homes and
sought a more hospitable environment in which to live.

a. partisans . . . denounced   c. hypocrites . . . vacated
b. oafs . . . devastated   d. inhabitants . . . forsook

5. The linesman's adverse calls so _____ one of the players in the
championship match that he began to shower the unfortunate official with an angry
_____ of verbal abuse.

a. infuriated . . . barrage   c. motivated . . . queue
b. pacified . . . dispatch   d. befuddled . . . strand

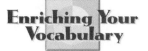

Enriching Your Vocabulary

Read the passage below. Then complete the exercise at the bottom of the page.

Compound Interest

Did you ever imagine that a dictionary and a laboratory had something in common? They have—both are full of compounds. The compounds in a laboratory are made by combining two or more chemical elements. The compounds in a dictionary are compound words. These come into the language when people put together two or more words to communicate a new idea.

In chemistry, the compound may be completely different from either of the elements from which it is made. Water, for example, is made of the gases hydrogen and oxygen. In the English language, compound words sometimes mean exactly what you'd think they'd mean when you put two words together. For instance, a *footbridge* is a bridge you'd walk over. A *rubber band* is a band made of rubber. The meaning of the compound word is

Creating compounds in chemistry class

often different from the words that make it up. Is a *butterfly* some kind of floating food? Do scalp exercises make you *headstrong* (Unit 5)? Is a *high school* a school on a mountaintop?

The English language grows and changes over time. New words come into use, and old-fashioned words hide inside old books. Compound words prove that the English language is flexible and alive.

In each row, it is possible to make two compound words. Match the parts correctly and write the words on the lines. Use a dictionary if you are not sure.

1. fire   wood   boat   saw   _____
_____

2. thunder   lightning   clap   storm   _____
_____

3. every   one   big   where   _____
_____

4. head   wall   light   ache   _____
_____

5. house   add   boat   warming   _____
_____

6. home   city   town   work   _____
_____

7. down   watch   play   load   _____
_____

Hear the words for this Unit pronounced, defined, and used in sentences at **www.vocabularyworkshop.com**.

Definitions

Note carefully the spelling, pronunciation, part(s) of speech, and definition(s) of each of the following words. Then write the word in the blank space(s) in the illustrative sentence(s) following. Finally, study the lists of synonyms and antonyms given at the end of each entry.

1. authorize
(ô' thə rīz)

(*v.*) to approve or permit; to give power or authority to

I wonder if Congress will someday _____ U. S. citizens to cast official votes over the Internet.

SYNONYMS: order, entitle, empower
ANTONYMS: forbid, ban, prohibit

2. culprit
(kəl' prit)

(*n.*) a person who has committed a crime or is guilty of some misconduct; an offender

Thanks to their efficient tracking methods, the police were able to catch the _____ red-handed.

SYNONYMS: lawbreaker, wrongdoer

3. dawdle
(dôd' əl)

(*v.*) to waste time; to be idle; to spend more time in doing something than is necessary

It's relaxing to _____ in the shower, but it wastes water.

SYNONYMS: delay, loiter, dillydally
ANTONYMS: hurry, hasten, speed up, bustle

4. dissect
(di sekt')

(*v.*) to cut apart in preparation for scientific study; to analyze with great care

I can't wait to _____ a frog in biology class next week.

SYNONYM: examine
ANTONYMS: sew together, fuse, weld

5. expend
(ek spend')

(*v.*) to pay out, spend; to use up

The most experienced long-distance runners learn not to _____ their energy too soon.

SYNONYMS: utilize, consume, disburse
ANTONYMS: save, hoard

6. fatality
(fā tal' ə tē)

(*n.*) an event resulting in death; an accidental death

The driver slammed on the brakes, but it was too late to prevent the traffic _____.

SYNONYMS: casualty, mortality
ANTONYM: injury

Hear the words for this Unit pronounced, defined, and used in sentences at **www.vocabularyworkshop.com**.

7

7. gullible
(gəl′ ə bəl)

(*adj.*) easily fooled, tricked, or cheated

Are you _____ enough to believe everything you hear on the radio?

SYNONYMS: trusting, innocent, naïve, credulous
ANTONYMS: suspicious, skeptical

8. illicit
(i lis′ it)

(*adj.*) not permitted, unlawful, improper

Students will be suspended for one week if they bring any _____ materials to school.

SYNONYMS: illegal, unauthorized, forbidden
ANTONYMS: legal, lawful, permissible, aboveboard

9. immerse
(i mərs′)

(*v.*) to plunge or dip into a fluid; to involve deeply

I find it's easier to _____ my entire body in a swimming pool than try to get used to the water slowly.

SYNONYMS: dunk, engross
ANTONYMS: dredge up, pull out

10. inflammatory
(in flam′ ə tôr ē)

(*adj.*) causing excitement or anger; leading to violence or disorder

The candidate made an _____ speech that incensed all those who heard it.

SYNONYMS: provoking, incendiary, provocative
ANTONYMS: calming, soothing, lulling, quieting

11. memorandum
(mem ə ran′ dəm)

(*n.*) a note to aid one's memory; an informal note or report (*pl.,* memorandums *or* memoranda)

The principal posts a weekly _____ to remind teachers of programs, deadlines, and special events.

SYNONYM: reminder

12. pathetic
(pə thet′ ik)

(*adj.*) marked by strong emotion, especially pity and sorrow; able to move people emotionally; worthy of pity; woefully inadequate

It was a _____ sight to see so many starving people desperately begging for food.

SYNONYMS: moving, distressing, pitiable, heartrending
ANTONYMS: funny, hilarious, frightening

13. persevere
(pər sə vēr′)

(*v.*) to keep doing something in spite of difficulties; to refuse to quit even when the going is tough

The patient needs to _____ with the painful exercises in order to be able to walk normally again.

SYNONYMS: plug away, pursue, stick to it
ANTONYMS: give up, despair, throw in the towel, quit

14. prevaricate
(pri var' ə kāt)

(v.) to lie, tell an untruth; to mislead on purpose

His reputation has suffered because of his unfortunate tendency to _____.

SYNONYMS: fib, stretch the truth, equivocate
ANTONYM: tell the truth

15. quash
(kwäsh)

(v.) to crush, put down completely

Swift military action was required to _____ the revolt before anyone was injured.

SYNONYM: suppress
ANTONYMS: start, kindle, ignite, encourage

16. relish
(rel' ish)

(n.) enjoyment or satisfaction; something that adds a pleasing flavor; (v.) to enjoy greatly

She opened the tiny box with _____, knowing that it contained a piece of jewelry.

Now that I've learned about Japan in class, I _____ the chance to travel there.

SYNONYMS: (n.) pleasure, gusto; (v.) take delight in
ANTONYMS: (v.) dislike, loathe, hate, despise

17. reminisce
(rem ə nis')

(v.) to recall one's past thoughts, feelings, or experiences

At the family reunion, we got to hear 94-year-old Tía Luzia _____ about life in old Havana.

SYNONYMS: remember, recollect

18. scour
(skaur)

(v.) to clean or polish by hard rubbing; to examine with great care; to move about quickly in search of

The pot roast was delicious, but it won't be any fun to _____ the burned roasting pan.

SYNONYMS: scrub, search, comb
ANTONYMS: dirty, soil

19. tribute
(trib' yüt)

(n.) something done or given to show thanks or respect; a payment

The best-selling author offered _____ to the teacher who inspired her.

SYNONYMS: praise, honor, homage, recognition, commendation, glorification, money, tax, levy
ANTONYMS: blame, criticism, reproach

20. writhe
(rīth)

(v.) to make twisting or turning movements in a way that suggests pain or struggle

It's so sad to see an injured bird _____ in pain.

SYNONYMS: twist, squirm, thrash

 **Completing
the Sentence**

*From the words for this unit, choose the one that best
completes each of the following sentences. Write the
word in the space provided.*

1. Our supervisor prepared a(n) _____ that reminded the
salespeople of the procedures to be followed during the holiday season.

2. The children won't _____ over their homework if they know they'll
be getting cheese and crackers as soon as they finish.

3. The dictator ordered his secret police to _____ any attempt to
organize a protest rally.

4. Is it wise to _____ so much of your hard-earned money on things
that you don't really want or need?

5. You may not _____ being told that your carelessness was
responsible for the accident even though it happens to be true.

6. Because he was seen near the scene of the crime at the time the deed was
committed, he was suspected of being the _____.

7. Many people were injured in the explosion, but luckily there was not a single
_____.

8. How can you adequately pay _____ to such an outstanding
individual?

9. We tried to hold Tom steady, but he _____ with pain as the doctor
put splints on his broken leg.

10. This pass _____ you to visit certain rooms in this museum that are
not open to the general public.

11. The story of the homeless child was so _____ that it moved us all
to tears.

12. Cracking down on _____ drug traffic is one of the biggest
problems facing law-enforcement agencies in the United States.

13. After we had _____ the animal, we had to point to each of its
important organs and explain its main function.

14. I love to listen to my grandfather _____ about his boyhood
adventures in Coney Island.

15. Before you _____ yourself in the bath, be sure to test the
temperature of the water.

16. Do you really think that I am _____ enough to believe his foolish
story about being a member of the Olympic team?

17. No matter how talented you may be, you will never be successful unless you learn
to _____ in what you undertake.

18. "Only a bigot would dare to make such a rude and _____ remark, even in jest," I replied.

19. You may be tempted to _____ , but in the long run it will be to your advantage to own up to the truth about your unfortunate error.

20. We had to _____ the walls for hours to get rid of the dirt and grease with which they were encrusted.

Synonyms

*Choose the word from this unit that is **the same** or **most nearly the same** in meaning as the **boldface** word or expression in the given phrase. Write the word on the line provided.*

1. upsetting to learn the **heartrending** details _____

2. targeted the most **innocent** people _____

3. their attempt to **suppress** all those wild rumors _____

4. will carefully **examine** their argument _____

5. **plug away** despite many setbacks _____

6. miracle that we suffered only one **casualty** _____

7. is certainly no time to **fib** _____

8. ideas for **disbursing** the remaining funds _____

9. desperate to **squirm** free from the ropes _____

10. should **dunk** it in cold water for one hour _____

11. a monthly **reminder** to all her patients _____

12. love to **recollect** about how we first met _____

13. responsible for the **forbidden** actions _____

14. will **comb** the shelves to find that book _____

15. no proof that he is the **wrongdoer** _____

Antonyms

*Choose the word from this unit that is **most nearly opposite** in meaning to the **boldface** word or expression in the given phrase. Write the word on the line provided.*

16. given **criticism** for his actions _____

17. encourages the children not to **hurry** _____

18. made **calming** gestures to the group _____

19. would **loathe** a weekend at the beach _____

20. to **forbid** taking this kind of risk _____

Choosing the Right Word

*Circle the **boldface** word that more satisfactorily completes each of the following sentences.*

1. His scheme to make money by preparing term papers for other students is not only completely (**gullible, illicit**) but immoral as well.

2. I am afraid that our ambitious plan to modernize the gym has become a (**memorandum, fatality**) of the School Board's economy drive.

3. Is there any sight more (**pathetic, illicit**) than a lonely old person peering out of a tenement window hour after hour?

4. We were amazed at the (**tribute, culprit**) that Edna received from the speaker who introduced her.

5. Although our coach can spend hours (**reminiscing, writhing**) about his victories, he doesn't have an equally good memory for his defeats.

6. The more he tried to protect himself by (**scouring, prevaricating**), the more he became entrapped in his own web of lies.

7. She was so deeply (**immersed, expended**) in the book she was reading that she did not even hear us enter the room.

8. In spite of all your talk about how hard it is to get into medical school, I intend to (**persevere, relish**) in my plans to become a doctor.

9. What good does it do for the president of the Student Council to issue (**fatalities, memorandums**) if no one takes the trouble to read them?

10. It was plain from the way that he (**dawdled, persevered**) over breakfast that he was in no hurry to visit the dentist.

11. Since the charges against the suspected mugger will probably not hold up in court, the district attorney has decided to (**authorize, quash**) them.

12. When the class comedian imitated my way of speaking, it was all I could do not to (**writhe, reminisce**) with embarrassment.

13. She (**expends, dawdles**) so much time and energy on small matters that she can't prepare properly for the things that are really important.

14. With the skill of a trained debater, she (**prevaricated, dissected**) her opponent's arguments one by one to reveal their basic weaknesses.

15. Dictators like Hitler and Mussolini used (**pathetic, inflammatory**) language to stir up the emotions of the crowds they addressed.

16. We learned in our social studies class that the Constitution (**dissects, authorizes**) the president to arrange treaties with foreign countries.

17. No one (**relishes, immerses**) being reminded of his or her mistakes, but if you are wise you will try to learn from such criticism.

18. She is so worried about appearing (**inflammatory, gullible**) that she sometimes refuses to believe things that are well supported by facts.

19. When it became known that four explorers were lost in the jungle, special search parties were sent out to (**quash, scour**) the area for them.

20. His sticky fingers and the crumbs around his mouth convinced us that he was the (**culprit, tribute**) in the Case of the Empty Cookie Jar.

*Read the following passage, in which some of the words you have studied in this unit appear in **boldface** type. Then complete each statement given below the passage by circling the letter of the item that is **the same** or **almost the same** in meaning as the highlighted word.*

Challenges of a Biographer

(Line)

It's likely that you have done research on the life of a famous person. If so, you probably **immersed** yourself in books and articles and put together facts and details into a report. But did you ever wonder how the works that guided you came to be? In many cases, they were written by professional biographers.

A biographer is, by turns, an explorer, a reporter, a judge, a psychologist, and a (5) storyteller. The biographer of a living person often interviews the subject, as well as his or her friends, family, and acquaintances. **Authorized** biographers may also get legal permission to examine the subject's personal papers, or attend private meetings. They may even live with the subject for a time for truly close-up study. (10)

A biographer who studies someone from the past has a harder task. This kind of biographer must **expend** another sort of energy—as a detective. He or she must dig into old documents, published articles, (15) personal diaries, or anything else that was written while the subject was alive. This type of first-hand material can be rare. The biographer **scours** public records for details about marriages, births, land purchases, (20) travel, legal cases, and so on. It's the biographer's job to link the data together in a sensible and accurate way.

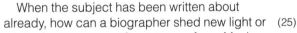
Carl Sandburg won a Pulitzer Prize in 1939 for *Lincoln—The War Years.*

When the subject has been written about already, how can a biographer shed new light or (25) offer new interpretations? Perhaps a long-lost **memorandum** may surface. Maybe an old diary will turn up in someone's attic. Perhaps a **tribute** to the subject may be unearthed. When the subject is little-known or rarely studied, the biographer may face a lack of information. In either case, the biographer's efforts enable us to learn about the lives of people we might not otherwise know. (30)

---

1. The meaning of **immersed** (line 2) is
  a. involved   c. confused
  b. exhausted   d. understood

2. Authorized (line 7) most nearly means
  a. impartial   c. approved
  b. forbidden   d. gifted

3. Expend (line 13) is best defined as
  a. save   c. choose
  b. utilize   d. gain

4. The meaning of **scours** (line 19) is
  a. polishes   c. photocopies
  b. borrows   d. examines

5. Memorandum (line 26) most nearly means
  a. relative   c. falsehood
  b. friend   d. report

6. Tribute (line 27) is best defined as
  a. homage   c. document
  b. criticism   d. report

Hear the words for this Unit pronounced, defined, and used in sentences at **www.vocabularyworkshop.com**.

UNIT 8

Definitions

Note carefully the spelling, pronunciation, part(s) of speech, and definition(s) of each of the following words. Then write the word in the blank space(s) in the illustrative sentence(s) following. Finally, study the lists of synonyms and antonyms given at the end of each entry.

1. affluence
(af′ lü əns)

(*n.*) wealth, riches, prosperity; great abundance, plenty

Education, hard work, and a very strong desire to succeed can raise a person from poverty to _____ .

SYNONYM: opulence
ANTONYMS: poverty, want, destitution, scarcity

2. arrears
(ə rērz′)

(*n., pl.*) unpaid or overdue debts; an unfinished duty

Bad spending habits and unexpected expenses left my aunt in _____ .

SYNONYMS: in default, in the red, late, overdue

3. cascade
(kas kād′)

(*n.*) a steep, narrow waterfall; something falling or rushing forth in quantity; (*v.*) to flow downward (like a waterfall)

We were thrilled when we hit the jackpot, which produced a _____ of loudly jangling coins.

I watched the clear, sparkling water _____ down the mountainside.

SYNONYMS: (*v.*) plunge, rush, tumble
ANTONYMS: (*n.*) drip, drop; (*v.*) trickle, ooze

4. cringe
(krinj)

(*v.*) to shrink back or hide in fear or submissiveness

My father told me to be brave and not to _____ when the doctor vaccinated me.

SYNONYMS: flinch, duck, cower, fawn
ANTONYMS: strut, swagger

5. crotchety
(kräch′ ə tē)

(*adj.*) cranky, ill-tempered; full of odd whims

It is unfortunate that the teacher asked me to work with the most _____ partner in the class.

SYNONYMS: grumpy, grouchy, crabby, disagreeable
ANTONYMS: sociable, friendly, agreeable, amiable

6. format
(fôr′ mat)

(*n.*) the size, shape, or arrangement of something

The clear _____ of the website makes it easy for users to find its key features.

SYNONYMS: layout, design .

7. immobile
(i mō′ bəl)

(*adj.*) not movable; not moving

Models must remain _____ for a long time in order for an artist to draw or paint them accurately.

SYNONYMS: fixed, stationary, unmoving, rooted
ANTONYMS: movable, portable, nimble, agile

8. impassable
(im pas′ ə bəl)

(*adj.*) blocked so that nothing can go through

Fallen trees formed an _____ barrier across the highway after the storm.

SYNONYMS: closed, impenetrable
ANTONYMS: unblocked, clear, open, fit for travel

9. innovation
(i nō vā′ shən)

(*n.*) something new, a change; the act of introducing a new method, idea, device, etc.

Our furnace has an energy-saving _____ that turns the heat on and off at certain intervals.

SYNONYMS: novelty, modernization, new wrinkle

10. jovial
(jō′ vē əl)

(*adj.*) good-humored, in high spirits; merry

My _____ friend is very entertaining and is always the life of the party.

SYNONYMS: jolly, cheerful, festive
ANTONYMS: gloomy, morose, melancholy, cheerless

11. manacle
(man′ ə kəl)

(*n., usually pl.*) a handcuff, anything that chains or confines; (*v.*) to chain or restrain (as with handcuffs)

The kidnappers clamped _____ on their hostages.

The guards were told to _____ the prisoner to the chair.

SYNONYMS: (*v.*) put in chains, fetter
ANTONYMS: (*v.*) unchain, set free, emancipate, release

12. martial
(mär′ shəl)

(*adj.*) warlike, fond of fighting; relating to war, the army, or military life

The army band plays _____ music as the troops formally march past the visiting general.

SYNONYMS: military, hostile, bellicose
ANTONYMS: peace-loving, peaceable, pacific, unwarlike

13. minimum
(min′ ə məm)

(*n.*) the smallest possible amount; (*adj.*) the lowest permissible or possible

I need to sleep a _____ of seven hours every night.

Sixteen is the _____ age to get a driver's license in this state.

SYNONYM: (*adj.*) least
ANTONYMS: (*n.*) maximum; (*adj.*) highest, most

Hear the words for this Unit pronounced, defined, and used in sentences at **www.vocabularyworkshop.com**.

8

14. nimble
(nim' bəl)

(*adj.*) quick and skillful in movement, agile; clever

As the _____ climber scaled Mount Everest, it looked as if she was barely exerting any energy at all.

SYNONYMS: lively, keen, flexible
ANTONYMS: awkward, clumsy, stiff, inflexible

15. onset
(än' set)

(*n.*) the beginning, start (especially of something violent and destructive); an attack, assault

At the _____ of the heavy storm, frightened people ran to find shelter.

SYNONYMS: outset, commencement
ANTONYMS: conclusion, close, end

16. partition
(pär tish' ən)

(*n.*) something that divides (such as a wall); the act of dividing something into parts or sections; (*v.*) to divide or subdivide into parts or shares

A cloth _____ in the study gave each of us some privacy.

We can _____ the backyard into four separate play areas.

SYNONYMS: (*n.*) divider, separation
ANTONYMS: (*v.*) join, combine, consolidate, merge

17. perishable
(per' ə shə bəl)

(*adj.*) likely to spoil or decay

You must keep _____ foods chilled or they will spoil.

SYNONYMS: short-lived, fleeting
ANTONYMS: long-lasting, durable, undying, permanent

18. retrieve
(ri trēv')

(*v.*) to find and bring back, get back; to put right, make good

I enjoy playing tennis, but I don't relish having to _____ tennis balls every time you hit them over the fence!

SYNONYMS: recover, regain, fetch, remedy, rectify

19. sinister
(sin' ə stər)

(*adj.*) appearing evil or dangerous; threatening evil or harm

A _____ message left on our answering machine made us wonder if we were safe at home.

SYNONYMS: frightening, menacing, ominous
ANTONYMS: cheering, encouraging, reassuring, benign

20. taut
(tôt)

(*adj.*) tightly drawn, tense; neat, in good order

A _____ chain kept the curious dog away from the swimming pool.

SYNONYMS: tight, strained, orderly, shipshape
ANTONYMS: loose, slack, drooping, messy, sloppy

Completing the Sentence

From the words for this unit, choose the one that best completes each of the following sentences. Write the word in the space provided.

1. Sherlock Holmes detected in the wicked scheme the _____ hand of the evil Professor Moriarty.

2. I know that my payments on the car are in _____, but I will catch up as soon as I get my next paycheck.

3. Unless you pull the ropes _____, the tennis net will sag.

4. The sunlight caught the waters of the stream as they _____ over the steep cliff and formed a brilliant rainbow.

5. The patients will have a much better chance to recover quickly if they receive treatment at the _____ of the fever.

6. The _____ mood of our cheerful little gathering changed abruptly to sorrow when news of the tragedy came over the radio.

7. Frank Lloyd Wright was a great American architect who was responsible for many _____ in the design of buildings.

8. I was able to _____ my baggage promptly after leaving the plane.

9. It's a pleasure to watch the expert typist's _____ fingers move swiftly over the keyboard.

10. The more we tried to humor the _____ crossing guard, the more irritable and demanding he seemed to become.

11. Today _____ foods are shipped in refrigerated trucks to prevent spoilage.

12. I don't expect you to be a hero, but do you have to _____ in that cowardly fashion whenever anyone so much as disagrees with you?

13. Although we are sure that the prisoners will make no attempt to escape, the law requires us to place _____ on them.

14. The feeling of _____ I had when I was paid lasted only until I had finished taking care of my bills.

15. As a result of the record-breaking snowstorm, all roads in the area became _____.

16. Can you explain why there is not only a maximum speed limit but also a(n) _____ speed limit on many modern highways?

17. His back injury was so severe that he has been placed in a cast and will have to remain _____ for months.

18. We made use of a(n) _____ to break up the floor space into a large number of small offices.

19. During the war years, the government tried by all kinds of propaganda to arouse the _____ spirit of the people.

20. We plan to change the _____ of our school magazine to make it more attractive and readable.

Synonyms

*Choose the word from this unit that is **the same** or **most nearly the same** in meaning as the **boldface** word or expression in the given phrase. Write the word on the line provided.*

1. recover data from my computer _____

2. in the **impenetrable** section of the cave _____

3. under strict **military** law _____

4. a **menacing** look in his eyes _____

5. installed to make it remain **stationary** _____

6. begged not to be **fettered** _____

7. in **default** after losing her job _____

8. so **short-lived** in this climate _____

9. as if confetti **tumbled** onto the stage _____

10. resisting the latest **modernization** _____

11. stack of books as a temporary **divider** _____

12. disagreeable because he was so tired _____

13. according to the most recent **design** _____

14. as **flexible** as a ballet dancer _____

15. to **cower** when the doctor approaches _____

Antonyms

*Choose the word from this unit that is **most nearly opposite** in meaning to the **boldface** word or expression in the given phrase. Write the word on the line provided.*

16. assigned the **maximum** penalty _____

17. reacting to our **melancholy** host _____

18. taken as a sure sign of **poverty** _____

19. at the **conclusion** of the program _____

20. massaging my **loose** muscles _____

Choosing the Right Word

*Circle the **boldface** word that more satisfactorily completes each of the following sentences.*

1. Of all the different types of writing, humor may be the most (**perishable, jovial**) because each generation has its own idea of what is funny.

2. I felt that there was something thoroughly (**sinister, immobile**) about the way he kept trying to duck questions on that subject.

3. In the moment of danger, my nerves were so (**taut, sinister**) that I would have screamed if someone had touched me.

4. The first thing the bankrupt firm must do with its funds is pay the (**arrears, formats**) due on the employees' wages.

5. Although we are proud of our high standard of living, we should not forget that there are those who do not share in this (**affluence, cascade**).

6. Robin Hood's faithful band of merry men were not only (**crotchety, jovial**) companions, but brave fighters as well.

7. Her mind is so (**impassable, nimble**) that she always seems to be one step ahead of us in any matter under discussion.

8. The self-styled "tough guy" (**cringed, manacled**) in terror and begged the police not to shoot.

9. A high school student looking for a vacation job usually can't expect to earn more than the (**perishable, minimum**) wage.

10. Normally, I'm very even tempered, but I can become a little (**crotchety, martial**) when I'm tired or hungry.

11. Her shimmering blond hair fell upon her pretty shoulders like a(n) (**onset, cascade**) of gold.

12. Although we all recognize that there must be changes, it is a mistake to think that every (**arrears, innovation**) is necessarily an improvement.

13. In the 18th century, Russia, Prussia, and Austria made a series of deals to (**partition, cringe**) and annex Poland right out of existence.

14. More than once, our skillful running backs managed to find a way through our opponents' supposedly (**impassable, affluent**) line.

15. Despite all his efforts, he was never able to (**retrieve, partition**) the fine reputation he had lost by that crooked deal.

16. The speed with which the boxer darted about the ring made his lumbering opponent seem utterly (**nimble, immobile**) by comparison.

17. If you spend much time watching TV, you will come to realize that all the news programs share the same basic (**format, minimum**).

18. We learned in our history class that the ancient Romans were very fine soldiers and excelled in all the (**martial, perishable**) arts.

19. Instead of acting as though you were permanently (**manacled, retrieved**) to your small circle of friends, you should try to meet new people.

20. With the (**affluence, onset**) of the heat wave, vast numbers of city dwellers began to stream toward the beaches and mountains.

Vocabulary in Context

*Read the following passage, in which some of the words you have studied in this unit appear in **boldface** type. Then complete each statement given below the passage by circling the letter of the item that is **the same** or **almost the same** in meaning as the highlighted word.*

Birth of a Puzzle

Line)

Crossword puzzles are so common that almost everyone knows how they work. Yet crosswords as we know them first appeared less than a hundred years ago. Before then, the only known word puzzles were simple British children's games. In these, letters could be arranged into connecting words. A clever child could read

(5) words both across and down.

In 1913, newspaper editor Arthur Wynne wanted a unique activity for the "Fun" page of his Sunday paper. He **retrieved** the old idea of the children's word puzzle. Wynne's **innovation** was to expand it into a larger written **format**. He drew interlocking boxes in a diamond shape. He gave clues to help solvers fill the

(10) boxes with letters to form linking words. Wynne's puzzle started a trend that others would perfect.

In 1924, Margaret Farrar published the first book of crossword puzzles. It became an instant best-seller. People did crossword puzzles to relax, to improve

(15) their vocabulary, and to keep their minds **nimble**.

Crossword puzzles quickly became a fad, and nearly every American newspaper featured them. In the days before television, people gathering to solve puzzles became a **jovial** social event.

Working together makes solving crossword puzzles even more fun.

(20) The fad grew into a familiar feature of daily life. Soon, serious puzzle solvers demanded more challenges. Puzzle makers began to develop larger diagrams with a **minimum** of blank spaces. They wrote hard clues based on obscure facts, current events, quotations, puns, and

(25) riddles. In 1942, the *New York Times* added a Sunday puzzle, edited by Mrs. Farrar. This happened at an opportune time—during World War II—when war-weary readers were glad for a break from bad news. Farrar's puzzles were wildly popular. Today, you will find crossword puzzles everywhere—in newspapers, magazines, books, at online interactive websites, and even on

(30) place mats.

. The meaning of **retrieved** (line 7) is
a. copied   c. brought back
b. researched   d. invented

. The meaning of **innovation** (line 8) is
a. change   c. outline
b. repetition   d. separation

. **Format** (line 8) most nearly means
a. contract   c. design
b. novel   d. box

4. **Nimble** (line 15) most nearly means
a. stiff   c. jolly
b. blocked   d. quick

5. **Jovial** (line 19) is best defined as
a. gloomy   c. crabby
b. cheerful   d. intellectual

6. **Minimum** (line 23) is best defined as
a. great number   c. equal number
b. small number   d. surplus

Hear the words for this Unit pronounced, defined, and used in sentences at **www.vocabularyworkshop.com**.

Definitions

Note carefully the spelling, pronunciation, part(s) of speech, and definition(s) of each of the following words. Then write the word in the blank space(s) in the illustrative sentence(s) following. Finally, study the lists of synonyms and antonyms given at the end of each entry.

1. avenge
(ə venj′)

(*v.*) to get revenge for, get even for, settle a score; to punish someone or get satisfaction for a wrong or injury

In Shakespeare's *Hamlet*, the title character vows to _____ his father's death.

SYNONYM: retaliate

2. cede
(sēd)

(*v.*) to give up, surrender; to hand over to another

Spain _____ territory to France.

SYNONYMS: yield, deliver up, transfer

3. deluge
(del′ yüj)

(*n.*) a great flood; a heavy fall of rain; anything that comes in vast quantity (like a flood); (*v.*) to flood

Owners are hoping this summer will bring a _____ of visitors to their new theme park in Minneapolis.

A torrential downpour _____ the entire town.

SYNONYMS: (*v.*) swamp, inundate
ANTONYMS: (*n.*) trickle, dribble

4. discretion
(dis kresh′ ən)

(*n.*) good judgment; care in speech and action; freedom to judge or choose

My teacher suggested I use _____ in dealing with my difficult classmate.

SYNONYMS: prudence, tact, discrimination

5. giddy
(gid′ ē)

(*adj.*) dizzy; light-headed; lacking seriousness

After the long race, the marathoner felt _____
SYNONYMS: faint, frivolous, flighty
ANTONYMS: levelheaded, serious, earnest, sober

6. impact
(*n.*, im′ pakt;
v., im pakt′)

(*n.*) the striking of one object against another; the shock caused by a collision; (*v.*) to affect, especially forcefully

The _____ of the car crash destroyed both vehicles, but miraculously no one was hurt.

Budget cuts will _____ the number of hours the public library can stay open.

SYNONYMS: (*n.*) collision, blow, effect

7. intimidate
(in tim′ ə dāt)

(*v.*) to make timid or frighten by threats; to use fear to get someone to do (or not to do) something

Hear the words for this Unit pronounced, defined, and used in sentences at **www.vocabularyworkshop.com**.

9

Bullies may try to _____ us, but if we stick together, we can stand up to their threats.
SYNONYMS: bully, browbeat, hector

8. liberate
(lib′ ə rāt)

(*v.*) to free from bondage or domination; to release
The police _____ the anxious hostages after sixteen hours of confinement.
SYNONYMS: untie, unshackle
ANTONYMS: imprison, fetter, shackle, bind

9. logical
(läj′ ə kəl)

(*adj.*) reasonable; making use of reason and good sense
Our parents are constantly encouraging us to look for
_____ solutions to our problems.
SYNONYMS: rational, sensible
ANTONYMS: absurd, ridiculous, unsound, preposterous

10. misrepresent
(mis rep ri zent′)

(*v.*) to give a false or untrue idea
If witnesses _____ the facts, the defense attorney has proof to support our story.
SYNONYMS: distort, falsify, twist, exaggerate

11. optional
(äp′ shə nəl)

(*adj.*) left to one's own choice; not required
The hotel will charge us for breakfast and dinner, but lunch is _____.
SYNONYMS: voluntary, elective, discretionary
ANTONYMS: required, mandatory, compulsory

12. outright
(aŭt′ rīt)

(*adj.*) complete; instantaneous; without reservation, thoroughgoing; (*adv.*) completely, instantaneously
When the teacher asked her why she didn't do her homework, she told an _____ lie.
Even though they had already heard it several times, the hilarious joke made them laugh _____.
SYNONYMS: (*adj.*) total, out-and-out; (*adv.*) utterly, instantly
ANTONYMS: (*adj.*) partial, incomplete; (*adv.*) by degrees

13. rendezvous
(rän′ dā vü)

(*v.*) to meet in accordance with a plan; (*n.*) a meeting by agreement; a meeting place
Let's all agree to _____ by the fountain on Saturday afternoon.
They kept their _____ a secret.
SYNONYMS: (*n.*) date, appointment, assignation

14. rotund
(rō tənd′)

(*adj.*) rounded and plump; full or rich in sound
My friends like to display the largest and most _____
pumpkin outside their front door.

SYNONYMS: round, plump, chubby, portly, sonorous
ANTONYMS: thin, angular, lean, lanky, skinny, gaunt

15. saunter
(sôn' tər)

(*v.*) to stroll; walk in an easy, leisurely way; (*n.*) a stroll

The star _____ past his adoring fans, pretending not to notice their cries of joy.

It's such a beautiful day to take a _____

SYNONYMS: (*v.*) ramble, amble; (*n.*) promenade
ANTONYMS: (*v.*) speed, race, hurry, dash, scurry, rush

16. sluggish
(sləg' ish)

(*adj.*) lazy; slow-moving; not active, dull

After a big lunch, I feel _____.

SYNONYMS: unhurried, lethargic, leisurely
ANTONYMS: active, energetic, lively, rapid, brisk

17. subordinate
(*adj., n.,* sə bôr' də nət; *v.,* sə bôr' də nāt)

(*adj.*) lower in rank or position, secondary; (*n.*) one who is in a lower position or under the orders of someone else; (*v.*) to put in a lower or secondary position

A corporal is _____ to a sergeant.

Let's ask a _____ to help us file.

Parents often _____ their own wishes for the sake of their children's needs.

SYNONYMS: (*n.*) assistant, helper
ANTONYMS: (*adj.*) superior, higher; (*n.*) chief, supervisor

18. tint
(tint)

(*n.*) a delicate color or hue; a slight trace of something; (*v.*) to give color to something; to dye

He wants to paint his room a darker _____ of blue

I hope my ophthalmologist can _____ my sunglass lenses pink.

SYNONYMS: (*n.*) shade, tone; (*v.*) color, stain
ANTONYMS: (*v.*) bleach, whiten

19. variable
(vâr' ē ə bəl)

(*adj.*) likely to undergo change; changeable; (*n.*) a value or quantity that varies; a symbol for such

Spring weather can be extremely _____

In mathematics, the letter x can stand for a _____

SYNONYMS: (*adj.*) fluctuating, shifting, inconstant
ANTONYMS: (*adj.*) constant, unchanging, steady

20. verge
(vərj)

(*n.*) the point at which something begins or happens; a border; (*v.*) to incline, tend toward, approach; to be in the process of becoming something else

I was on the _____ of tears toda

That chatter _____ on baby talk.

SYNONYMS: (*n.*) brink, threshhold, edge

Completing the Sentence

From the words for this unit, choose the one that best completes each of the following sentences. Write the word in the space provided.

1. By late September the leaves on the trees in my neck of the woods have begun to take on their normal autumn _____.

2. Our "truth in advertising" laws are designed to discourage manufacturers from _____ the virtues of their products.

3. Next year, when we have a stronger, more experienced team, we hope to _____ the crushing defeat we have just suffered.

4. The two groups of hikers, setting out from different points, have planned a(n) _____ at four o'clock at Eagle Rock.

5. After being defeated in a war that lasted from 1846 to 1848, Mexico was forced to _____ vast territories to the United States.

6. You may like to live where the sun shines all the time, but I prefer a more _____ climate.

7. According to the Bible, Noah and his family were the only human beings to survive the great _____ that once engulfed the world.

8. Even fans sitting high in the stands could hear the _____ when the big fullback crashed into the line.

9. We believe that the world is now on the _____ of new and exciting developments that may dramatically change the way we live.

10. Her argument was so _____ that she convinced us that her solution to the math problem was the correct one.

11. Uncle Eddie, with his _____ figure, is often called on to play Santa Claus.

12. Every eye was on us as we _____ down Main Street in our new outfits.

13. As a young and inexperienced employee, you cannot expect to hold more than a(n) _____ job in that big company.

14. After the heavy meal, we felt so _____ that we just sat in the living room and watched whatever was on television.

15. The impact of the head-on collision was so severe that the drivers of both vehicles were killed _____.

16. We can hold down the cost of the new car we want to buy by not ordering _____ features.

17. When they realized that sweet talk and flattery were getting them nowhere, they tried to _____ me into doing what they wanted.

18. Many older residents of Paris can still recall the day in 1944 when Allied troops _____ the city from German occupation.

19. Because of the lawyer's long experience in legal matters, we left it to his _____ how to proceed with the case.

20. Many people say that they become quite _____ when they look down from the top of a tall building.

Synonyms

*Choose the word from this unit that is **the same** or **most nearly the same** in meaning as the **boldface** word or expression in the given phrase. Write the word on the line provided.*

1. as **inconstant** as the latest fad   _____

2. an **assistant** to the vice principal   _____

3. on the **brink** of a new beginning   _____

4. made **total** fools of themselves   _____

5. could **bully** us into giving in   _____

6. kissed the baby's **chubby** cheek   _____

7. the jarring sound of the **collision**   _____

8. as if they made an **appointment** with danger   _____

9. had to **yield** that point in the debate   _____

10. decided to **stain** my T-shirt a pastel shade   _____

11. taught two **elective** classes after school   _____

12. spent a **lethargic** morning in bed   _____

13. thought of ways to **retaliate**   _____

14. her **tact** with difficult customers   _____

15. not to **distort** the facts of the case   _____

Antonyms

*Choose the word from this unit that is **most nearly opposite** in meaning to the **boldface** word or expression in the given phrase. Write the word on the line provided.*

16. gave a **preposterous** explanation   _____

17. a **trickle** of information   _____

18. to **shackle** the young falcons   _____

19. couldn't comprehend the **sober** mood   _____

20. as they **scurry** through the mall   _____

Choosing the Right Word

Circle the **boldface** word that more satisfactorily completes each of the following sentences.

1. We held a meeting to discuss why the sale of tickets to the class dance has been so (**sluggish, rotund**) and what we can do about it.

2. At the State Fair, we separated to visit different exhibits, but we agreed to (**saunter, rendezvous**) at the refreshment stand at five o'clock.

3. Only the (**optional, outright**) repeal of this unfair nuisance tax will satisfy the voters.

4. Many people, unhappy with what nature has given them, seek to improve their appearance by (**tinting, ceding**) their hair.

5. It is sad to see how, in just a few years, the lean young athlete has allowed himself to become flabby and (**giddy, rotund**).

6. In times of crisis, we may be called on to (**deluge, subordinate**) our personal interests to the needs of the nation as a whole.

7. Many Western films include a character who is out to (**intimidate, avenge**) a wrong done to a close friend or relative.

8. Letters of protest (**deluged, tinted**) the Mayor's office when he proposed an increase in the sales tax.

9. It is good for you to "stand up for your rights," but you should not do so in a way that (**verges, subordinates**) on discourtesy.

10. There are times in life when you should be guided more by your feelings, without trying to be strictly (**outright, logical**) about everything.

11. I plan to write a term paper that will discuss the different ways in which television has had a major (**impact, verge**) on American life.

12. We had regarded her as a rather (**logical, giddy**) young girl, but in this tough situation she showed that she had courage and good sense.

13. If you know that you are late for school, why do you (**saunter, rendezvous**) along as though you had all the time in the world?

14. This biased editorial has deliberately (**misrepresented, avenged**) the stand of our candidate on the important issues of the election.

15. The invitation to the party said that formal wear was (**optional, variable**).

16. I look forward to the time when my parents will agree that I have reached the "age of (**discretion, misrepresentation**)."

17. He soon learned that the moods of a youngster—happy one moment, miserable the next—can be as (**variable, sluggish**) as the winds.

18. Modern household appliances have done much to (**liberate, deluge**) homemakers from tedious and time-consuming chores.

19. The aged millionaire, wishing to spend his last years in peace and quiet, (**ceded, impacted**) all his business interests to his sons.

20. A fastball pitcher will often try to (**intimidate, liberate**) an opposing batter by "shaving" him with an inside pitch.

Read the following passage, in which some of the words you have studied in this unit appear in **boldface** type. Then complete each statement given below the passage by circling the letter of the item that is **the same** or **almost the same** in meaning as the highlighted word.

Exaggerated Kings

(Line)

For centuries, people have regarded the lion as a noble creature. But have lions been **misrepresented** as the king of beasts? The truth about lions may surprise you.

Without a doubt, lions are handsome, powerful cats. The male lion's rich, thick mane makes it both beautiful and fierce looking. It would be a **logical** conclusion, then, to view the male as a great hunter and protector. But this is (5)

Why is this lion winking? Perhaps it is because he knows the truth!

not the case. Female lions do most of the hunting, often at night and in teams. Male lions rest or sleep up to twenty hours a day. The so-called "king" is actually a **sluggish** monarch much of the time. (10)

Lions generally live in groups known as *prides*, which are like family units. Females of several generations may stay in the same pride for life. Male lions wander away or are forced out by new, stronger males. A pride may have a **variable** number of (15) members, from as few as three to as many as thirty or more, depending on the amount of food in their territory. More food means larger prides.

These meat-eaters often feed on fresh kill that they bring down. However, some lions are **outright** (20) thieves. They steal meat from other predators to save themselves the effort of hunting. That doesn't seem like noble behavior! Nor does the fact that after female lions have made a kill, males chase them away so they can take the finest morsels for themselves.

Lions were once common to many parts of Europe, Asia, India, and Africa. (25) But human hunters and farmers, as well as widespread development in regions where lions once roamed, have all had a serious **impact** on the wild lion population. Today, wild lions are found only in parts of Africa, and in a protected wildlife preserve in India. Neither an endangered nor threatened species, the lion continues to occupy its throne. (30)

---

1. The meaning of **misrepresented** (line 2) is
  a. judged   c. construed
  b. liberated   d. falsified

2. Logical (line 4) most nearly means
  a. compulsory   c. senseless
  b. sensible   d. ridiculous

3. Sluggish (line 9) is best defined as
  a. royal   c. lazy
  b. energetic   d. plump

4. The meaning of **variable** (line 15) is
  a. changeable   c. constant
  b. superior   d. large

5. Outright (line 20) most nearly means
  a. devious   c. total
  b. accidental   d. partial

6. Impact (line 27) is best defined as
  a. hazard   c. damage
  b. effect   d. support

Vocabulary for Comprehension

*Read the following passage, in which some of the words you have studied in Units 7–9 appear in **boldface** type. Then answer questions 1–12 on page 106 on the basis of what is <u>stated</u> or <u>implied</u> in the passage and in the introductory statement.*

Once upon a time, a strange-looking bird called the dodo lived on an island in the Indian Ocean. This passage describes what became of it.

(Line)

Alas, the dodo bird is no more. None of these funny-looking relatives of pigeons and doves exist today. In fact, dodos have been extinct for
(5) over three centuries.

The **pathetic** dodo never got much respect in its time. People said it was "disgusting." The clumsy-looking bird looked a bit like a deformed pigeon,
(10) but larger. Others thought it might be a kind of **rotund** turkey. Its hooked bill led still others to think it might be a flightless cockatoo. Had the dodo understood what people said about
(15) it, it probably wouldn't have **cringed** a bit. That's because of its strangely docile nature.

The dodo was slow moving and unusually trusting. Little would
(20) **intimidate** the easygoing bird. Its natural home was Mauritius, a small island in the Indian Ocean. Dutch and Portuguese sailors who visited Mauritius in their travels were
(25) fascinated by the dodo. Its odd looks made it seem almost fantastic, appealing to artists, naturalists, and writers.

But the dodo's trusting nature left it
(30) vulnerable. Several categories of **culprits** contributed to the extinction of the dodo. Enterprising sailors began to steal dodos from Mauritius.

They sold them to eager collectors,
(35) who would pay handsomely for the homely birds. Also, the dodo was dinner for the colonists of and visitors to the island and for the animals that they brought with them. By 1681, no
(40) more dodos lived on Mauritius or anywhere else. The ones that had been held in captivity were never bred. They left no descendants.

Lack of scientific evidence led
(45) nineteenth-century naturalists to ask whether the dodo ever existed at all. With no bodies to **dissect** and few bones to examine, skeptics came to denounce the dodo as a fraud. Later
(50) research proved that the dodo had indeed existed but that its lack of natural enemies and overly trusting nature probably cost it a lasting place in the animal world.

1. The primary purpose of this passage is to identify several
   a. causes of the dodo's extinction
   b. effects of the dodo's extinction
   c. characteristics of the dodo's nature
   d. characteristics of the island of Mauritius
   e. animals that have become extinct

2. The meaning of **pathetic** (line 6) is
   a. gullible
   b. pitiable
   c. repulsive
   d. aggressive
   e. shy

3. Rotund (line 11) most nearly means
   a. huge
   b. skinny
   c. tall
   d. plump
   e. flighty

4. Cringed (line 15) is best defined as
   a. minded
   b. strutted
   c. flinched
   d. wept
   e. argued

5. Paragraph 2 focuses primarily on the dodo bird's
   a. extinction
   b. appearance
   c. temperament
   d. history
   e. environment

6. The meaning of **intimidate** (line 20) is
   a. imprison
   b. avenge
   c. pursue
   d. anger
   e. bully

7. You can tell from the first sentences in paragraphs 1 and 2 that the tone of the passage will be somewhat
   a. scientific
   b. humorous
   c. objective

d. skeptical
e. critical

8. All of the following describe the dodo EXCEPT
   a. strange-looking
   b. docile
   c. trusting
   d. easygoing
   e. imaginary

9. Culprits (line 31) most nearly means
   a. people
   b. thieves
   c. wrongdoers
   d. merchants
   e. causes

10. Dissect (line 47) is best defined as
   a. bury
   b. weigh
   c. dig up
   d. analyze
   e. compare

11. You can infer that the "later research" mentioned in lines 49–54 involved
   a. skeletal or fossil remains of the dodo
   b. paintings and drawings of the dodo
   c. stories and songs about the dodo
   d. eyewitness testimony about the dodo
   e. photographs of the last dodos in captivity

12. Which of the following generalizations would the author agree with?
   a. The dodo had many natural enemies.
   b. The only enemy of the dodo bird was human beings.
   c. If the dodo had been more trusting, it might still exist today.
   d. The dodo bird was beautiful.
   e. The dodo bird was intelligent.

Grammar in Context

In the sentence "None of these funny-looking relatives of pigeons and doves exist today" (lines 2–3 on page 105), the author uses the adjective "funny-looking" to describe "relatives." An **adjective** is a word that modifies a noun or a pronoun. Adjectives can appear either before or after the noun or pronoun. They answer questions such as *What kind? How many? How much?* and *Which one?* "Dutch" and "Portuguese" in the sentence on lines 22–25 are *proper adjectives*. The indefinite articles *a* and *an* are also adjectives; so is the definite article *the.* An adjective may appear after a linking verb, as "extinct" does in the sentence "In fact, dodos have been extinct for over three centuries" (lines 3–5).

Do not confuse adjectives with **adverbs**, which modify verbs, adjectives, other adverbs, and prepositional phrases (as in "<u>almost</u> to the end"). Adverbs can also modify complete sentences and subordinate clauses. They tell *how, when, where, to what extent, in what manner,* or *how much.* Negatives, such as *not, never,* and *hardly* are adverbs, too, as in the sentence "They should <u>never</u> have stolen that dodo."

When you need to decide whether to use an adjective or an adverb, use what you have learned thus far plus the following ideas and rules: (1) Don't count on the *–ly* ending to identify a modifier as an adverb; words like *friendly* and *elderly* are adjectives. (2) *Good* and *bad* are always adjectives. (3) *Badly* and *well* are adverbs, although *well* can be used as an adjective to describe a person's health.

Choose the modifier in parentheses that correctly completes each sentence, and write it on the line provided.

1. My puppy is (**particular, particularly**) trusting, just as the dodo was.

_____

2. The scientists searched the island (**careful, carefully**) for nests.

_____

3. The dodo stews that the islanders ate tasted (**delicious, deliciously**).

_____

4. I felt (**anxious, anxiously**) as we approached the iguanas and other wild creatures on the island.

_____

5. The dodo did not make enemies (**easy, easily**).

_____

6. While the flightless bird was (**happy, happily**) going about its business, the predator watched it intently from behind the bush.

_____

7. I (**sure, surely**) would have loved to have seen a dodo.

_____

8. The dodo was trusting and docile, and sailors treated it (**bad, badly**).

_____

 **Two-Word Completions** *Circle the pair of words that best complete the meaning of each of the following passages.*

1. The Emancipation Proclamation _____ Southern blacks once and for all from the _____ that bound them to a life of servitude and humiliation.
   a. immersed . . . arrears
   b. liberated . . . manacles
   c. subordinated . . . memoranda
   d. retrieved . . . tints

2. During "Operation Dragnet," the police _____ the entire city in search of the two _____ who had pulled off the daring bank robbery.
   a. immersed . . . fatalities
   b. quashed . . . innovators
   c. scoured . . . culprits
   d. deluged . . . subordinates

3. Joan of Arc spent most of her brief career as the "warrior maiden of France" attempting to _____ lands that the French had been forced to _____ to England as a result of English victories in the initial stages of the Hundred Years' War.
   a. partition . . . expend
   b. avenge . . . authorize
   c. liberate . . . misrepresent
   d. retrieve . . . cede

4. The _____ of their sudden collision left one of the players _____ on the ice in agony, while the other was hurled five feet into the air.
   a. format . . . cringing
   b. impact . . . writhing
   c. fatality . . . verging
   d. onset . . . scouring

5. The bully down the block is so big and so _____ that I find myself unconsciously _____ in fear every time he looks in my direction.
   a. intimidating . . . cringing
   b. rotund . . . prevaricating
   c. sinister . . . dawdling
   d. martial . . . sauntering

6. After Grandpa _____, then lost, half of his nest egg in an obviously crooked scheme, I stressed that he could no longer be so _____ when it came to taking the advice of financial "wizards."
   a. reminisced . . . jovial
   b. intimidated . . . taut
   c. deluged . . . giddy
   d. invested . . . gullible

Choosing the Right Meaning

Read each sentence carefully. Then circle the item that best completes the statement below the sentence.

Not only was Abraham Lincoln a master of English prose, but by all accounts he possessed a keen sense of humor and relished a good story. (2)

1. The word **relished** in line 2 is used to mean

    a. enjoyed   b. told   c. collected   d. concocted

Our teacher wrote "$x + 9$" on the board to give an example of a mathematical expression containing a variable. (2)

2. In line 2 the word **variable** is best defined as

    a. difficult problem   b. mistake   c. unknown value   d. solution

With the death of Stonewall Jackson in May of 1863, Confederate commander Robert E. Lee lost his ablest subordinate. (2)

3. In line 2 the word **subordinate** is best defined as

    a. adviser   b. strategist   c. ally   d. lieutenant

By the time of Lee's surrender at Appomattox in April 1865, the war-making capacity of the South had been destroyed outright. (2)

4. The word **outright** in line 2 most nearly means

    a. quickly   b. completely   c. gradually   d. partially

Over the years countless students have recited the rotund lines of Edgar Allan Poe's famous poem "The Raven." (2)

5. The word **rotund** in line 1 most nearly means

    a. plump   b. stout   c. round   d. sonorous

Antonyms

*In each of the following groups, circle the word or expression that is most nearly the **opposite** of the word in **boldface** type.*

1. manacle
a. emancipate
b. delete
c. befuddle
d. expand

2. illicit
a. permissible
b. explicit
c. illegal
d. coarse

3. optional
a. new
b. interesting
c. required
d. difficult

4. expend
a. spend
b. avoid
c. save
d. require

5. perishable
a. foreign
b. expensive
c. colorful
d. durable

6. liberate
a. shackle
b. study
c. rule
d. visit

7. relish
a. consider
b. loathe
c. examine
d. invent

8. gullible
a. rich
b. silly
c. tall
d. suspicious

9. persevere
a. pursue
b. quit
c. reply
d. spend

11. sluggish
a. thoughtful
b. friendly
c. active
d. sleepy

13. rotund
a. round
b. dark
c. frightening
d. lanky

15. crotchety
a. new
b. agreeable
c. former
d. overworked

10. pathetic
a. funny
b. unusual
c. inadequate
d. sad

12. affluence
a. wealth
b. poverty
c. heaviness
d. confusion

14. minimum
a. only
b. latest
c. usual
d. most

16. scour
a. dirty
b. cower
c. hide
d. believe

Word Families

A. *On the line provided, write the word you have learned in Units 7–9 that is related to each of the following nouns.*
EXAMPLE: intimidation—**intimidate**

1. retrieval, retriever, retrievability _____

2. dissection, dissector _____

3. immersion _____

4. nimbleness _____

5. joviality _____

6. avenger _____

7. misrepresentation _____

8. liberation, liberator, liberationist _____

9. perseverance, perseveration _____

10. authorization _____

11. dawdler _____

12. prevarication, prevaricator _____

13. logic _____

14. reminiscence _____

15. gullibility _____

16. option _____

B. *On the line provided, write the word you have learned in Units 7–9 that is related to each of the following verbs.*
EXAMPLE: inflame—**inflammatory**

17. innovate _____

18. perish _____

19. minimize _____

20. vary _____

Word Associations

In each of the following groups, circle the word that is best defined or suggested by the given phrase.

1. read the report
a. culprit   b. innovation   c. memorandum   d. affluence

2. will not allow ourselves to be bullied
a. avenged   b. impacted   c. immersed   d. intimidated

3. a highway death
a. deluge   b. memorandum   c. onset   d. fatality

4. enjoyed the military music
a. gullible   b. martial   c. illicit   d. jovial

5. pulled the rope tight
a. taut   b. nimble   c. crotchety   d. immobile

6. the effect of the new factory
a. innovation   b. manacle   c. subordinate   d. impact

7. on the brink of collapse
a. verge   b. manacle   c. variable   d. tribute

8. put down a revolt
a. quash   b. deluge   c. expend   d. partition

9. get even for a wrong
a. authorize   b. avenge   c. dawdle   d. cringe

10. the layout of the catalog
a. affluence   b. format   c. impact   d. memorandum

11. showed outstanding judgment
a. onset   b. discretion   c. relish   d. tint

12. divide the country
a. liberate   b. cascade   c. partition   d. reminisce

13. dye the canvas
a. cede   b. deluge   c. immerse   d. tint

14. a flood of letters
a. deluge   b. manacle   c. parcel   d. tribute

15. the blocked country road
a. inflammatory   b. illicit   c. jovial   d. impassable

16. in a merry mood
a. pathetic   b. jovial   c. sluggish   d. wholesome

17. the start of flu symptoms
a. onset   b. cascade   c. impact   d. encounter

18. a heartfelt commendation
a. memorandum   b. format   c. subordinate   d. tribute

19. a memorable date
a. fatality   b. rendezvous   c. impact   d. onset

20. strolling along
a. avenging   b. writhing   c. sauntering   d. immersing

Building with Classical Roots

log, logue—speech, word, discourse

This Greek root appears in **logical** (page 99). Some other words in which this root appears are listed below.

apology	**dialogue**	**eulogy**	**neologism**
decalogue	**epilogue**	**monologue**	**prologue**

From the list of words above, choose the one that corresponds to each of the brief definitions below. Write the word in the blank space in the illustrative sentence below the definition.

1. a long speech made by one person; a speech that monopolizes conversation; a series of jokes or comedic stories delivered by one comedian

The opening _____ given by talk-show hosts, consisting of light banter and political humor, has become a staple of late-night television.

2. a conversation between two or more people or characters; the lines in a script that are to be spoken; an airing of ideas or views

Abbott and Costello's wacky routine "Who's on first?" is one of the funniest baseball _____ in American comedy.

3. a speech or written tribute composed to honor someone who has died

Lincoln's Gettysburg Address was delivered on November 19, 1863, to dedicate a national cemetery and as a _____ to those who died at the Battle of Gettysburg.

4. words of regret to express remorse and ask pardon for an accident, fault, failure, or offense; an explanation, defense, or excuse

"If you'd like me to accept your _____," he explained, "I need to believe that you know what you did wrong and that you will strive to do better."

5. an introductory statement, act, or event; a preface; opening remarks

The novel's _____ offers background on the main character so that the action can begin immediately in Chapter 1.

6. a concluding section at the end of a play or literary work, intended to provide further comment, interpretation, or information; an afterword

After the curtain fell, a narrator gave a brief _____ to tie up loose ends.

7. a newly invented word, expression, or usage; new meaning for an old word

Evolving technology has led to many _____, such as CD-ROM, that have become part of our everyday language.

8. a set of ten authoritative rules or laws; (*usu. cap.*) the Ten Commandments (in the Bible)

The stained-glass window shows Moses holding the _____ above his head.

From the list of words on page 112, choose the one that best completes each of the following sentences. Write the word in the blank space provided.

1. The man scolded us with an angry _____ about the decline of manners.

2. The best way to achieve lasting peace is for both parties to engage in ongoing, meaningful_____ to address their fundamental desires and demands.

3. The acting governor delivered a heartfelt _____ at the funeral of her former boss.

4. An authentic _____ should be more than a bunch of meaningless words.

5. The author included a _____ to clarify her intentions in writing her latest book.

6. Stay tuned until the very end or you will miss the surprising _____.

7. Many _____ first achieve notice when they are introduced by popular culture's trendsetters.

8. The board of directors drafted a _____ to specify the fundamental rules and procedures for the organization.

---

*Circle the **boldface** word that more satisfactorily completes each of the following sentences.*

1. The intensely dramatic (**monologue, decalogue**) lasted for nearly an hour—a stunning success for one actor alone on a bare stage.

2. What an unexpectedly productive (**eulogy, dialogue**) between the anti-war protesters and the police officers who were assigned to protect them!

3. The ushers have been instructed not to seat anyone who arrives at the theater after the (**epilogue, prologue**) has begun.

4. No one who heard the inspiring (**eulogy, neologism**) given for the young hero will ever forget the deeply felt emotions of that sad moment.

5. The first British edition of *Moby Dick* accidentally omitted the (**epilogue, apology**), which tells how Ishmael alone survived, and justifies his first-person narrative.

6. The Biblical source of the (**Decalogue, Dialogue**) is Chapter 20 of the Book of Exodus.

7. Today's most original (**monologue, neologism**) may one day become woven into conventional standard usage.

8. When he realized that he had forgotten his mother's birthday, he drafted a thoughtful and loving (**apology, prologue**), which he tucked into a bouquet of roses for her.

Analogies *In each of the following, circle the item that best completes the comparison.*

1. nimble is to **agility** as
a. immobile is to liveliness
b. gross is to sensitivity
c. arid is to variety
d. limber is to flexibility

2. taut is to **leeway** as
a. variable is to change
b. cramped is to elbowroom
c. global is to area
d. optional is to choice

3. highwayman is to **waylay** as
a. assailant is to assault
b. inhabitant is to manipulate
c. culprit is to idolize
d. oaf is to forsake

4. crotchety is to **amiable** as
a. famished is to ravenous
b. mortal is to perishable
c. immediate is to instantaneous
d. sluggish is to energetic

5. jovial is to **merriment** as
a. sage is to joy
b. serene is to bliss
c. martial is to peace
d. sinister is to contentment

6. apparel is to **wear** as
a. equipment is to read
b. entertainment is to live
c. food is to eat
d. furniture is to break

7. synopsis is to **compress** as
a. memorandum is to discredit
b. ovation is to depict
c. commentary is to dissect
d. dispatch is to reimburse

8. manacle is to **constrain** as
a. spur is to motivate
b. leash is to liberate
c. chain is to generate
d. handcuff is to designate

9. setback is to **discourage** as
a. victory is to delight
b. loss is to please
c. triumph is to sadden
d. defeat is to thrill

10. maximum is to **minimum** as
a. immense is to petty
b. giddy is to eerie
c. pathetic is to pitiful
d. disinterested is to impartial

Choosing the Right Meaning *Read each sentence carefully. Then circle the item that best completes the statement below the sentence.*

Tacitus tells us in *The Annals* that Emperor Nero ordered the dispatch of scores of his enemies—both real and imagined. (2)

1. In line 1 the word **dispatch** is best defined as
a. promptness   b. communication   c. execution   d. conviction

Among those who perished at Nero's bidding was the philosopher and dramatist Lucius Annaeus Seneca, who had been the emperor's tutor. (2)

2. The word **perished** in line 1 most nearly means
a. profited
b. informed on others
c. died
d. were exiled

No visit to Paris is complete without a saunter down its most famous boulevard, the Champs-Elysees. (2)

3. In line 1 the word **saunter** is best defined as
  a. scamper   b. stroll   c. race   d. hike

A brief scan of the rugged terrain that lay ahead was enough to tell us that a long, difficult hike was in store. (2)

4. In line 1 the word **scan** most nearly means
  a. exploration   b. examination   c. discussion   d. mapping

Instructing an actor how to play a part, Prince Hamlet advises, "Let your own discretion be your tutor." (2)

5. The word **discretion** in line 2 is used to mean
  a. judgment   b. freedom   c. choice   d. talent

Two-Word Completions

Circle the pair of words that best complete the meaning of each of the following sentences.

1. Though surrounded on all sides by superior forces, the inhabitants of the _____ city were able to keep the enemy at bay for a long time by maintaining a steady _____ of missiles from their walls and towers.
  a. encompassed . . . rendezvous   c. restricted . . . oracle
  b. partitioned . . . repast   d. besieged . . . barrage

2. "Despite all the problems and _____ we have experienced in recent months, we must _____ in our endeavor to achieve the goals we have set for the company this year," I said.
  a. revocations . . . verge   c. keepsakes . . . cringe
  b. setbacks . . . persevere   d. vocations . . . tarry

3. During the lengthy dry spell that the area experiences every summer, the vegetation _____ completely away, and the landscape takes on a surprising resemblance to the kind of _____ found on the moon.
  a. frays . . . format   c. blusters . . . tribute
  b. withers . . . terrain   d. cedes . . . duration

4. When the volcano erupted, huge quantities of molten lava and boiling mud _____ like some fiery waterfall down the steep sides of the mountain, _____ the region round about.
  a. cascaded . . . devastating   c. billowed . . . vacating
  b. deluged . . . befuddling   d. writhed . . . stranding

5. Though many of the hardships that the peoples of the world face today are purely local, the _____ of those suffering from hunger and malnutrition is of truly _____ proportions.
  a. enigma . . . incomprehensible   c. plight . . . global
  b. queue . . . adverse   d. maze . . . acute

Read the passage below. Then complete the exercise at the bottom of the page.

The Right to a Fair Trial

There have always been rules about how people should treat one another. And there have always been folks who break the rules. So societies have come up with methods to keep order and to insure justice.

What can United States citizens do when they think someone has wronged them? The *plaintiff,* the person with the complaint, accuses the *defendant.* Sometimes the case is decided in court and is tried before a *judge* and a *jury.* The plaintiff and the *defendant* are both represented by an attorney. Both sides may present *evidence* to support their case and call witnesses to *testify* for them. A *jury* of twelve citizens and a *judge* hear the evidence.

After all the arguments are heard, the jury discusses the evidence and comes to a *verdict,* a formal decision about the case. If the verdict is "not guilty," the defendant has been *acquitted* (Unit 4). If the verdict is "guilty," the judge decides on a penalty for the *culprit* (Unit 7), who may have to pay a fine, do community service, or serve time in jail.

Our legal system is complicated and detailed. However, it is one of the most important benefits that American citizens have.

Lady of Justice in front of Supreme Court

In Column A below are 8 more legal terms. With or without a dictionary, match each word with its meaning in Column B.

Column A

_____ **1.** oath
_____ **2.** arraign
_____ **3.** affidavit
_____ **4.** statute
_____ **5.** sequester
_____ **6.** judicial
_____ **7.** indict
_____ **8.** mistrial

Column B

a. to accuse someone based on evidence
b. to call a defendant before a court of law to hear and answer charges
c. a trial that is ruled invalid because there was a problem with evidence or how it was presented
d. a solemn promise
e. a law that has been passed by a legislative body such as Congress
f. a written statement made under oath
g. to set apart, as members of a jury
h. having to do with judges, courts, and law

Hear the words for this Unit pronounced, defined, and used in sentences at **www.vocabularyworkshop.com**.

UNIT 10

Definitions

Note carefully the spelling, pronunciation, part(s) of speech, and definition(s) of each of the following words. Then write the word in the blank space(s) in the illustrative sentence(s) following. Finally, study the lists of synonyms and antonyms given at the end of each entry.

1. abominable
(ə bäm′ ə nə bəl)

(*adj.*) arousing hatred; disgusting, detestable

Unfortunately there are many _____ ideas circulating on the Internet.

SYNONYMS: hateful, despicable, loathsome
ANTONYMS: praiseworthy, delightful, charming

2. bumbling
(bəm′ bliŋ)

(*adj.*) blundering and awkward; (*n.*) clumsiness

The _____ burglars were so inept that they actually left some of their own money at the home they were planning to rob!

The old cartoon character Mr. Magoo was well known for his _____.

SYNONYMS: (*adj.*) clumsy, stumbling
ANTONYMS: (*adj.*) forceful, effective, skillful, adroit

3. consequence
(kän′ sə kwens)

(*n.*) a result, effect; importance

Does he truly comprehend the _____ of his actions?

SYNONYMS: outcome, significance
ANTONYMS: cause, source

4. delude
(di lüd′)

(*v.*) to fool, deceive; to mislead utterly

Don't _____ yourself into thinking that you will become a famous concert pianist just because you played one song at the school's talent show.

SYNONYMS: trick, hoodwink

5. dole
(dōl)

(*v.*) to give out in small amounts; (*n.*) money, food, or other necessities given as charity; a small portion

Let's _____ out scraps of food to the hungry dogs.

The homeless people lined up to receive their weekly _____ at the shelter.

SYNONYMS: (*v.*) ration, allot, distribute; (*n.*) handout

6. engulf
(en gəlf′)

(*v.*) to swallow up, overwhelm, consume

The truck was _____ in flames after its fuel tank exploded.

SYNONYMS: envelop, encompass, immerse

7. foil
(foil)

(v.) to defeat; to keep from gaining some end; (n.) a thin sheet of metal; a light fencing sword; a person or thing serving as a contrast to another

We hope that good police work will _____ the criminals' plot.

Glum characters make a good _____ for the upbeat star of that new comedy.

SYNONYMS: (v.) frustrate, thwart, counter; (n.) rapier
ANTONYMS: (v.) aid, abet, assist, advance, promote

8. formulate
(fôr' myə lāt)

(v.) to express definitely or systematically; to devise, invent; to state as a formula

The town board is working to _____ a more economical energy policy for its citizens.

SYNONYMS: define, articulate, frame, specify

9. initiative
(i nish' ə tiv)

(n.) the taking of the first step or move; the ability to act without being directed or urged from the outside

Dad was proud that I took the _____ to rake the leaves without being asked.

SYNONYMS: leadership, enterprise
ANTONYMS: laziness, sloth, shiftlessness

10. memento
(mə men' tō)

(n.) something that serves as a reminder

This cap is a _____ of our trip this past summer.

SYNONYMS: remembrance, keepsake, souvenir, token

11. nonconformist
(nän kən fôr' mist)

(n.) a person who refuses to follow established ideas or ways of doing things; (adj.) of or relating to the unconventional

Jake is a _____ who is never swayed by other people's opinions or expectations.

Her _____ poetry appears in many small literary magazines.

SYNONYMS: (n.) maverick, individualist, bohemian
ANTONYMS: (n., adj.) traditionalist, conventionalist; (adj.) traditional, conventional, conservative

12. null and void
(nəl and void)

(adj.) without legal force or effect; no longer binding

This contract becomes _____ at noon tomorrow.

SYNONYMS: canceled, invalid, repealed, abolished
ANTONYMS: in effect, binding, valid

13. panorama
(pan ə ram' ə)

(n.) a wide, unobstructed view of an area; a complete survey of a subject; a continuously passing or changing scene; a range or spectrum

Hear the words for this Unit pronounced, defined, and used in sentences at **www.vocabularyworkshop.com**.

10

Displays of old picture postcards present an entertaining
_____ of twentieth-century life.
SYNONYMS: vista, overview

14. posterity
(pä ster′ ət ē)

(*n.*) all of a person's offspring, descendants; all future generations
Let's keep the family photo album for _____.
ANTONYMS: ancestry, ancestors, forebears, the past

15. pry
(prī)

(*v.*) to pull loose by force; to look at closely or inquisitively; to be nosy about something
We can use this tool to _____ the lid off a can of paint.
SYNONYMS: snoop, meddle

16. refurbish
(ri fər′ bish)

(*v.*) to brighten, freshen, or polish; to restore or improve
Every five years, the hotel _____ the décor of its elegant lobby.
SYNONYMS: remodel, renew, spruce up
ANTONYMS: dilapidate, run down

17. resourceful
(ri sôrs′ fəl)

(*adj.*) able to deal promptly and effectively with all sorts of problems; clever in finding ways and means of getting along
A _____ guide will know how to handle any questions or surprises that come up on the tour.
SYNONYMS: inventive, ingenious, skillful
ANTONYMS: uninventive, incompetent, dull-witted

18. rigorous
(rig′ ər əs)

(*adj.*) severe, harsh, strict; thoroughly logical
"Boot camp" is the nickname for the place where new soldiers receive _____ basic training.
SYNONYMS: tough, trying, challenging, stringent
ANTONYMS: easy, lax, indulgent, undemanding

19. subsequent
(səb′ sə kwent)

(*adj.*) coming after; following in time, place, or order
The country enjoyed peace and prosperity in the years _____ to the war.
SYNONYMS: following, later, next, succeeding, ensuing
ANTONYMS: previous, prior, preceding

20. unerring
(ən er′ iŋ)

(*adj.*) making no mistakes, faultless, completely accurate
Even a pilot with _____ judgment can be surprised by sudden changes in the weather.
SYNONYMS: sure, certain, unfailing
ANTONYMS: faulty, fallible, unreliable

Completing the Sentence

From the words for this unit, choose the one that best completes each of the following sentences. Write the word in the space provided.

1. Professional baseball players get themselves into shape for the upcoming season by undergoing a _____ training period each spring.

2. Anyone who _____ into someone else's business runs the risk of opening a can of worms.

3. Huge clouds of smoke and ash from the angry volcano _____ the sleepy little villages that nestled on its flanks.

4. The alert employee _____ an attempted robbery by setting off the alarm promptly.

5. Like so many other young people, he has been _____ into the false belief that there is an easy way to success.

6. You may think that the crude way he has behaved is slightly amusing, but I think it is _____ and inexcusable.

7. A truly _____ administrator always seems to be able to find an effective way of dealing with any problem that may come up.

8. At the time it occurred, that mistake didn't seem to be too important, but it had _____ that still hurt me today.

9. From the observation deck of the skyscraper one may enjoy a sweeping _____ of the city.

10. These old photographs may not look like much, but I treasure them as a(n) _____ of the last summer my entire family spent together.

11. We must _____ a detailed response that leaves no doubt about our position on this important issue.

12. The first meeting will be in the school auditorium, but all _____ meetings will be held in the homes of our members.

13. Rather than sit back and wait for the enemy to attack him, the general took the _____ and delivered the first blow.

14. What a disappointment to hear that dull and _____ speech when we were expecting a clear, forceful, and interesting statement!

15. Many an artist whose work has been overlooked in his or her own lifetime has had to trust to _____ for appreciation.

16. The term "_____" was first applied in the 1660s to English Protestants who dissented from the Church of England.

17. As a tennis player, Sue doesn't have much speed or power, but she hits the ball with _____ accuracy.

18. During World War II, food became so scarce in Great Britain that the government
_____ it out to consumers in very small amounts.

19. All that you will need to _____ that dilapidated old house is lots of
time, lots of skill, lots of enthusiasm, and lots of money.

20. Since I was able to prove in court that the salesperson had lied to me, the contract
I had signed was declared _____.

Synonyms

*Choose the word from this unit that is **the same** or **most nearly the same** in meaning as the **boldface** word or expression in the given phrase. Write the word on the line provided.*

1. the only **maverick** in the group   _____

2. to discuss it at our **next** meeting   _____

3. **inventive** use of leftover materials   _____

4. must pass a **challenging** exam   _____

5. if they can **define** their goals   _____

6. a dramatic **vista** of red rock formations   _____

7. established for **future generations**   _____

8. a precious **keepsake** of Sally's childhood   _____

9. if we decide to **spruce up** the kitchen   _____

10. huge waves that **envelop** the tiny beach   _____

11. carefully **ration** out the medicine   _____

12. no longer **meddle** into my affairs   _____

13. judging the **significance** of this change   _____

14. **hoodwink** them into believing his story   _____

15. a **clumsy** attempt at an apology   _____

Antonyms

*Choose the word from this unit that is **most nearly opposite** in meaning to the **boldface** word or expression in the given phrase. Write the word on the line provided.*

16. declared **valid** by the courts   _____

17. to **promote** that wicked plot   _____

18. due to my **faulty** sense of direction   _____

19. **charming** behavior for a twelve-year-old   _____

20. anticipating your **laziness**   _____

*Circle the **boldface** word that more satisfactorily completes each of the following sentences.*

1. With his serious face and his dignified way of speaking, he is an excellent (**foil, memento**) for the clownish comedian.

2. The war that began with Germany's invasion of Poland in 1939 spread until it had (**pried, engulfed**) almost the entire world.

3. It is too late to attempt to (**refurbish, formulate**) the old city charter; we must have a completely new plan for our city government.

4. Brad is the kind of (**rigorous, resourceful**) quarterback who can always come up with something new when it is a matter of victory or defeat.

5. If you think that you can get away with selling overpriced products to the people of this town, you are (**deluding, refurbishing**) yourself.

6. One of the signs of a truly democratic nation is that it gives protection and freedom to (**initiatives, nonconformists**) who espouse unpopular views.

7. She hopes to win the election by convincing voters that the city's troubles result from the (**bumbling, unerring**) policies of the present Mayor.

8. Do you think the United States should take the (**initiative, dole**) in trying to bring about a compromise peace in the region?

9. In devising the Constitution, the Founding Fathers sought to "secure the blessings of liberty to ourselves and our (**posterity, foils**)."

10. Since you have failed to carry out your promises, I must tell you that the agreement between us is now (**resourceful, null and void**).

11. "We must (**engulf, formulate**) a plan to deal with this new situation and carry it out as quickly as possible," the president said.

12. He may look like an ordinary man, but he is in fact a figure of real (**panorama, consequence**) in the state government.

13. The lawyer made the point that her client had been at the scene of the crime before the murder but not (**subsequent, null and void**) to it.

14. By coaxing and questioning hour after hour, Tom finally managed to (**pry, delude**) the big secret from his sister.

15. What we lightly refer to as our "foreign policy" in fact embraces a vast (**panorama, consequence**) of aims and objectives, problems and concerns.

16. Why is it that such hardworking, self-reliant people now have to depend on a (**posterity, dole**) of food and other necessities from charitable agencies?

17. Perhaps he doesn't seem to be very bright, but he has an (**abominable, unerring**) instinct for anything that may make money for him.

18. All these things in the attic may seem like a lot of junk to you, but to me they are priceless (**mementos, nonconformists**) of childhood.

19. We all know that it is a long time since the speeding laws in our community have been (**subsequently, rigorously**) enforced.

20. Here I am on my first vacation in three years, and I have to put up with this (**abominable, bumbling**) weather day after day!

Read the following passage, in which some of the words you have studied in this unit appear in **boldface** type. Then complete each statement given below the passage by circling the letter of the item that is **the same** or **almost the same** in meaning as the highlighted word.

Annie Smith Peck: A Woman of Firsts

(Line)

Mountain climbing has always been a **rigorous** activity, even without today's high-tech gear. So imagine how rare it was when Annie Smith Peck climbed Mount Shasta in California in 1888. Peck became interested in mountain climbing when she first saw the Swiss Alps. Once she made that first climb in California

(5) and saw the marvelous **panorama** from the top, she was hooked for life.

Always a **nonconformist**, Peck refused to let the days' common prejudices against women keep her from her lofty goals. Born in 1850, she graduated from the University of Michigan with honors. Pursuing her interest in Greek and the

(10) Classics, she **subsequently** went on to study at the American School of Classical Studies in Athens, Greece, and was the school's first female student. She worked as a teacher, writer, and scholar, but it is as a mountain

(15) climber that **posterity** remembers her.

When she climbed Mount Orizaba in Mexico in 1897, Annie Smith Peck became the first woman in the Americas to climb a mountain over 18,000 feet high. By 1900,

(20) she had climbed twenty major mountains. Eight years later, she became the first person, man or woman, to climb the north peak of Mount Huarascan in Peru. Its summit, at 21,812 feet, marked the highest

The Swiss Alps, mountains that inspired Annie Smith Peck and countless others

(25) point ever reached in the Western Hemisphere. As a **consequence** of her accomplishments, the north peak of the mountain was renamed in her honor: *Cumbre Aña Smith.*

This spirited woman never let age hold her back. At sixty-one, Peck became the first person to climb Peru's Mount Coropuna. At the top she planted a flag that said,

(30) "Votes for Women." Peck climbed her last mountain in New Hampshire when she was eighty-two. Her death three years later marked the end of a long and remarkable life.

---

1. The meaning of **rigorous** (line 1) is
a. challenging
b. unpleasant
c. undemanding
d. enjoyable

2. Panorama (line 5) is best defined as
a. clouds
b. rocks
c. mountains
d. view

3. Nonconformist (line 6) most nearly means
a. follower
b. individualist
c. leader
d. feminist

4. Subsequently (line 10) is best defined as
a. suddenly
b. previously
c. surprisingly
d. later

5. Posterity (line 15) most nearly means
a. the past
b. the present
c. the future
d. the media

6. The meaning of **consequence** (line 25) is
a. cause
b. reminder
c. result
d. memory

Hear the words for this Unit pronounced, defined, and used in sentences at **www.vocabularyworkshop.com**.

Note carefully the spelling, pronunciation, part(s) of speech, and definition(s) of each of the following words. Then write the word in the blank space(s) in the illustrative sentence(s) following. Finally, study the lists of synonyms and antonyms given at the end of each entry.

1. alias
(ā′ lē əs)

(*n.*) an assumed name, especially as used to hide one's identity; (*adv.*) otherwise called

Mr. Plante was just one _____ used by the elusive spy.

Superman, _____ Clark Kent, began as a comic book character created in 1938.

SYNONYM: (*n.*) pseudonym
ANTONYMS: (*n.*) real name, given name, legal name

2. amble
(am′ bəl)

(*v.*) to walk slowly, stroll; (*n.*) an easy pace; a leisurely walk

It's a lovely day to _____ to work and enjoy the many sights and sounds along the way.

When we woke to see the sun shining, we planned a long _____ in the park.

SYNONYMS: (*v.*) saunter; (*n.*) ramble
ANTONYMS: (*v., n.*) gallop, dash, sprint, run, race, rush

3. burly
(bər′ lē)

(*adj.*) big and strong; muscular

That guy is as _____ as a lumberjack, so he would be the perfect one to help me move my furniture.

SYNONYMS: strapping, hefty, beefy, brawny
ANTONYMS: weak, puny, delicate, frail

4. distort
(dis tôrt′)

(*v.*) to give a false or misleading account of; to twist out of shape

A magazine known to _____ the facts would be an unreliable source of information.

SYNONYMS: disfigure, misshape, falsify

5. dogged
(dôg′ əd)

(*adj.*) persistent, stubbornly determined, refusing to give up

The troops fought with _____ determination and courage.

SYNONYM: untiring
ANTONYMS: wishy-washy, faltering, irresolute

6. dumbfounded
(dəm′ faúnd əd)

(*adj.*) so amazed that one is unable to speak, bewildered

When the shocking news finally reached us, we were completely _____.

SYNONYMS: speechless, stunned, flabbergasted
ANTONYMS: unsurprised, expectant

Hear the words for this Unit pronounced, defined, and used in sentences at **www.vocabularyworkshop.com**.

II

7. extinct
(ek stiŋkt′)

(*adj.*) no longer in existence; no longer active; gone out of use

The _____ volcano no longer threatens the area, but it changed the landscape forever.

SYNONYMS: died out, vanished
ANTONYMS: still alive, surviving, extant

8. fossil
(fäs′ əl)

(*n.*) the petrified remains or traces of an animal or plant that lived in the past; an extremely old-fashioned person or thing; (*adj.*) having qualities that belong to a remote past

This fish _____ is a million years old yet is amazingly well preserved.

Workers discovered _____ remains of an ancient beast.

SYNONYM: (*n.*) relic

9. grit
(grit)

(*n.*) very fine sand or gravel; courage in the face of hardship or danger; (*v.*) to grind; to make a grating sound

Cars stall if _____ clogs a fuel line.

It upsets me to see Dad get angry and _____ his teeth.

SYNONYMS: (*n.*) dirt, mettle
ANTONYMS: (*n.*) timidity, cowardice, faintheartedness

10. inevitable
(in ev′ ə tə bəl)

(*adj.*) sure to happen, unavoidable

Is it _____ that all comedies have happy endings?

SYNONYMS: inescapable, fated
ANTONYMS: avoidable, escapable, preventable

11. ingrained
(in grānd′)

(*adj.*) fixed deeply and firmly; working into the grain or fiber; forming a part of the inmost being

My habit of biting my lower lip when I'm nervous is so _____ that I don't notice doing it.

SYNONYMS: deep-seated, deep-rooted, indelible
ANTONYMS: superficial, shallow, skin-deep

12. meteoric
(mē tē ôr′ ik)

(*adj.*) resembling a meteor in speed; having sudden and temporary brilliance similar to a meteor's

The young actor's _____ rise to fame was legendary.

SYNONYMS: brilliant, blazing
ANTONYMS: slow, sluggish, gradual

13. parody
(par′ ə dē)

(*n.*) a humorous or ridiculous imitation; (*v.*) to make fun of something by imitating it

The audience roared with laughter at the hilarious

_____ .

Unit 11 ■ *125*

The comedy film _____ political life in England.

SYNONYMS: (*n.*) satire, travesty; (*v.*) lampoon, burlesque

14. prevail
(pri vāl′)

(*v.*) to triumph over; to succeed; to exist widely, be in general use; to get someone to do something by urging

We hope to _____ over all obstacles we may encounter on this project.

SYNONYMS: win, rule, reign, overcome, conquer
ANTONYMS: be defeated, go under, succumb

15. rend
(rend)

(*v.*) to tear to pieces; split violently apart (*past tense*, rent)

The abominable tactics of this trial could _____ public confidence in the legal system.

SYNONYMS: cleave, dismember, splinter, tear asunder

16. replenish
(ri plen′ ish)

(v.) to fill again, make good, replace

Airport crews work quickly to _____ a plane's supply of food, water, and safety supplies.

SYNONYMS: refill, restock, refresh, restore
ANTONYMS: empty, drain, deplete, sap

17. rummage
(rəm′ əj)

(*v.*) to search through, investigate the contents of; (*n.*) an active search; a collection of odd items

It can be an adventure to _____ around our garage for remnants of our childhood.

She found an old saddle in the _____.

SYNONYMS: (*v.*) delve into, sift through, poke around

18. skimp
(skimp)

(*v.*) to save, be thrifty; to be extremely sparing with; to give little attention or effort to

If you _____ on regular meals, you may be tempted to snack on too much junk food.

SYNONYMS: be stingy, scrimp, cut corners
ANTONYMS: be extravagant, splurge, lavish

19. sleuth
(slüth)

(*n.*) a detective

A skilled _____ can find hidden clues in unusual places.

SYNONYMS: investigator, gumshoe

20. vandalism
(van′ dəl iz əm)

(*n.*) deliberate and pointless destruction of public or private property

The city needs to create tougher laws to discourage

_____.

SYNONYMS: willful destruction, malicious defacement

Completing the Sentence

From the words for this unit, choose the one that best completes each of the following sentences. Write the word in the space provided.

1. There is an old saying that nothing is really _____ except death and taxes.

2. We were nothing less than _____ when we saw the immense damage that the hurricane had done in so brief a time.

3. As the buffalo began to decrease sharply in numbers, conservationists feared that it might become totally _____ .

4. Whenever our team needs a few yards to make a first down, we call on our big, _____ fullback to crash through the line.

5. The cruise ship stopped at the port both to give the passengers a chance to go ashore and to _____ the water supply.

6. If you truly want to improve your math grades, you should not continue to _____ so often on your homework.

7. We saw a bolt of lightning _____ a huge limb from the mighty oak tree.

8. The old con artist had used so many _____ over the course of his criminal career that he sometimes forgot his real name!

9. After our furious gallop across the countryside, we allowed our tired horses to _____ back to the stable.

10. We greatly admired the _____ determination and patience that the disabled veteran showed in learning to master a wheelchair.

11. The rock singer enjoyed a sudden _____ rise in popularity, but his career faded just as quickly as it had blossomed.

12. Since coal was formed from the decayed bodies of plants that lived many millions of years ago, it is considered a kind of _____ fuel.

13. The grime on the mechanic's hands was so deeply _____ that even a thorough scrubbing couldn't entirely remove it.

14. In the late 19th century, Sir Arthur Conan Doyle created one of the most famous _____ in literature, Sherlock Holmes.

15. The old custom of celebrating the Fourth of July with a fireworks display still _____ in many American towns.

16. Even though so many people were criticizing and ridiculing him, he had the _____ to continue doing what he felt was right.

17. Isn't it a shame that our School Board must spend thousands of dollars every year just to repair the damage caused by _____ ?

18. Her face was so _____ with pain and suffering that at first I did not recognize her.

19. Her ability to _____ the words and gestures of prominent Americans makes her an excellent comic impressionist.

20. Isn't it fun on a rainy day to _____ about in the attic and look for interesting odds and ends?

1. deep-rooted sense of right and wrong _____

2. ways to **falsify** the evidence _____

3. tried to **lampoon** the governor _____

4. memoirs of her **brilliant** career _____

5. where science **reigns** over superstition _____

6. greedily **dismember** its prey _____

7. protected by a **brawny** bodyguard _____

8. untiring faith in technology _____

9. admiring the **mettle** of those hardy pioneers _____

10. sift through the old catalogues _____

11. left the guide totally **flabbergasted** _____

12. a valuable **relic** of life in the past _____

13. observing the sharp-witted **investigator** _____

14. broken apart by **malicious defacement** _____

15. to sign the document using a **pseudonym** _____

16. whether that outcome is **avoidable** _____

17. after **depleting** the ice _____

18. photographs of the **surviving** species _____

19. dash along the scenic river _____

20. usually **splurge** on the desserts _____

Choosing the Right Word

*Circle the **boldface** word that more satisfactorily completes each of the following sentences.*

1. The defenders of the Alamo put up such a (**burly, dogged**) resistance that the enemy had a hard time capturing it.

2. To avoid a lot of unwanted attention, the famous rock star registered in the hotel under a(n) (**rummage, alias**).

3. An art historian who is trying to verify the authenticity of a painting acts more like a (**sleuth, fossil**) than a critic.

4. His (**dogged, meteoric**) success at such an early age left him unprepared to handle the disappointments and failures that came to him later in life.

5. It may be, as you say, that this volcano has been (**extinct, dumbfounded**) for many years, but isn't there some danger that it may come to life again?

6. Whether the window was broken accidentally or as an act of (**parody, vandalism**), the fact remains that it is broken and must be paid for.

7. I hope to pick up some real bargains at the (**rummage, grit**) sale being held in our civic center.

8. Although it is sometimes hard, we must have faith that in the long run justice and decency will (**skimp, prevail**).

9. Visiting the school I had attended so many years before made me feel like a creature from the far past—a living (**alias, fossil**).

10. "I'll have two franks with all the fixings," I said to the vendor, "and don't (**prevail, skimp**) on the mustard!"

11. I am exhausted now, but all I need is a satisfying meal, a hot shower, and a good night's sleep to (**replenish, rend**) my energies.

12. Is there anything more romantic than a nighttime (**amble, vandalism**) upon the moonlit decks of a mighty ocean liner?

13. No, I wasn't (**ingrained, dumbfounded**) to be chosen the most popular member of the class, but maybe I was just a little surprised!

14. The aging actor trying to play the part of a young man seemed no more than a (**sleuth, parody**) of the great performer he once was.

15. The prejudices of a bigot are sometimes so (**ingrained, alias**) that it is very difficult to get rid of them.

16. Isn't it foolish to think that just because of his (**meteoric, burly**) physique he has no interest in art or music?

17. We scorn all those who would deliberately bend the truth and (**distort, amble**) history in order to suit the political needs of their day.

18. Since it is possible for nations to settle their disagreements in a reasonable way, we refuse to believe that war is (**inevitable, dumbfounded**).

19. I know that you don't like the idea of working in a gas station, but you'll just have to (**replenish, grit**) your teeth and do it.

20. Suddenly, the stillness of the early morning hours was (**rent, rummaged**) by a single shot!

Vocabulary in Context

Read the following passage, in which some of the words you have studied in this unit appear in **boldface** type. Then complete each statement given below the passage by circling the letter of the item that is **the same** or **almost the same** in meaning as the highlighted word.

Delving into Dinosaur Truths

(Line)

Bone hunters first began to find, identify, and speculate about dinosaur **fossils** in the early 1800s. Since then, people the world over have offered a wide range of ideas and opinions about life in the age of dinosaurs. These great creatures have inspired painters, cartoonists, writers, filmmakers, musicians, and others. But not all ideas reflected scientific reality. (5)

Whether on purpose or out of ignorance, generations of misinformation have **distorted** our view of dinosaurs, which have been portrayed as stupid, vicious, and slow-moving creatures. Recent evidence now shows that some could run very fast and with grace. Many had well-developed brains. We now know that some were fierce predators, (10) while others were peaceful vegetarians.

In nature's great time line, dinosaurs were **extinct** long before human beings first appeared. Scenes of primitive people battling dinosaurs could never really have happened. Plots that may make for (15) absorbing entertainment, bold comedy, or gripping adventure should not be confused with reality.

It may be **inevitable** that creatures as big and as mystifying as dinosaurs would inspire art and invention. This is just what science fiction is—a (20) blend of fact and fantasy that entertains and stirs thought. Famous sci-fi adventures, such as *King Kong, Journey to the Center of the Earth, The Land That Time Forgot,* and the *Tarzan* tales, have become part of popular culture. They amuse both (25) scientists and escapists. Even a cartoon like "The Flintstones," in which sitcom cave families have cute dinosaurs as pets and as **burly** beasts of burden, amuses us. Must cartoons be accurate?

The fearsome tyrannosaurus rex: What was this huge creature *really* like?

Maybe truth should **prevail** over entertainment value. To combat imaginative fiction being taken as truth, we need to do detailed research and ask probing questions. (30)

---

1. The meaning of **fossils** (line 1) is
a. remains   c. herds
b. eggs   d. movies

2. The meaning of **distorted** (line 7) is
a. encouraged   c. proved
b. twisted   d. shaped

3. Extinct (line 12) most nearly means
a. existent   c. born
b. studied   d. gone

4. Inevitable (line 18) most nearly means
a. understandable   c. unavoidable
b. surprising   d. avoidable

5. Burly (line 27) is best defined as
a. clever   c. amazing
b. misshapen   d. muscular

6. Prevail (line 29) most nearly means
a. win   c. draw
b. lose   d. prepare

Hear the words for this Unit pronounced, defined, and used in sentences at **www.vocabularyworkshop.com**.

UNIT 12

Definitions

Note carefully the spelling, pronunciation, part(s) of speech, and definition(s) of each of the following words. Then write the word in the blank space(s) in the illustrative sentence(s) following. Finally, study the lists of synonyms and antonyms given at the end of each entry.

1. abduct
(ab dəkt′)

(*v.*) to kidnap, carry off by force

Some people with vivid imaginations fear that hostile aliens will come to Earth to _____ humans.

SYNONYMS: seize, snatch

2. ambiguous
(am big′ yü əs)

(*adj.*) not clear; having two or more possible meanings

The purpose of a test is to determine whether students learned the material, not to confuse them with

_____ questions.

SYNONYMS: vague, uncertain, unclear, equivocal
ANTONYMS: obvious, plain, clear, unequivocal

3. balk
(bôk)

(*v.*) to stop short and refuse to go on; to refuse abruptly; to prevent from happening; (*n.*) (in baseball) an illegal motion made by a pitcher

My horse _____ when I urged it to go up the steep mountain slope.

The opposing team scored an additional run because of the pitcher's _____.

SYNONYM: (*v.*) resist, hesitate, block

4. compact
(*v., adj.,* kəm pakt′;
n., käm′ pakt)

(*adj.*) closely and firmly packed together; small; (*v.*) to squeeze together; (*n.*) an agreement between parties; a small case containing a mirror and face powder; a small car

Computers are much more _____ now than they were a generation ago.

Workers at the town dump were asked to _____ the trash to save space.

SYNONYMS: (*adj.*) dense; (*v.*) compress
ANTONYMS: (*adj.*) oversize, enormous, humongous, bulky

5. confer
(kən fər′)

(*v.*) to consult, talk over, exchange opinions; to present as a gift, favor, or honor

The committee will _____ before taking any action on the proposed new contract.

SYNONYMS: deliberate, award, bestow
ANTONYMS: withdraw, take away, withhold, deny

6. earmark
(ir′ mark)

(*v.*) to set aside for a special purpose; to mark an animal's ear for identification; (*n.*) an identifying mark or feature

Let's _____ the money we received for the new building fund.

SYNONYMS: (v.) reserve; (n.) trait, attribute

7. frigid
(frij' id)

(adj.) extremely cold; lacking in warmth or feeling

Antarctica has a very _____ climate.

SYNONYMS: freezing, unresponsive
ANTONYMS: hot, balmy, torrid, warm, friendly

8. implement
(im' plə mənt)

(n.) an instrument, tool; (v.) to put into effect

The harrow is a farm _____ that is used to pulverize and smooth soil.

The highway patrol will _____ the new speed limit as of July 1 of this year.

SYNONYMS: (n.) device, utensil; (v.) fulfill, accomplish, achieve, apply, carry out

9. incalculable
(in kal' kyə lə bəl)

(adj.) too great to be counted; unpredictable, uncertain

Concerned scientists worry that global warming may cause _____ damage to our environment.

SYNONYMS: countless, measureless
ANTONYMS: measurable, countable, predictable

10. indisputable
(in dis pyüt' ə bəl)

(adj.) beyond question or argument, definitely true

With such _____ evidence, Judge Lee must rule to drop all charges against my client.

SYNONYMS: irrefutable, undeniable, incontestable, inarguable
ANTONYMS: questionable, debatable, arguable

11. intensive
(in ten' siv)

(adj.) thorough, deep; showing great effort; concentrated

It took _____ physical therapy for the injured athlete to regain her strength and speed.

SYNONYMS: thoroughgoing, heightened, exhaustive
ANTONYMS: relaxed, easygoing, laid-back

12. maneuver
(mə nü' vər)

(n.) a planned movement; a skillful plan; a scheme; (v.) to perform or carry out such a planned movement

The troops carried out a night _____ as part of the training mission.

It takes a steady hand to _____ the high-speed power drill.

SYNONYMS: (n.) move, tactic; (v.) guide, manipulate

13. sabotage
(sab' ə täzh)

(n.) an action taken to destroy something or to prevent it from working properly; (v.) to take such destructive action

Foreign embassies worry about _____

Hear the words for this Unit pronounced, defined, and
used in sentences at **www.vocabularyworkshop.com**.

12

Angry workers decided to _____
the factory to protest its poor working conditions.

SYNONYMS: (*v.*) vandalize, cripple, subvert, destroy

14. scant
(skant)

(*adj.*) not enough; barely enough; marked by a small or
insufficient amount

Somehow, we made the _____
supply of food stretch for nearly a week.

SYNONYMS: inadequate, meager, skimpy, bare
ANTONYMS: abundant, plentiful, profuse, excessive

15. stealthy
(stel' thē)

(*adj.*) done in a way so as not to be seen or observed; sneaky,
underhanded

The nervous robber took _____
glances at the cash register.

SYNONYMS: sly, furtive
ANTONYMS: open, direct, aboveboard, forthright

16. strapping
(strap' iŋ)

(*adj.*) tall, strong, and healthy

That _____ young man will make
a very good wrestler.

SYNONYMS: sturdy, husky, brawny, athletic, hefty
ANTONYMS: weak, frail, fragile, delicate, puny

17. strident
(strīd' ənt)

(*adj.*) harsh, shrill; unpleasant sounding

The group's _____ laughter
represented harsh ridicule, not cheery amusement.

SYNONYMS: piercing, grating
ANTONYMS: mellow, soothing, musical, honeyed

18. thrive
(thrīv)

(*v.*) to grow vigorously; to grow in wealth and possessions

Angela remains hopeful that her business will

_____ in today's Internet culture.

SYNONYMS: flourish, blossom, prosper
ANTONYMS: wither, die, fade, fail

19. titanic
(tī tan' ik)

(*adj.*) of enormous size, strength, power, or scope

The movie plot explores the _____
struggle between the forces of good and evil.

SYNONYMS: gigantic, huge, mighty, immense
ANTONYMS: tiny, miniature, diminutive, pint-size

20. valiant
(val' yənt)

(*adj.*) possessing or acting with bravery or boldness

Sir Galahad was a _____ knight
of King Arthur's Round Table.

SYNONYMS: brave, bold, courageous, gallant, heroic
ANTONYMS: timid, cowardly, fainthearted, "chicken"

Completing the Sentence

From the words for this unit, choose the one that best completes each of the following sentences. Write the word in the space provided.

1. No doubt our antipollution program will be expensive, but the cost of doing nothing would be simply _____ .

2. At first the zebras did not notice the _____ movements of the lions inching their way closer to the herd.

3. The millionaire has hired special guards to make sure that his children will not be

_____ .

4. When the winds begin to turn _____ in November, our thoughts turn to our warm and sunny island off the coast of Florida.

5. Each year a portion of the school budget is _____ for the purchase of new books for the library.

6. When our team saw their _____ 200-pound defensive linemen, we realized that we would have a hard time running against them.

7. In your training to become a dental assistant, you will become familiar with many of

the _____ that dentists use.

8. I prefer the _____ edition of the dictionary because it is so much lighter and less bulky than the unabridged version.

9. Even mighty warships were endangered by the _____ waves that loomed like mountains above them.

10. The new recruits were rudely awakened from their peaceful sleep by the _____ voice of the sergeant barking commands.

11. Why must you always be so _____ when I want you to give me a straight yes-or-no answer?

12. In Shakespeare's words, "Cowards die many times before their deaths; the

_____ never taste of death but once."

13. I was amazed to see how skillfully Felicia _____ that huge car through the heavy downtown traffic.

14. For a person who loves to argue as much as Gene does, there is nothing that is

really _____ .

15. The president will _____ well-deserved honors on the retiring ambassador.

16. The cactus is an example of a plant having natural adaptations that enable it to

_____ even in a very dry climate.

17. Since I'm afraid of heights, I usually _____ at the idea of sitting in the first row of the topmost balcony in a theater.

18. The breakdown of all these machines at the same time cannot simply be a coincidence; we suspect deliberate _____ .

19. Since the time we have to prepare for the final exams is exceedingly _____ , we had better make the best of every hour.

20. As the day of the big game approached, our practice sessions became more and more _____ .

Synonyms

*Choose the word from this unit that is **the same** or **most nearly the same** in meaning as the **boldface** word or expression in the given phrase. Write the word on the line provided.*

1. forced to try dangerous **tactics** _____

2. **resist** because of fear _____

3. lending us **measureless** support _____

4. its **small** motor _____

5. the **inarguable** star of the team _____

6. a most **unresponsive** welcome _____

7. a plot to **kidnap** the king for ransom _____

8. to interpret that **vague** remark _____

9. as they put forth an **immense** effort _____

0. a **courageous** fight against the disease _____

1. may use that **device** to move the baggage _____

2. made a **furtive** grab for the jewels _____

3. all the **attributes** of a rascal _____

4. tries to **cripple** the communications system _____

5. the **heightened** search for the missing child _____

Antonyms

*Choose the word from this unit that is **most nearly opposite** in meaning to the **boldface** word or expression in the given phrase. Write the word on the line provided.*

6. to **deny** the award _____

7. its **abundant** natural resources _____

8. met a **delicate** peasant girl _____

9. spoken in **soothing** tones _____

0. expected to **wither** in that environment _____

Choosing the Right Word

*Circle the **boldface** word that more satisfactorily completes each of the following sentences.*

1. Truthfulness and sincerity are the (**earmarks, compacts**) of an honest person.

2. As election day gets closer, the tone of the candidates' political oratory becomes more and more (**titanic, strident**).

3. What do you think the United States should do when its representatives are (**sabotaged, abducted**) and held for ransom?

4. I don't think democracy can (**balk, thrive**) in an atmosphere of racial and religious hatred.

5. Of all the evergreens that tower in America's forests, none can surpass the height and girth of the (**titanic, indisputable**) California redwoods.

6. Though the odds were greatly against them, the brave defenders of the fort waged a (**valiant, scant**) battle against the enemy's troops.

7. Because her condition was so poor after the operation, she was placed in the hospital's (**stealthy, intensive**) care unit.

8. The future is indeed (**incalculable, strapping**) but we must face it with faith and confidence.

9. After straining and sweating in the hot sun for an hour, we realized that we had pushed the stalled car only a(n) (**scant, intensive**) quarter mile.

10. Since *presently* means both "right now" and "in the future," any statement containing it must be considered (**strident, ambiguous**).

11. When we made our appeal for funds, their response was so (**incalculable, frigid**) that we realized we would have to find other ways of raising money.

12. Although our club is run more or less democratically, we don't have the time to (**confer, abduct**) about every minor detail.

13. Creeping (**stealthily, ambiguously**) through the underbrush, the enemy came within a few yards of the stockade before the guards saw them.

14. When their pitcher committed the (**balk, earmark**), the umpire advanced our runner from first to second base.

15. When a country has been overrun by a conquering army, the only way the people may have to strike back is by acts of (**ambiguity, sabotage**).

16. Before landing on the shore of New England, the first Pilgrim settlers signed an agreement called the "Mayflower (**Compact, Maneuver**)."

17. Why is that big, (**strapping, frigid**) fellow in the ad always kicking sand into the face of the 98-pound weakling?

18. In her floor exercise, the champion gymnast performed some of the most amazing (**earmarks, maneuvers**) I have ever seen.

19. We have worked out a good plan on paper; now we must decide how we are going to (**implement, balk**) it.

20. When he says that his analysis of the problem is (**indisputable, valiant**), all he means is that he's not willing to listen to anyone else's ideas.

Vocabulary in Context

Read the following passage, in which some of the words you have studied in this unit appear in **boldface** type. Then complete each statement given below the passage by circling the letter of the item that is **the same** or **almost the same** in meaning as the highlighted word.

Navajo Code Talkers

(Line)

In war, survival may depend on an army's ability to pass data in secret. Armies make **intensive** efforts to break each other's communication codes. Each wants to uncover what its enemy plans to do. During World War II, no intelligence group was more valuable to American troops in the South Pacific than the Navajo Code Talkers.

(5)   The Navajo Code Talkers were a remarkable group of Navajo soldiers who used their native language to create an unbreakable code. The Navajo language has many **earmarks** of a successful code: it is unwritten, complicated, and known only by a **scant** number of non-Navajos. The Japanese could never crack it. During (10) the terrible battle of Iwo Jima, six Navajo Code Talkers sent and received 800 vital messages without a single error.

Philip Johnston got the idea of using the Navajo language for a code in 1941. (15) He had grown up among the Navajo and spoke their language fluently. He believed that any code based on Navajo would be secure. After months of testing and training, the first group of twenty-nine (20) Navajo Code Talkers **implemented** their distinctive system. They matched Navajo words to common military terms. For example, the Navajo word for

Navajo code talkers in the Pacific relay orders over a field radio during World War II.

"hummingbird" stood for fighter plane; "iron fish" meant submarine; "turtle" meant (25) tank. They also created a secondary code in which Navajo words stood for English letters. Code Talkers could then spell specific words by stringing words together.

Some people found it odd that Native Americans made such **valiant** efforts to help a nation that had a history of harming them. Yet Navajo Code Talkers never **balked** at the chance to serve the United States. Their code remains one of the few in all of military (30) history that was never broken. In 1982, President Ronald Reagan declared August 14 as Navajo Code Talkers Day to honor the contributions of these brave soldiers.

. The meaning of **intensive** (line 2) is
a. concentrated   c. truthful
b. vague   d. half-hearted

. The meaning of **earmarks** (line 7) is
a. sounds   c. benefits
b. actions   d. attributes

. **Scant** (line 8) most nearly means
a. meager   c. sturdy
b. plentiful   d. clever

4. **Implemented** (line 20) most nearly means
a. withheld   c. manipulated
b. applied   d. destroyed

5. **Valiant** (line 27) is best defined as
a. timid   c. heroic
b. harsh   d. sly

6. **Balked** (line 28) is best defined as
a. spoke   c. hesitated
b. insisted   d. gave up

Vocabulary for Comprehension

*Read the following passage, in which some of the words you have studied in Units 10–12 appear in **boldface** type. Then answer questions 1–10 on page 139 on the basis of what is <u>stated</u> or <u>implied</u> in the passage and in the introductory statement.*

This passage explains why the icy continent of Antarctica is a truly international scientific laboratory.

(Line)

"Science lab" usually means a clean, bright room in which researchers work with high-tech equipment. Antarctica, the fifth
(5) largest of Earth's seven continents, is itself an enormous, ice-cold science lab. It has no native population. Few living things can survive in its brutal climate. But scientists are attracted
(10) to the rare features of this desolate continent.

Antarctica is more than 95% ice-covered all year long. It has had the lowest air temperature ever
(15) measured, as well as some of the highest winds. Because it has no industrial pollution, its ice and snow are pure. All that ice makes it doubtful that any settlement or
(20) economic development will ever take place. But many tiny outposts have sprung up since the 1950s.

In that decade, twelve nations set up research stations all over Antarctica.
(25) Representatives of those nations got together to draft a **compact** devoting the continent to peaceful study. This pact went into effect in 1961. It forbids military action and nuclear weapons. It
(30) promotes a free exchange of ideas.

Antarctic scientists devise and carry out a wide range of tests. They study glaciers, weather patterns and

conditions, icebergs, magnetism,
(35) volcanoes, the movement of rock plates, and animal and plant biology. They openly share their findings with the global scientific community.

Life in such a difficult place
(40) demands planning, special gear, and **grit**. Scientists must figure out how to do their research safely and effectively. They must guard their health and well-being. Internet and
(45) satellite technologies surely help. Researchers so far from home can **confer** with the family, friends, and coworkers they left behind. They can stay up-to-date on world events.
(50) But they cannot easily come and go. Scientists often arrive before the Antarctic winter, when near-total darkness **engulfs** the area. They typically stay for six to ten long, cold,
(55) lonely months.

1. The "rare features" of Antarctica that the author refers to in lines 9–11
   a. are never identified
   b. are identified in paragraph 2
   c. are identified in paragraph 4
   d. are not so rare or unusual
   e. have vanished as weather conditions have changed

2. **Compact** (line 26) most nearly means
   a. dense
   b. reminder
   c. agreement
   d. small car
   e. speech

3. The compact that went into effect in 1961 had all of the following purposes EXCEPT
   a. to divide Antarctica among twelve nations
   b. to share the results of all scientific research
   c. to prevent any kind of military action
   d. to ban all nuclear weapons
   e. to promote peaceful study

4. The meaning of **grit** (line 41) is
   a. gravel
   b. power
   c. courage
   d. grind
   e. persistence

5. **Confer** (line 47) most nearly means
   a. consult
   b. study
   c. argue
   d. present gifts
   e. play

6. **Engulfs** (line 53) is best defined as
   a. empties
   b. divides
   c. endangers
   d. envelops
   e. avoids

7. Paragraph 5 (lines 39–55) focuses on the
   a. difficulties faced by scientists who work on Antarctica
   b. future of Antarctica

   c. likelihood that the research stations will remain on Antarctica
   d. kinds of tests scientists conduct on Antarctica
   e. weather conditions on Antarctica

8. Which of the following best states the main idea of the passage?
   a. Antarctica, the fifth-largest continent, has no native population.
   b. It is easy to do scientific research on Antarctica
   c. Scientists from twelve countries share information from research on Antarctica.
   d. Antarctica is almost totally covered with ice all year.
   e. Scientists on Antarctica depend on the Internet for communication.

9. Which of the following conclusions can you draw from the passage?
   a. There is discord among the nations that signed the 1961 agreement.
   b. Antarctica is a difficult place to live and work.
   c. Antarctica is one of the most valuable resources on this planet.
   d. In the future, nations will build colonies on Antarctica, and businesses will exploit it.
   e. The numerous scientific outposts on Antarctica have severely damaged the continent's native plants and animals.

10. What can you infer about the author's attitude toward the scientists who live and work on Antarctica?
   a. The author thinks they are foolish for getting stuck on Antarctica.
   b. The author wishes he were one of them.
   c. The author thinks that the scientists from twelve nations are destined for conflict.
   d. The author admires and respects them.
   e. The author thinks they have an easy, comfortable life.

Grammar in Context

Read the sentences "Antarctica is more than 95% ice-covered all year long. It has had the lowest air temperature ever measured, as well as some of the highest winds" (lines 12–16 on page 138). The **pronoun** "it" that begins the second sentence agrees in number and gender with its **antecedent** "Antarctica" in the first sentence. Pronouns and antecedents must agree in number. They must also agree in gender, as in the sentence "Captain Robert Scott led his men on a treacherous journey."

Learn a few rules to avoid errors in **pronoun-antecedent agreement**. (1) Singular antecedents and singular antecedents linked by *or* or *nor* require singular pronouns. (2) Indefinite pronoun antecedents such as *everybody*, *nobody*, *each*, and *neither* are singular. They, too, require singular pronouns. (3) Singular antecedents linked by *and* and plural antecedents linked by *and*, *or*, or *nor* require plural pronouns. (4) Indefinite pronoun antecedents such as *several*, *both*, *few*, and *many* are plural and therefore also require plural pronouns. In addition to keeping these rules in mind, remember that sometimes groups of words (such as "living in the frigid Antarctic wilderness") can be a singular subject. Refer to them with a singular pronoun. (5) When you are deciding whether to use the personal pronoun *me* or *I*, eliminate everything from the subject except the personal pronoun, and then read the sentence.

For each of the following sentences, choose the pronoun from the pair in parentheses that agrees with its antecedent, and write it on the line provided.

1. One of the scientists stated his opinion in a letter that (**he, they**) wrote to his colleagues.

_____

2. The scientist in charge took my assistant and (**me, I**) on a tour of the Antarctic weather station.

_____

3. Anyone who has worked in Antarctica will say that (**he or she, they**) is lucky to have had the experience.

_____

4. Both the frigid temperatures and the strong, chilling winds made (**its, their**) effects felt.

_____

5. An environmentalist from Stanford and a meteorologist from Yale made (**his, their**) first visit to our station.

_____

6. The group of scientists who studied the animals and plants of the icy region shared (**its, their**) remarkable findings with the international scientific community.

_____

7. Neither the scientists who studied the weather conditions nor those who focused on glaciers were finished with (**his or her, their**) work by the time I arrived.

_____

Two-Word Completions

Circle the pair of words that best complete the meaning of each of the following passages.

1. "Although we have devised a plan to deal with the situation," the official said, "we will not be able to _____ it until we get the funds that the government has _____ for the project."
a. replenish . . . conferred
b. implement . . . earmarked
c. refurbish . . . maneuvered
d. formulate . . . rummaged

2. Though such animals as the saber-toothed tiger and the woolly mammoth have been _____ since the close of the last Ice Age, many thousands of years ago, their _____ remains have been found in various parts of the world.
a. extinct . . . fossilized
b. scant . . . earmarked
c. skimpy . . . distorted
d. indisputable . . . unerring

3. When we saw the breathtaking _____ on that lovely autumn morning, we decided to _____ rather than rush and miss the impact of that stunning vista.
a. parody . . . maneuver
b. panorama . . . amble
c. fossil . . . balk
d. grit . . . compact

4. Kidnappers had made plans to _____ the official and hold him for ransom. Fortunately, however, the police were able to _____ the plot after an informant tipped them off about it.
a. delude . . . balk
b. abduct . . . foil
c. sabotage . . . distort
d. parody . . . pry

5. When I asked her where I could find the old book, her reply was so _____ that I had to spend over an hour _____ around the attic until I finally found it.
a. indisputable . . . earmarking
b. bumbling . . . abducting
c. intensive . . . prevailing
d. ambiguous . . . rummaging

6. The way in which the nimble little star quarterback _____ around the _____ linebackers attempting to sack him reminded me of a bicycle weaving through heavy midtown traffic.
a. engulfed . . . compact
b. abducted . . . strapping
c. maneuvered . . . burly
d. foiled . . . frigid

7. I am always _____ by the amazing powers of observation and deduction exhibited by my favorite _____, the legendary Sherlock Holmes.
a. deluded . . . fossil
b. ingrained . . . foil
c. dogged . . . vandal
d. dumbfounded . . . sleuth

Read each sentence carefully. Then circle the item that best completes the statement below the sentence.

Rather than retire from public life as he had hoped, George Washington was prevailed upon in 1789 to accept the presidency of the United States. (2)

1. The best definition for the phrase **prevailed upon** in line 2 is

a. commonly expected   c. reluctantly allowed
b. successfully urged   d. secretly ordered

It is no exaggeration to compare with canned sardines the thousands of commuters compacted in rush-hour subway cars. (2)

2. The word **compacted** in line 2 is best defined as

a. fleeing work   c. squeezed together
b. making deals   d. going home

Dr. Watson is often reminded by Sherlock Holmes that his astonishing solutions stem from observation and rigorous deduction, not hunches or gut feelings. (2)

3. In line 2 the word **rigorous** is used to mean

a. severe   b. logical   c. harsh   d. trying

One of the chief aims of American foreign policy in the period following World War II was to balk Soviet attempts to "export" communism to the Third World. (2)

4. In line 2 the word **balk** most nearly means

a. reverse   b. shy away from   c. monitor   d. block

New York City's Greenwich Village has long been a favorite destination for people whose nonconformist views set them apart from the mainstream. (2)

5. The word **nonconformist** in line 2 most nearly means

a. bohemian   b. revolutionary   c. foreign   d. quaint

Antonyms *In each of the following groups, circle the word or expression that is most nearly the **opposite** of the word in **boldface** type.*

1. consequences
a. aims
b. criticisms
c. causes
d. results

2. frigid
a. balmy
b. icy
c. wasted
d. busy

3. strapping
a. sharp
b. strong
c. frail
d. husky

4. prevail
a. win
b. succumb
c. participate
d. campaign

5. subsequent
a. odd
b. prior
c. funny
d. disturbing

6. dumbfounded
a. astonished
b. saddened
c. amazed
d. expectant

7. indisputable
a. new
b. proven
c. debatable
d. strong

8. null and void
a. meaningless
b. illegal
c. vague
d. in effect

9. compact
a. efficient
b. enormous
c. modern
d. costly

11. ambiguous
a. wordy
b. strange
c. clear
d. brief

13. strident
a. loud
b. mellow
c. strong
d. harsh

15. inevitable
a. costly
b. avoidable
c. desired
d. foolish

10. replenish
a. empty
b. count
c. budget
d. increase

12. burly
a. delicate
b. fat
c. tough
d. muscular

14. skimp
a. splurge
b. plan
c. annoy
d. decorate

16. nonconformist
a. clever
b. conventional
c. radical
d. severe

Word Families

A. On the line provided, write the word you have learned in Units 10–12 that is related to each of the following nouns.
EXAMPLE: compactness—**compact**

1. stealthiness, stealth _____

2. formula, formulation, formulator _____

3. extinction _____

4. refurbisher, refurbishment _____

5. rigor, rigorousness _____

6. stridency _____

7. distortion, distorter _____

8. resource, resourcefulness _____

9. titan _____

10. burliness _____

11. conference _____

12. meteor, meteorite _____

13. delusion, deluder _____

14. inevitability, inevitableness _____

15. scantness, scantiness _____

B. On the line provided, write the word you have learned in Units 10–12 that is related to each of the following verbs.
EXAMPLE: dispute—**indisputable**

16. vandalize _____

17. abominate _____

18. initiate _____

19. fossilize _____

20. bumble _____

Word Associations

In each of the following groups, circle the word that is best defined or suggested by the given phrase.

1. said of someone who seems to be incapable of making a mistake
   a. titanic   b. unerring   c. bumbling   d. ambiguous

2. what one of King Arthur's knights would probably be
   a. abominable   b. null and void   c. valiant   d. inevitable

3. "This paperweight reminds me of the wonderful time I had last summer."
   a. panorama   b. memento   c. parody   d. foil

4. rightly said of a dinosaur
   a. extinct   b. rigorous   c. scant   d. ingrained

5. a trait that is fixed within a person
   a. ingrained   b. ambiguous   c. intensive   d. null and void

6. "He seems to have a gift for doing the wrong thing, at the wrong time, in the wrong way."
   a. strapping   b. bumbling   c. indisputable   d. rigorous

7. what might be done to a garment to express grief
   a. confer   b. rend   c. grit   d. balk

8. so shocked and amazed that I couldn't speak
   a. dumbfounded   b. resourceful   c. subsequent   d. meteoric

9. what a flood would probably do
   a. dole   b. skimp   c. amble   d. engulf

10. an extinct fish found in a rock
    a. rummage   b. fossil   c. alias   d. balk

11. food given in small amounts
    a. balk   b. dole   c. earmark   d. grit

12. what we did when our water supply began to run out
    a. formulate   b. thrive   c. replenish   d. prevail

13. what troops go out on to train for warfare
    a. panoramas   b. parodies   c. maneuvers   d. initiatives

14. describing study that is thorough
    a. dogged   b. intensive   c. strapping   d. subsequent

15. those who come after us, especially our descendants
    a. foils   b. nonconformists   c. sleuths   d. posterity

16. said of a person who is moving about very carefully in order to escape attention
    a. stealthy   b. intensive   c. strident   d. dogged

17. a phony name that a con artist might use to avoid detection
    a. initiative   b. consequence   c. alias   d. earmark

18. someone who is good at tracking down clues
    a. sleuth   b. foil   c. fossil   d. nonconformist

19. what a nosy person is likely to do
    a. delude   b. balk   c. confer   d. pry

20. "They claim to be our friends but are deliberately trying to make our program fail."
    a. vandalism   b. sabotage   c. rummage   d. compact

co, col, com, con, cor—with, together

This prefix appears in **consequence** (page 117), **compact** (page 131), and **confer** (page 131). Some other words in which this prefix appears are listed below.

coincidence	**colleague**	**compute**	**confide**
collaborate	**composure**	**concurrent**	**correspond**

From the list of words above, choose the one that corresponds to each of the brief definitions below. Write the word in the blank space in the illustrative sentence below the definition.

1. occurring at the same time; agreeing

The convicted felon was sentenced to _____ prison terms.

2. the chance occurrence of two things at the same time or place

"What a _____ to bump into you here at the passport office!" she exclaimed.

3. to determine by arithmetic, calculate

The mechanic used a calculator to _____ the total repair bill.

4. to exchange letters; to be in agreement

My cousin and I decided to _____ by e-mail after he moved to Montana.

5. calmness of mind, bearing, or appearance; self-control

Even the car alarms wailing outside did not ruffle the speaker's _____.

6. to work with others; to aid or assist an enemy of one's country

They agreed to _____ on the science project so they could pool their resources and ideas.

7. to tell something as a secret; to entrust a secret

I would never _____ such details to anyone but a close friend.

8. a fellow worker, associate

The proud retiree was honored by her longtime _____ at the library.

From the list of words above, choose the one that best completes each of the following sentences. Write the word in the space provided.

1. The composer George Gershwin often _____ with his brother Ira to write some of America's best-loved songs.

2. The gossip columnist's success stemmed from her amazing ability to get even the most reclusive celebrities to _____ in her.

3. Sherlock Holmes was often assisted in his investigations by his trusted friend and _____ Dr. Watson.

4. The abacus is still widely used in China to _____ sums.

5. The culprits rehearsed their alibi until their stories _____ in every detail.

6. For a rookie making his first World Series appearance, the young pitcher showed remarkable _____ and maturity on the mound.

7. Powers exercised at one and the same time by states and the federal government—for example, the power to tax—are said to be _____.

8. By the strangest _____, two of our nation's founders, Thomas Jefferson and John Adams, died on exactly the same day—July 4, 1826.

---

*Circle the **boldface** word that more satisfactorily completes each of the following sentences.*

1. In terms of anatomical function, the wings of birds may be said to (**correspond, collaborate**) to the fins of fish.

2. To get recommendations for fine arts camp, she scheduled (**coincidental, concurrent**) appointments with her guidance counselor and her drama teacher.

3. One can sense how candidates may react under pressure by noticing their degree of (**composure, coincidence**) during unscripted town meetings and press conferences.

4. The architects, engineers, and designers found creative ways to (**collaborate, confide**) on a brilliant renovation of the old city hall.

5. What an amusing (**composure, coincidence**) that the newlyweds received as gifts three types of coffee makers—and neither of them even drinks the stuff!

6. "I'm not qualified to advise you on wallpapering," said the sales clerk at the home store, "but my (**colleague, concurrence**) over there is quite the expert."

7. The teacher showed us several strategies to help us mentally (**correspond, compute**) a tip at a restaurant.

8. The apprentice refused to (**confide, compute**) his anxieties to anyone but his older brother.

Analogies

In each of the following, circle the item that best completes the comparison.

1. dumbfounded is to **shock** as
a. befuddled is to confusion
b. irked is to pleasure
c. pacified is to disgust
d. infuriated is to satisfaction

2. thrive is to **wither** as
a. skimp is to restrict
b. idolize is to detest
c. reminisce is to recall
d. refute is to disprove

3. gory is to **sight** as
a. sinister is to taste
b. meteoric is to feel
c. strident is to sound
d. martial is to smell

4. deluge is to **engulf** as
a. blizzard is to bake
b. earthquake is to devastate
c. drought is to swamp
d. avalanche is to fry

5. serene is to **ruffle** as
a. dogged is to persevere
b. gullible is to delude
c. resourceful is to motivate
d. valiant is to intimidate

6. culprit is to **commit** as
a. nonconformist is to obey
b. oaf is to foil
c. sage is to bungle
d. sleuth is to solve

7. global is to **world** as
a. cosmic is to universe
b. lunar is to sun
c. aquatic is to star
d. colonial is to planet

8. partisan is to **defend** as
a. hypocrite is to pry
b. pacifist is to attack
c. vagabond is to tarry
d. oracle is to predict

9. vandalism is to **destroy** as
a. initiative is to harm
b. fossil is to foil
c. sabotage is to wreck
d. memento is to injure

10. keepsake is to **memento** as
a. agenda is to decision
b. fidelity is to treachery
c. fatality is to death
d. debut is to journey

Choosing the Right Meaning

Read each sentence carefully. Then circle the item that best completes the statement below the sentence.

After the Emancipation Proclamation of 1863, Union victories in the South were often occasions for the mass liberation of slaves. (2)

1. The word **liberation** in line 2 is used to mean
a. freeing　　b. arrest　　c. transportation　　d. migration

From a nearby hilltop scouts could see an enemy regiment drawn up in a long battle line at the forest's verge. (2)

2. The word **verge** in line 2 most nearly means
a. path　　b. clearing　　c. edge　　d. center

Riflemen preparing for battle thoroughly cleaned their weapons to make sure they were free of grit. (2)

3. The best definition for the word **grit** in line 2 is
a. courage　　b. determination　　c. mettle　　d. dirt

Packing winds in excess of 100 miles per hour, Hurricane Andrew tore through
Florida in 1992, leaving wholesale devastation in its wake. (2)

4. In line 2 the word **devastation** most nearly means

a. grief b. destruction c. flooding d. misery

In fencing matches the two competitors bring the tips of their foils together to signal
that they are ready to commence. (2)

5. In line 1 the word **foils** is best defined as

a. weapons b. pistols c. daggers d. swords

Two-Word Completions

Circle the pair of words that best complete the meaning of each of the following sentences.

1. Though a number of people claim to have spotted his tracks or even sighted him, the
yeti, or "_____ snowman," has proved to be one of nature's most
_____ creatures, and may not even exist!

a. burly . . . pathetic
b. abominable . . . elusive
c. immobile . . . incomprehensible
d. ingenious . . . ambiguous

2. "In the frozen wastes of Antarctica," the world-famous explorer remarked,
"temperatures are so _____ that a person's hands and feet can
become _____ with cold after only a brief exposure to the elements."

a. frigid . . . numb
b. acute . . . extinct
c. gross . . . sluggish
d. rigorous . . . null and void

3. "I wouldn't go near that particular joint," I warned them, "because it is known to be a
favorite _____ of hoods, pushers, and other _____
or disreputable characters."

a. terrain . . . smug
b. rendezvous . . . sinister
c. earmark . . . affluent
d. queue . . . petty

4. Though the storm itself was of very brief _____, it dumped so
much snow on the city while it lasted that roads and highways all over town were
virtually _____ for a week.

a. format . . . indisputable
b. onset . . . inflammatory
c. duration . . . impassable
d. stamina . . . incalculable

5. That terrible _____ of war, like the atomic bomb, should in fact
prove to be our most reliable guardians of the peace is one of the most puzzling
_____ of modern life.

a. misgivings . . . consequences
b. vows . . . innovations
c. illusions . . . facets
d. implements . . . enigmas

Enriching Your Vocabulary

Read the passage below. Then complete the exercise at the bottom of the page.

You Name It!

Everybody and everything has a name. There are names that describe one's achievements, that explain where we are from, and that hide our true identities.

What words do we use to describe types of names? Your pet Chihuahua puppy is named Spike. He only has one name, but you, his owner, also have a *surname*, or last name. One type of surname is the *patronymic*, which is formed by adding a prefix or a suffix to the name of an ancestor. Peterson or "son of Peter" and O'Neal or "of Neal" are patronymics.

Someone who wants to hide his true identity could adopt an *alias* (Unit 11), a false name. A performer may choose a *stage name* that is more catchy or glamorous than her real name. That's what Caryn Johnson did. (You know her as Whoopi Goldberg.) Authors are famous for using *pen names*. Samuel Clemens—Mark Twain—is one of the best known.

Pennsylvania, Rome, and America all have something in common. These place names are based on the names of real or legendary people. Pennsylvania is named after William Penn. Rome is named after Romulus, one of its mythical founders. America is named after the explorer Amerigo Vespucci. Such place names are called *eponyms*.

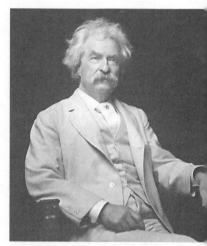

Mark Twain (1835–1910), famous American humorist

Here is a questionnaire about names. Read each question and write the answer on the lines. Use a dictionary if you need to.

1. What is your *appellation*? _____

_____

2. Do you have a *nickname?* If not, think of one you would like. Write it here. _____

_____

3. Do you have a *title*? Do you think you might have a title at some time in the future? If so, write it here. _____

_____

4. Are you someone's *namesake*? If so, write that person's name here. If not, use your imagination and write the name of someone you could be named for. _____

_____

_____

5. What would it mean if someone called you by a *misnomer*? _____

_____

6. Do you ever use a *pseudonym* or a *nom de plume*? If so, what is it? If not, which one would you choose? _____

_____

Hear the words for this Unit pronounced, defined, and used in sentences at **www.vocabularyworkshop.com**.

Definitions

Note carefully the spelling, pronunciation, part(s) of speech, and definition(s) of each of the following words. Then write the word in the blank space(s) in the illustrative sentence(s) following. Finally, study the lists of synonyms and antonyms given at the end of each entry.

1. adhere
(ad hēr′)

(*v.*) to stick to, remain attached; to be devoted or loyal as a follower or supporter

Things will work out better if we _____ to our original plan.

SYNONYMS: cling, hold fast
ANTONYMS: unfasten, unglue, abandon, betray

2. affirm
(ə fərm′)

(*v.*) to declare to be true, state positively; to confirm

Unexpected kindness from a stranger during a time of need can _____ one's faith in human nature.

SYNONYMS: assert, ratify
ANTONYMS: deny, disavow, reject, veto, disallow

3. atrocity
(ə träs′ ət ē)

(*n.*) an extremely wicked, brutal, or cruel act; something very bad or unpleasant

The Nazis took great pains to keep detailed records of each kind of _____ they committed.

SYNONYMS: outrage, enormity, monstrosity
ANTONYMS: good deed, kindness, kind act

4. audition
(ô dish′ ən)

(*n.*) a trial hearing for a performer; (*v.*) to conduct or perform such a hearing

Kent will hold the final _____ for Ibsen's *The Doll House* today.

Will you _____ for the lead role in the school play?

SYNONYMS: (*n.*) tryout, screen test

5. cope
(kōp)

(*v.*) to struggle successfully against; to prove to be a match for, deal with satisfactorily; (*n.*) a long religious cloak; a canopy

Education and experience provide us with the skills we need to _____ with difficult situations.

We exchanged wedding vows under a blue _____.

SYNONYMS: (*v.*) make do, manage, get along, handle

6. deter
(di tər′)

(*v.*) to discourage, scare off, or prevent through fear or doubt

Traffic jams won't _____ us from coming to your birthday party.

ANTONYMS: encourage, urge on

Hear the words for this Unit pronounced, defined, and
used in sentences at **www.vocabularyworkshop.com**.

13

7. disquieting
(dis kwī'ət iŋ)

(*adj.*) causing uneasiness or worry

A _____ incident at school put all
the teachers and students on edge.

SYNONYMS: troubling, disturbing, alarming
ANTONYMS: calming, reassuring, soothing, comforting

8. empower
(em paú' ər)

(*v.*) to give power or authority to; to enable; to permit

Signing this legal paper will _____
me to set up my own bank account.

SYNONYMS: authorize, license
ANTONYMS: forbid, prohibit, ban, disqualify

9. fluent
(flü' ənt)

(*adj.*) speaking or writing easily and smoothly, flowing gracefully

Susannah can speak _____
Japanese, French, and Russian.

SYNONYMS: eloquent, articulate, glib
ANTONYMS: halting, tongue-tied, choppy

10. lag
(lag)

(*v.*) to move slowly or fall behind; to bring up the rear; (*n.*) a
falling behind; the amount by which someone or something is
behind; an interval

Please try not to _____ behind
the others.

There is a three-hour _____ from
the time I send you an e-mail until you receive it.

SYNONYMS: (*v.*) trail, straggle; (*v., n.*) delay
ANTONYMS: (*v.*) keep up, outstrip, outdo

11. mangle
(maŋ' gəl)

(*v.*) to injure very seriously by cutting, tearing, crushing, etc.; to
bring to ruin

Workers could _____ their hands
in this equipment if they don't pay attention to what they're
doing.

SYNONYMS: damage, mutilate, butcher, disfigure, rend

12. misapprehension
(mis ap ri hen' shən)

(*n.*) a wrong idea, misunderstanding

A lingering _____ may cause ill
will between friends.

SYNONYM: misconception

13. optimist
(äp' tə mist)

(*n.*) one who expects things to turn out for the best; someone
who looks on the bright side of things

An _____ holds a rosy view of life.

ANTONYMS: pessimist, prophet of doom

14. prowl
(praúl)

(*v.*) to roam about stealthily in search of something

A panther can _____ freely at night because its dark fur prevents it from being seen.

SYNONYMS: rove, skulk, slink, lurk

15. stupefy
(stü′ pə fī)

(*v.*) to make stupid, dull, or groggy; to surprise or astonish

The vet used a powerful tranquilizer to _____ the animal.

SYNONYMS: stun, daze, shock, amaze, astound
ANTONYMS: awaken, arouse, stimulate, enliven

16. sulky
(səl′ kē)

(*adj.*) in a bad or nasty mood, resentful; gloomy

A _____ child does not make a very good playmate.

SYNONYMS: grouchy, sullen, peevish, petulant
ANTONYMS: cheerful, sociable, sunny, amiable

17. supplement
(səp′ lə ment)

(*n.*) something added to complete a thing or make up for a lack; a section added to a book or document; (*v.*) to provide such an addition or completion

The sports _____ is my favorite part of this magazine.

Many people _____ their regular diet by taking daily vitamins.

SYNONYMS: (*n.*) addition, extension; (*v.*) add to

18. surge
(sərj)

(*v.*) to have a heavy, violent, swelling motion (like waves); (*n.*) a powerful forward rush

Runners who train hard and who have good stamina often _____ ahead of the pack.

A sudden _____ of electrical current could make a computer crash.

SYNONYMS: (*v.*) flood, rush, burst, gush; (*n.*) wave
ANTONYMS: (*v.*) recede, ebb; (*n.*) recession, slowdown

19. trait
(trāt)

(*n.*) a quality or characteristic (especially of personality); a distinguishing feature

Your most appealing _____ is your unfailing sense of humor.

20. unscrupulous
(ən skrü′ pyə ləs)

(*adj.*) dishonest; not guided or controlled by moral principles

Avoid dealing with _____ merchants whenever possible.

SYNONYMS: crooked, corrupt, shady
ANTONYMS: fair, honest, trustworthy, aboveboard

Completing the Sentence

From the words for this unit, choose the one that best completes each of the following sentences. Write the word in the space provided.

1. He is so careless in handling his textbooks that by the end of the term he has practically _____ all of them.

2. The Constitution _____ the president to name the people who will fill many of the most important positions in the government.

3. As soon as the doors were opened, the shoppers, eager for the advertised bargains, _____ into the store in great waves.

4. If you are having so much trouble with a program of four major courses, how do you expect to _____ with a fifth course?

5. Do you think that it is possible to become _____ in a foreign language without actually living in a country where it is spoken?

6. Since she has a large family, she finds it necessary to _____ her income by working at a second job at night and on weekends.

7. We were so _____ by the bad news that for a few moments we just sat there without moving or speaking.

8. In spite of our best efforts, collections for the Community Fund this year have _____ far behind last year's figures.

9. As the robber _____ the streets looking for victims, he was unaware that undercover police officers were watching his every move.

10. Throughout her long and noble career, her outstanding _____ has been her deep love for her fellow human beings.

11. In spite of all his talents, he will never gain high public office because so many voters feel that he is _____ and cannot be trusted.

12. Now that the job has been completed, I have finally become skillful in hanging the paper so that it _____ firmly to the wall.

13. It is hard to be a(n) _____ when nothing works out for you.

14. Naturally we were upset when we received the _____ news that our uncle had been taken to the hospital.

15. On Broadway, _____ that are open to any performer who just walks in off the street are referred to as "cattle calls."

16. The witness solemnly _____ that the evidence she was about to give was true.

17. If you think that I would go to a party without being invited, you are under a complete _____.

18. The unfavorable weather reports did not _____ us from holding the picnic that we had planned for so long.

19. When he gets in one of those _____ moods, he is as unreasonable and unpleasant as a cranky child.

20. Drunken soldiers roamed the streets of the fallen city, committing one _____ after another on the terrified population.

Synonyms

*Choose the word from this unit that is **the same** or **most nearly the same** in meaning as the **boldface** word or expression in the given phrase. Write the word on the line provided.*

1. while they **damaged** the stolen bicycle _____

2. did not welcome her **peevish** attitude _____

3. **outrage** that stunned the world _____

4. the most unique **feature** of the breed _____

5. hikers who **straggle** behind the group _____

6. clinging to that **misconception** _____

7. as the crowds **rush** forward _____

8. which contained some **troubling** news _____

9. scheduled **tryouts** for the chorus _____

10. unsure how to **manage** with the sick puppy _____

11. hoping that the special effects will **amaze** you _____

12. a special **addition** to the regular menu _____

13. to **skulk** along the corridor _____

14. **authorized** to make major decisions _____

15. able to **cling** to slippery surfaces _____

Antonyms

*Choose the word from this unit that is **most nearly opposite** in meaning to the **boldface** word or expression in the given phrase. Write the word on the line provided.*

16. as only the **pessimist** would believe _____

17. attempted to **encourage** their mission _____

18. their reputation as **trustworthy** mechanics _____

19. **halting** public-speaking skills _____

20. to **deny** that we were there _____

Choosing the Right Word

*Circle the **boldface** word that more satisfactorily completes each of the following sentences.*

1. Shortly after World War II, Japan began the great economic (**surge, trait**) that has put her among the world's top industrial nations.

2. All those smooth words and vague promises are not going to (**adhere, deter**) us from doing what we know is needed to improve conditions.

3. The City Council has approved funds for a new playground, but we expect a (**lag, surge**) of several months before construction begins.

4. There is no one (**optimist, trait**) that makes him so likable; it is the overall effect of his personality.

5. It is far better to know you are ignorant of something than to act on the basis of wrong information and (**misapprehensions, auditions**).

6. Come what may, I will (**adhere, affirm**) to the great ideas and ideals for which our ancestors suffered so much.

7. My definition of a(n) (**optimist, misapprehension**) is someone who looks at an almost empty bottle of juice and says, "This bottle is one-quarter full."

8. The worst way to deal with disappointments is to become (**fluent, sulky**); the best way is to smile and make up your mind to try again.

9. When everything went wrong for Stan, and he saw absolutely no way out of his troubles, he muttered to himself, "I just can't (**mangle, cope**)!"

10. After the conductor (**auditioned, supplemented**) all the candidates for the position of first violinist, he made his final choice.

11. Everything that I have learned about Abraham Lincoln from history books (**stupefies, affirms**) my reverence for this great president.

12. I agree fully with what the previous speaker has said, but I should like to (**cope, supplement**) his ideas with a few remarks of my own.

13. Who (**prowled, empowered**) you to speak for everyone in our class?

14. Although José has been living in this country for only a few years, I would love to be half as (**fluent, sulky**) in Spanish as he is in English.

15. The play went along smoothly until it came to Mark Antony's funeral oration, which Fred (**empowered, mangled**) beyond all recognition.

16. Jackals and other scavengers now (**prowl, deter**) through the ruins of what was once a great city.

17. A loud groan went through the class when we got the (**unscrupulous, disquieting**) news that there would be a full-period test later in the week.

18. My friend took one look at the statue I fashioned from stray pieces of junk and exclaimed, "That's not a sculpture; it's a(n) (**lag, atrocity**)!"

19. A true friend would not have been so (**sulky, unscrupulous**) as to take unfair advantage of your trust and confidence.

20. Have all these years of peace and good living (**disquieted, stupefied**) us to such an extent that we are not even prepared to defend ourselves?

Read the following passage, in which some of the words you have studied in this unit appear in **boldface** *type. Then complete each statement given below the passage by circling the letter of the item that is* **the same** *or* **almost the same** *in meaning as the highlighted word.*

Mary Cassatt

(Line)

Throughout her life, American painter Mary Cassatt demonstrated several important **traits** that contributed to her success. A passion for painting, hard work, and extensive study **empowered** her to achieve success in an age when few women had careers. She first studied art in Pennsylvania, where she was born in 1844. To **supplement**

her training, she traveled to Europe and (5) visited great art museums in Rome and Madrid. Above all, she spent time in Paris, then the center of the modern art world.

Her confidence **surged** when, in 1868, her painting *A Mandolin Player* was accepted for (10) exhibit in a famous Paris art show. She decided to settle in Paris and to devote herself to a life of art. Degas saw Cassatt's work, and in 1877 he asked her to join the Impressionists, a group of artists who used (15) shimmering color and bold brush strokes and experimented with light, shadow, and form. Cassatt's prestigious colleagues included Monet, Renoir, Cezanne, and Van Gogh.

In Mary Cassatt's day, most women (20) married and raised families; few women had careers. That did not **deter** her. Cassatt decided not to marry, making the conscious choice of art over family.

Mary Cassatt's *Maternal Kiss* (1897) hangs in the Philadelphia Museum of Art.

At first, Mary Cassatt painted typical scenes: social events, nightlife, people at (25) work, and scenes of the theatre. Eventually, she decided not to **adhere to** these themes alone. She chose instead to portray domestic life. Although she did not have a family of her own, her tender mother-and-child portraits became her most beloved pictures. Cassatt produced over 200 works during her career. When her vision began to fail in 1911, she was forced to give up art. She died near Paris in 1926. (30)

---

1. The meaning of **traits** (line 2) is
a. features
b. talents
c. ideas
d. trials

2. Empowered (line 3) most nearly means
a. forced
b. told
c. enabled
d. disabled

3. Supplement (line 4) is best defined as
a. hurry
b. cut back
c. repeat
d. add to

4. The meaning of **surged** (line 9) is
a. began
b. ended
c. rushed
d. receded

5. Deter (line 22) is best defined as
a. encourage
b. discourage
c. wake
d. shake

6. Adhere to (line 26) most nearly means
a. paint
b. stick to
c. abandon
d. avoid

Hear the words for this Unit pronounced, defined, and used in sentences at **www.vocabularyworkshop.com**.

UNIT 14

Definitions

Note carefully the spelling, pronunciation, part(s) of speech, and definition(s) of each of the following words. Then write the word in the blank space(s) in the illustrative sentence(s) following. Finally, study the lists of synonyms and antonyms given at the end of each entry.

1. abstain
(ab stān')

(*v.*) to stay away from doing something by one's own choice

I find it hard to _____ from these tempting and delicious desserts.

SYNONYMS: avoid, decline, resist, refrain from
ANTONYMS: yield to, give in to, indulge in

2. accommodate
(ə käm' ə dāt)

(*v.*) to do a favor or service for, help out; to provide for, supply with; to have space for; to make fit or suitable

That van is the ideal vehicle for carpooling because it can _____ nine passengers.

SYNONYMS: oblige, lodge, house, adapt
ANTONYMS: disoblige, inconvenience, trouble

3. allegiance
(ə lēj' əns)

(*n.*) the loyalty or obligation owed to a government, nation, or cause

At a festive yet solemn ceremony, fifty new citizens swore _____ to their adopted nation.

SYNONYMS: obedience, devotion, fidelity

4. amalgamate
(ə mal' gə māt)

(*v.*) to unite; to combine elements into a unified whole

Two small companies will _____ into one large corporation on June 1.

SYNONYMS: merge, consolidate
ANTONYMS: divide, separate, carve up, break up

5. append
(ə pend')

(*v.*) to attach, add, or tack on as a supplement or extra item

We were dismayed when our teacher decided to _____ an additional assignment to our already huge load of homework.

ANTONYMS: detach from, disconnect

6. commemorate
(kə mem' ə rāt)

(*v.*) to preserve, honor, or celebrate the memory of

Each May we _____ Grandpa's life by lighting a special candle for him that burns for 24 hours.

SYNONYM: memorialize
ANTONYMS: dishonor, forget, overlook

7. enumerate
(i nü' mə rāt)

(*v.*) to count; to name one by one, list

These booklets _____ and compare all the high-tech features that new televisions can offer.

SYNONYMS: check off, spell out, specify

8. exalt
(eg zôlt')

(v.) to make high in rank, power, character, or quality; to fill with pride, joy, or noble feeling; to praise, honor

Let us now _____ the heroes for their courage and character in the face of all this adversity.

SYNONYMS: elevate, raise, uplift
ANTONYMS: lower, cast down, humble, degrade, demote, depose

9. extort
(ek stôrt')

(v.) to obtain by violence, misuse of authority, or threats

The kidnappers tried to _____ a huge sum of money in return for releasing their prisoners safely.

SYNONYMS: blackmail, coerce, bilk, "shake down"

10. far-fetched
(fär fecht')

(adj.) strained or improbable (in the sense of not being logical or believable), going far afield from a topic

No one will believe the _____ excuse you just gave!

SYNONYMS: unlikely, hard to swallow
ANTONYMS: likely, probable, plausible, credible

11. glum
(gləm)

(adj.) depressed, gloomy

The losing team wore _____ expressions on their faces as the final buzzer sounded.

SYNONYMS: dejected, morose, melancholy
ANTONYMS: cheerful, merry, rosy, sunny

12. replica
(rep' lə kə)

(n.) a copy, close reproduction

We visited a life-size _____ of the *Mayflower*, the Pilgrim ship docked near Plymouth, Massachusetts.

SYNONYMS: duplicate, imitation
ANTONYMS: original, prototype

13. responsive
(ri spän' siv)

(adj.) answering or replying; reacting readily to requests, suggestions, etc.; showing interest and understanding

The host of the charming inn was _____ to our every wish.

SYNONYMS: sympathetic, open, receptive
ANTONYMS: insensitive, unsympathetic

14. sanctuary
(saŋk' chə wer ē)

(n.) a sacred or holy place; refuge or protection from capture or punishment; a place of refuge or protection

The exhausted refugees found _____ in a local church.

SYNONYMS: shrine, haven

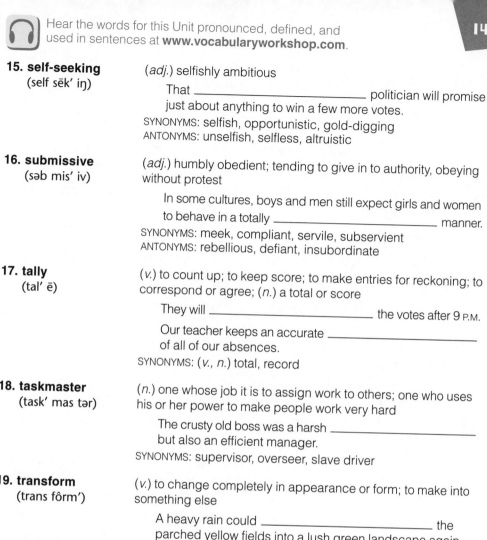
Hear the words for this Unit pronounced, defined, and used in sentences at **www.vocabularyworkshop.com**.

14

15. self-seeking
(self sēk′ iŋ)

(*adj.*) selfishly ambitious

That _____ politician will promise just about anything to win a few more votes.

SYNONYMS: selfish, opportunistic, gold-digging
ANTONYMS: unselfish, selfless, altruistic

16. submissive
(səb mis′ iv)

(*adj.*) humbly obedient; tending to give in to authority, obeying without protest

In some cultures, boys and men still expect girls and women to behave in a totally _____ manner.

SYNONYMS: meek, compliant, servile, subservient
ANTONYMS: rebellious, defiant, insubordinate

17. tally
(tal′ ē)

(*v.*) to count up; to keep score; to make entries for reckoning; to correspond or agree; (*n.*) a total or score

They will _____ the votes after 9 P.M.

Our teacher keeps an accurate _____ of all of our absences.

SYNONYMS: (*v., n.*) total, record

18. taskmaster
(task′ mas tər)

(*n.*) one whose job it is to assign work to others; one who uses his or her power to make people work very hard

The crusty old boss was a harsh _____ but also an efficient manager.

SYNONYMS: supervisor, overseer, slave driver

19. transform
(trans fôrm′)

(*v.*) to change completely in appearance or form; to make into something else

A heavy rain could _____ the parched yellow fields into a lush green landscape again.

SYNONYMS: alter, convert
ANTONYMS: maintain, preserve

20. upheaval
(əp hēv′ əl)

(*n.*) a sudden, violent upward movement; great disorder or radical change

The sudden change in leadership caused dramatic social and economic _____.

SYNONYMS: confusion, disruption, chaos
ANTONYMS: tranquility, peace and quiet

Completing the Sentence

From the words for this unit, choose the one that best completes each of the following sentences. Write the word in the space provided.

1. Every entertainer likes a(n) _____ audience that shows it appreciates and enjoys a performance.

2. Good employees don't need a(n) _____ to keep them working.

3. I would like to _____ you, but I don't think it is right to allow you to copy my homework.

4. We learned in our science class how _____ of the earth's crust has resulted in the formation of mountains.

5. When we visited New York City, we bought a small _____ of the Statue of Liberty as a memento of our trip.

6. In just a few years, she was _____ from an awkward tomboy into a charming young woman.

7. A portion of the forest has been set aside as a bird _____ for the protection of endangered species in the area.

8. I love basketball games, but I have decided to _____ from attending them until I can get my grades up to where they should be.

9. On Memorial Day, Americans gather in ceremonies across the country to _____ the nation's war dead.

10. Imagine how _____ we felt when a sudden wave of warm weather melted all the snow and ruined our plans for a winter carnival!

11. Under the U.S. Constitution, officials are never _____ to a point where they are more important or more powerful than the law.

12. Anne usually seems to be quiet and _____, but she has a way of flaring up when she feels that anyone is being unfair to her.

13. Is there anything more despicable than trying to _____ money from innocent people by threatening them with bodily harm?

14. When Ben Franklin said, "God helps those who help themselves," he did not mean that the most important thing in life is to be _____.

15. I enjoyed the first part of the detective story, but the surprise ending was so _____ that I couldn't accept it.

16. I know that Mother has given you all kinds of instructions before you leave for camp, but let me _____ some extra advice of my own.

17. Can you see why it was logical for various labor unions in the clothing and textile industries to _____ into a single organization?

18. Though an injured hand kept Larry from actually bowling, he took part in the tournament by keeping a careful _____ of the scores.

19. Remember that the Pledge of _____ is not a formula to be repeated mechanically but a summary of our sacred duty to our country.

20. The driving instructor _____ carefully the bad habits and practices that are likely to lead to accidents.

Synonyms

*Choose the word from this unit that is **the same** or **most nearly the same** in meaning as the **boldface** word or expression in the given phrase. Write the word on the line provided.*

1. elevated as a standard of beauty _____

2. as **specified** on the packing slip _____

3. that **imitation** of a Picasso sculpture _____

4. an arrogant and **opportunistic** person _____

5. lit candles in the quiet **shrine** _____

6. fear of displeasing the **overseer** _____

7. has clearly proven his **devotion** _____

8. chose to **refrain** from voting _____

9. to **house** an exchange student from Senegal _____

10. forgotten amidst the **disruption** of moving _____

11. how to **coerce** innocent victims _____

12. made her feel so **dejected** _____

13. may **convert** it into a family resort _____

14. if we **total** up all the book orders _____

15. always **receptive** to new ideas _____

Antonyms

*Choose the word from this unit that is **most nearly opposite** in meaning to the **boldface** word or expression in the given phrase. Write the word on the line provided.*

16. questioning such a **likely** conclusion _____

17. separate the two chemical elements _____

18. meant to be **detached** _____

19. as they usually **overlook** the holiday _____

20. reputation of being a **rebellious** student _____

Choosing the Right Word *Circle the **boldface** word that more satisfactorily completes each of the following sentences.*

1. Each member of the basketball team was awarded a trophy to (**transform, commemorate**) the championship season.

2. Ms. Wilentz is the kind of manager who does not try to (**extort, exalt**) cooperation from the people under her, but earns it by being a real leader.

3. The detective's suspicion was aroused when the suspect's story failed to (**tally, commemorate**) with the known facts of the case.

4. If you look so (**far-fetched, glum**) just because you can't go to the party, how are you going to react when something really bad happens?

5. In Robert Louis Stevenson's classic story, a chemical potion (**tallies, transforms**) the good Dr. Jekyll into the evil Mr. Hyde.

6. Isn't it a little (**far-fetched, self-seeking**) to suggest that the pollution of our environment is mainly caused by creatures from outer space?

7. Unless the poor people of the country see some hope of improving their lives, there will probably soon be a great social (**sanctuary, upheaval**) there.

8. The Mayor had to choose between (**allegiance, tally**) to his political party and his judgment of what was best for the city.

9. The new hotel is spacious enough to (**accommodate, extort**) large groups of people attending conventions and banquets.

10. Experience has taught me that people who constantly boast about their unselfishness are often secretly quite (**submissive, self-seeking**).

11. Financiers are planning to (**accommodate, amalgamate**) various businesses in the United States and England into one huge multinational corporation.

12. The United States has a long history of providing (**upheaval, sanctuary**) to those fleeing persecution abroad.

13. He enjoys (**abstaining, enumerating**) all the factors that enabled him to rise from poverty to great wealth, but he always omits the very important element of good luck.

14. Since she sets extremely high standards for herself and is always pushing herself to do better, she is her own most severe (**taskmaster, replica**).

15. We cannot have a peaceful and just society so long as any one race is required to be (**responsive, submissive**) to another.

16. I didn't have time to write a letter to Lucy, but I (**appended, enumerated**) a few sentences to my sister's letter, expressing my congratulations.

17. Instead of working so hard to prepare (**replicas, allegiances**) of famous works of art, why don't you try to create something original?

18. Only seven members of the Security Council voted on the resolution; the others (**abstained, appended**).

19. When he felt low, he found that singing (**exalted, amalgamated**) his spirits.

20. It remains to be seen how (**responsive, glum**) the students will be to the new method of teaching mathematics.

Vocabulary in Context

*Read the following passage, in which some of the words you have studied in this unit appear in **boldface** type. Then complete each statement given below the passage by circling the letter of the item that is **the same** or **almost the same** in meaning as the highlighted word.*

"Let the Good Times Roll!"

(Line)

Most American pop music can trace its roots to folk music from many cultures. *Zydeco* music **amalgamates** aspects of French, Native American, German, African, and Caribbean musical styles into a unique new whole. It emerged in Southwest Louisiana as a separate style in the 1940s, but it owes much to the
(5) Creole and Cajun music that came hundreds of years earlier.

Creoles are French-speaking blacks from Louisiana. Creole music was played on fiddle and accordion. Cajuns descended from French settlers—the Acadians— who came to Canada in the 1600s. These pioneers sang old French folk music. When the
(10) British forced the Acadians out of Canada in 1755, many moved to Louisiana. Cajuns, as they became known, settled in the swampy delta. They eked out meager lives fishing and logging.

Clifton Chenier, the late King of Zydeco, coined
(15) the term *zydeco. Les haricots,* pronounced "lay- zariko," is the French word for green beans. An old French saying, "Les haricots sont pas salées" (the beans aren't salty), referred to times when people were so poor they even had to **abstain from** using
(20) salt pork to flavor their beans. Circumstances may have been difficult, but the mood certainly wasn't **glum**! Families would gather for a "La La" (house dance) to celebrate a harvest, a wedding, or any

Buckwheat Zydeco (r.) plays the accordion in Lafayette, Louisiana, while another musician plays a washboard, or *zydeco frottoir.*

other event. One couldn't help but be **responsive** to the peppy music played on
(25) spoons, fiddles, accordions, washboards, animal bones, and triangles. Adults and children danced and celebrated long into the night.

Zydeco **accommodates** old Cajun and Creole dance tunes and homey instruments, but was **transformed** by the post-World War II elements of rhythm and blues. Chenier introduced the use of drums and guitars. Zydeco now borrows from country-western,
(30) disco, hip-hop, and reggae. Lyrics now include English along with, or instead of, French. As Zydeco musicians say, "Le bons temps roulez," or "Let the good times roll!"

---

1. The meaning of **amalgamates** (line 2) is
  a. rejects   c. combines
  b. copies   d. borrows

2. Abstain from (line 19) is best defined as
  a. avoid   c. indulge in
  b. escape   d. stop

3. Glum (line 22) most nearly means
  a. bored   c. depressed
  b. restless   d. cheery

4. The meaning of **responsive** (line 24) is
  a. indifferent   c. opposed
  b. receptive   d. insensitive

5. Accommodates (line 27) is best defined as
  a. combines   c. enjoys
  b. respects   d. adapts

6. Transformed (line 28) most nearly means
  a. changed   c. mocked
  b. produced   d. judged

UNIT 15

 Hear the words for this Unit pronounced, defined, and used in sentences at **www.vocabularyworkshop.com**.

Definitions

Note carefully the spelling, pronunciation, part(s) of speech, and definition(s) of each of the following words. Then write the word in the blank space(s) in the illustrative sentence(s) following. Finally, study the lists of synonyms and antonyms given at the end of each entry.

1. beacon
(bē′ kən)

(*n.*) a light or other signal that warns and guides; a lighthouse; anything that guides or inspires

Sailors returning to port on a dark night search for the glow of a familiar _____.

SYNONYMS: beam, flare

2. berserk
(bər sərk′)

(*adj., adv.*) violently and destructively enraged

A _____ gunman terrified the crowd of subway riders.

The wounded lion went _____ in his cage.

SYNONYMS: (*adj.*) mad, deranged
ANTONYMS: (*adj.*) sane, rational

3. celestial
(sə les′ chəl)

(*adj.*) having to do with the sky or heavens; heavenly; yielding great bliss or happiness

The sun is the brightest _____ body in our solar system.

SYNONYMS: ethereal, stellar, blissful
ANTONYMS: earthly, terrestrial, infernal

4. chasten
(chā′ sən)

(*v.*) to punish (in order to bring about improvement in behavior, attitude, etc.); to restrain, moderate

Dad knows how to _____ the stubborn child with a firm but soothing voice.

SYNONYMS: discipline, temper
ANTONYMS: praise, commend, reward

5. confiscate
(kän′ fə skāt)

(*v.*) to seize by authority; to take and keep

The police will _____ that car.

SYNONYMS: commandeer, expropriate
ANTONYMS: return, restore

6. data
(dā′ tə)

(*pl. n.*) information; facts, figures, statistics

For math class, we collected _____ on the Internet sites students visited during the past week.

7. detract
(di trakt′)

(*v.*) to take away from; reduce in value or reputation

Nothing can _____ from your beauty!

SYNONYMS: subtract from, lower
ANTONYMS: increase, heighten, enhance

Hear the words for this Unit pronounced, defined, and used in sentences at **www.vocabularyworkshop.com**.

15

8. encounter
(en kaùn' tər)

(*n.*) a meeting (especially one that is unplanned); a meeting of enemies, battle; (*v.*) to meet or come upon

Remember our _____ with that skunk?

We might _____ other curious visitors to the Crystal Caverns in Virginia.

SYNONYMS: (*n.*) confrontation; (*v.*) happen upon
ANTONYMS: (*v.*) avoid, sidestep

9. epic
(ep' ik)

(*n.*) a long narrative poem (or other literary composition) about the deeds of heroes; an event or movement of great sweep; (*adj.*) on a grand scale, vast, titanic

Beowulf, the English _____, was written around the year 700.

It describes _____ struggles between the forces of good and evil.

SYNONYMS: (*n.*) saga, chronicle

10. pantomime
(pan' tə mīm)

(*n.*) a play or story performed without words by actors using only gestures; (*v.*) to express in this way

The very outspoken street performer amused us when she suddenly included _____ in her routine.

We _____ when we're unable to speak.

SYNONYMS: (*n.*) charade, mime show, dumb show

11. pessimist
(pes' ə mist)

(*n.*) one who believes or expects the worst; prophet of doom

A _____ sees a glass as half empty.

SYNONYM: killjoy
ANTONYMS: optimist, Pollyanna

12. precaution
(pri kô' shən)

(*n.*) care taken beforehand; a step or action taken to prevent something from happening

I advise you to take every _____ necessary to prevent a household fire.

SYNONYMS: foresight, prudence, safeguard
ANTONYMS: recklessness, heedlessness

13. prosecute
(präs' ə kyüt)

(*v.*) to bring before a court of law for trial; to carry out

She was told she would not be _____ if she restored the money.

SYNONYMS: put on trial, pursue
ANTONYMS: defend, abandon, give up

14. puncture
(pəŋk' chər)

(*n.*) a small hole made by a sharp object; (*v.*) to make such a hole, pierce

He used a needle to make a small _____ in the balloon.

I tried not to wince as the hypodermic needle _____ my skin.

SYNONYM: (*n.*) perforation

15. retaliate
(ri tal′ ē āt)

(*v.*) to get revenge; to strike back for an injury

I would _____ for that cheap insult, but I fear it may only make matters worse.

SYNONYMS: avenge, pay back, get even with
ANTONYMS: pardon, forgive, turn the other cheek

16. sham
(sham)

(*adj.*) fake, not genuine; (*n.*) something false pretending to be genuine; a pretender; a decorated pillow covering; (*v.*) to pretend

The play includes a _____ fight scene.

Her claim that she's a princess is a _____ .

Don't _____ an illness in order to miss a day of school.

SYNONYMS: (*adj.*) phony, counterfeit; (*n.*) fraud
ANTONYMS: (*adj.*) authentic, bona fide

17. uncouth
(ən küth′)

(*adj.*) unrefined, crude; awkward or clumsy

Although the quality of his work was good, his _____ attitude cost him the job.

SYNONYMS: boorish, graceless
ANTONYMS: refined, polished, graceful, genteel

18. underscore
(ən′ dər skôr)

(*v.*) to draw a line under; to put special emphasis on; (*n.*) a line drawn under something

The dire situation in the hospital's emergency room _____ the importance of having enough doctors and nurses available.

The word with the _____ is in Spanish.

SYNONYMS: (*v.*) underline, stress, emphasize, accent
ANTONYMS: (*v.*) downplay, de-emphasize, soft-pedal

19. wholesome
(hōl′ səm)

(*adj.*) healthy; morally and socially sound and good; helping to bring about or preserve good health

He always eats _____ foods.

SYNONYMS: nourishing, beneficial
ANTONYMS: harmful, unhealthy, baneful

20. wistful
(wist′ fəl)

(*adj.*) full of melancholy yearning or longing, sad, pensive

Her _____ look made me sad.

ANTONYMS: cheerful, happy, contented, satisfied

Completing the Sentence

From the words for this unit, choose the one that best completes each of the following sentences. Write the word in the space provided.

1. The police have done their job in arresting the suspect; now it is up to the district attorney to _____ him and prove his guilt.

2. Though many people doubted that the new program would do any real good, I thought it was a very _____ development.

3. Late that afternoon, one of the inmates went _____ and totally wrecked the infirmary.

4. Isn't it remarkable that a(n) _____ poem such as the *Iliad*, written almost 3,000 years ago, still has interest for readers today?

5. Now that we have gathered a vast amount of _____, it is up to us to draw some useful conclusions from all this information.

6. After the war, all the property that had been _____ by the government was turned back to its former owners.

7. Little did I realize when I _____ that old man on a lonely beach that this chance meeting would change my life.

8. With a(n) _____ expression on his face, the prisoner looked through his cell window at the patch of sky that meant freedom to him.

9. When she said she would "turn the other cheek," she simply meant that she would not _____ for the injury done to her.

10. Freedom of speech is a(n) _____ and a mockery if it does not apply to people whose opinions are very unpopular.

11. In the old days, whippings and other forms of physical punishment were used to _____ student misbehavior, even in college.

12. Nothing can _____ from the fact that he stood by us in our hour of greatest need.

13. So there I was with a(n) _____ in one of my rear tires, on a lonely road, on a dark night, and during a violent rainstorm!

14. In polite society it is considered _____ to balance peas on your knife at the dinner table.

15. My definition of a(n) _____ is someone who worries about the hole in the doughnut and forgets about the cake surrounding it.

16. In ancient times, people gazed at the sky and studied the planets and other _____ bodies to predict the future.

17. Before we use the blowtorch in our industrial arts class, we are required to take the _____ of wearing goggles.

18. Although he could speak no English, he made us understand by the use of _____ that he was extremely thirsty.

19. The workbook directions instruct the user to _____ the subject of each sentence in red and the predicate in blue.

20. Over the years, a great many ships have been saved from destruction by that tall _____ standing on the rocky coast.

Synonyms

*Choose the word from this unit that is **the same** or **most nearly the same** in meaning as the **boldface** word or expression in the given phrase. Write the word on the line provided.*

1. if it might **subtract** from its value _____

2. a brief but awkward **confrontation** _____

3. should **emphasize** its safety features _____

4. crowds enjoying the **charade** _____

5. sure to certify the **statistics** _____

6. a convincing, yet **phony** excuse _____

7. due to a small **perforation** _____

8. with a strong desire to **avenge** _____

9. took a **beneficial** family vacation _____

10. kept an emergency **flare** in the trunk _____

11. had to **discipline** the rookie officer _____

12. a sprawling **saga** of pioneer life _____

13. reasonable **safeguard** against theft _____

14. might **commandeer** our boat _____

15. embarrassed by their **boorish** behavior _____

Antonyms

*Choose the word from this unit that is **most nearly opposite** in meaning to the **boldface** word or expression in the given phrase. Write the word on the line provided.*

16. anticipated your **rational** behavior _____

17. forced to **abandon** the case _____

18. watching the family's **cheerful** encounter _____

19. **optimists** who always share their views _____

20. decorated with **earthly** figures _____

Choosing the Right Word

*Circle the **boldface** word that more satisfactorily completes each of the following sentences.*

1. The youth center that the charity organized was like a (**precaution, beacon**) to many young people desperately needing help and guidance.

2. The child gazed (**wistfully, wholesomely**) at the shiny toys in the store window.

3. Is it right to (**retaliate, confiscate**) against an evil act by performing evil acts of one's own?

4. Marie is not really pretty, but her sparkling personality and (**wholesome, berserk**) charm make her very attractive.

5. Many a perfectly healthy employee has been known to (**retaliate, sham**) illness to avoid going to work.

6. For some strange reason, the photocopier suddenly went (**berserk, wistful**) and started spewing vast quantities of paper all over the floor.

7. The report that he sent to the president of the company (**underscored, retaliated**) the need for better planning and more careful use of funds.

8. The settlement of the American West is one of the great (**pantomimes, epics**) of world history.

9. Our driving instructor has emphasized that the use of seat belts is not a "silly" (**encounter, precaution**) but a surefire way of saving lives.

10. The Bible tells us that the Lord is like a stern but loving parent, and that "whom He loveth, He (**chasteneth, detracteth**)."

11. During the long years of defeat, Lincoln searched for a general who would (**prosecute, underscore**) the war fearlessly until the Union was saved.

12. Her writing style is a little (**celestial, uncouth**), but what it lacks in polish and refinement is more than made up for by its wonderful humor.

13. The trouble with being a(n) (**underscore, pessimist**) is that you are so taken up with what is going wrong that you are unaware of what is going right.

14. It does not (**prosecute, detract**) in the least from his reputation as a great player to say that all the team members deserve equal credit.

15. Before we can plan properly for the upcoming school year, we must have accurate (**beacons, data**) on the results of last year's programs.

16. The news that I had been dropped from the football squad (**detracted, punctured**) my dream of becoming a great gridiron hero.

17. She had such a (**celestial, sham**) expression on her face that I thought she'd seen a vision of heaven.

18. As I watched through the soundproof hospital window, the skaters on the pond seemed to be carrying out a colorful (**pantomime, epic**).

19. If you try to smuggle goods into this country without paying the customs duties, the inspectors may (**puncture, confiscate**) the goods and fine you.

20. I knew that it would be difficult to raise funds for the recycling program, but I never expected to (**chasten, encounter**) so many tough problems.

Read the following passage, in which some of the words you have studied in this unit appear in **boldface** type. Then complete each statement given below the passage by circling the letter of the item that is **the same** or **almost the same** in meaning as the highlighted word.

Making a Difference

(Line)

Old-timers in Everett, Washington grew **wistful** when they recalled Pigeon Creek running "red with salmon." The fish once swam freely through its clear, fresh waters. But over the years, people threw dirt, garbage, and old motor oil into it, making Pigeon Creek into a muddy trash dump.

Students and teachers at Jackson Elementary School, near Pigeon Creek, (5) decided to do something. They were determined to **prosecute** an ambitious project they named Operation Pigeon Creek. They vowed to clean up the creek. They hauled garbage, posted "No Dumping" signs, wrote letters, handed out leaflets, and worked to make the community aware of their mission. They hoped

Silver salmon in Tongass National Forest, Alaska

that one day Pigeon Creek would become the (10) **wholesome** waterway it once was.

The entire school took part. Younger kids studied the life cycle of salmon. They learned how water gets polluted and how it can be made cleaner. Older students did research on fresh water ecology (15) and learned to use water-testing equipment. They studied scientific **data** from Pigeon Creek.

Not everyone in the area supported Operation Pigeon Creek. Some believed that it was a waste of school time, energy, and funds. Even if Pigeon (20) Creek did get cleaner, it would never stay that way long enough for salmon to return, according to local **pessimists**. But the students would not give up. They tended a large fish tank in which they hatched and raised young salmon to release into Pigeon Creek. The project lasted the entire school year. (25)

One day, after more than twenty years as a nearly dead stream, Pigeon Creek welcomed back salmon. The first student to **encounter** a returning salmon nearly burst with excitement! News spread fast. The success story appeared on television, in magazines, and in newspapers. You can read about it in the Sierra Club book, *Come Back, Salmon,* by Molly Cone. (30)

---

1. The meaning of **wistful** (line 1) is
a. satisfied   c. angry
b. ashamed   d. sad

2. Prosecute (line 6) most nearly means
a. punish   c. pursue
b. emphasize   d. abandon

3. Wholesome (line 11) is best defined as
a. healthy   c. harmful
b. partial   d. complete

4. The meaning of **data** (line 17) is
a. meetings   c. papers
b. facts   d. lessons

5. Pessimists (line 23) most nearly means
a. believers   c. killjoys
b. dreamers   d. officials

6. Encounter (line 27) is best defined as
a. catch   c. raise
b. come upon   d. describe

Vocabulary for
Comprehension

Read the following passage, in which some of the
words you have studied in Units 13–15 appear in
boldface type. Then answer questions 1–11 on
page 172 on the basis of what is <u>stated</u> or <u>implied</u>
in the passage and in the introductory statement.

*Modern scientists have a theory that explains why
the great Spanish painter Francisco de Goya, the
subject of this passage, was often ill.*

Line)

The masterful Spanish painter
Francisco de Goya (1746–1828)
coped with strange bouts of illness
at various times in his life. Might his
(5) illness have explained the dramatic
changes in his work? His early
paintings were gentle and bright.
His graceful portraits were lovely.
But over time, his work grew dark
(10) and moody. He began to paint
angry scenes in thick, dark colors.
Art historians have long debated
the reasons for this shift in Goya's
style. Could it have been his
(15) health?

Modern science has evidence to
suggest that Goya may have had a
severe case of lead poisoning. High
levels of lead in the bloodstream
(20) can cause muscle and joint pains,
headaches, hearing loss, dizziness,
mental distress, nausea, deranged
conduct, personality changes, and
finally, death. This list **tallies** with
(25) the catalog of symptoms that Goya
suffered.

Goya's **disquieting** symptoms
forced him to take breaks from
painting. When he felt well enough to
(30) return to painting, he would rush
back to his studio. There he would
grind pigments again and paint
enthusiastically to make up for the
lag in his output.

(35) Like most artists of the past, Goya
made his paints himself. Grinding the
pigments put him at risk to inhale
lead dust and to get it in his eyes,
mouth, and ears and on his skin.
(40) Goya was known to use an unusual
amount of a pigment called *lead
white*. It gave his works their
characteristic pearly glow. But it also
made him sick. Although other artists
(45) risked lead poisoning, few used as
much lead white as Goya did.

It no longer seems **far-fetched** to
think that Goya's physical condition
changed his artistic vision. One can
(50) only wonder how modern medical
knowledge might have prevented his
illness and allowed him to express
his later genius.

1. The author's primary purpose is to prove that
   a. Goya was an inferior artist
   b. Goya's later paintings are superior to his early work
   c. Goya's severe lead poisoning caused great changes in his work
   d. Goya is Spain's greatest genius
   e. Goya had a number of physical symptoms

2. The meaning of **coped with** (line 3) is
   a. laughed at
   b. dealt with
   c. suffered from
   d. avoided
   e. discovered

3. The two rhetorical questions in paragraph 1 (lines 4–6 and 13–14) provide the focus for
   a. paragraph 1
   b. paragraph 2
   c. paragraph 3
   d. paragraph 4
   e. the entire passage

4. In paragraph 1 the sentence about art historians (lines 12–14) implies that
   a. art historians are argumentative
   b. not everyone believes there was a definite shift in Goya's style
   c. there are other theories to explain Goya's change in style
   d. the theory stated in this passage is definitely true
   e. the theory stated in this passage is definitely false

5. **Tallies** (line 24) is best defined as
   a. degrades
   b. agrees
   c. merges
   d. totals
   e. conflicts

6. What is the main purpose of paragraph 2?
   a. to describe Goya's various symptoms
   b. to prove that Goya's symptoms are the same as those of severe lead poisoning

   c. to warn readers to watch out for symptoms of lead poisoning
   d. to make readers feel sorry for Goya
   e. to show the conflict between modern science and art historians

7. The meaning of **disquieting** (line 27) is
   a. unusual
   b. painful
   c. hidden
   d. surprising
   e. disturbing

8. **Lag** (line 34) most nearly means
   a. delay
   b. belief
   c. inconsistencies
   d. glut
   e. disappointment

9. **Far-fetched** (line 47) is best defined as
   a. shocking
   b. plausible
   c. sympathetic
   d. improbable
   e. selfish

10. Which of the following best states the author's attitude in this passage?
    a. matter-of-fact
    b. outraged
    c. disbelieving
    d. optimistic
    e. humorous

11. Which of the following best outlines the organization of this passage?
    a. Goya's biography, lead poisoning
    b. Goya's later work, lead poisoning, Goya's symptoms
    c. changes in Goya's work, symptoms, grinding own pigments, lead poisoning
    d. art historians' views, modern science's views
    e. grinding own pigments, lead poisoning

In the sentence "Goya's disquieting symptoms forced him to take breaks from painting" (lines 27–29 on page 171), the author of the passage has taken care to place the **modifier** "disquieting" where it correctly belongs. But if the author had written "Goya's symptoms forced him to take breaks from painting, which were disquieting," it would appear that the artist's breaks from painting, not his symptoms, were disquieting. That is because the modifier is in the wrong place.

A **misplaced modifier** is a word, phrase, or clause that is in the wrong place in a sentence. Because it is incorrectly placed, it does not modify the word for which it is intended; it modifies another instead—sometimes with comical results. To correct a misplaced modifier, move it as close as possible to the word it is meant to modify, or reword the sentence.

On the lines provided, rewrite each of the following sentences in which the modifier is misplaced. Write "correct" if the sentence is correct.

1. I took the paintbrush from my assistant with thin bristles.

_____

_____

2. The sculptor found an early work of hers looking through the collection of works in her basement.

_____

_____

3. She donated that early work to the art museum she found in her basement.

_____

_____

4. The painter gave his old easel to the art school which he no longer used.

_____

_____

5. The artist was known to create paintings for collectors working at the rate of three per week.

_____

_____

6. The art student studied the model sitting on the chair with her pad and charcoal in hand.

_____

_____

7. The young, talented painter bought a studio along with his father.

_____

_____

8. With a welcoming smile, the photographer approached the art dealer.

_____

_____

Two-Word Completions

Circle the pair of words that best complete the meaning of each of the following passages.

1. The _____ who had been lurking very suspiciously around the neighborhood was caught in the act of breaking into our house. The police _____ the set of burglar's tools that he had with him as evidence to back up the charges against him.

a. prowler . . . confiscated
b. optimist . . . underscored
c. sham . . . mangled
d. pessimist . . . enumerated

2. It's difficult to _____ all the reasons I like him because he has so many excellent _____.

a. pantomime . . . epics
b. enumerate . . . traits
c. puncture . . . data
d. amalgamate . . . lags

3. To say our new boss is a _____ is one thing. But you are wrong to say that you believe she is making us work very hard to _____ for past wrongs that were done to her.

a. sham . . . prosecute
b. atrocity . . . mangle
c. pessimist . . . exhort
d. taskmaster . . . retaliate

4. There's a wise old saying that a(n) _____ sees a partially filled glass of water as half full, while a _____ sees the same glass of water as half empty.

a. taskmaster . . . sham
b. optimist . . . pessimist
c. replica . . . tally
d. trait . . . beacon

5. The *Iliad*, Homer's famous _____ poem about the Trojan War, opens with the hero, Achilles, _____ moodily in his tent because he has not been accorded the proper reward for his brave deeds.

a. celestial . . . prowling
b. disquieting . . . shamming
c. epic . . . sulking
d. berserk . . . lagging

6. "The only way we are going to _____ people from driving a car while drunk," the speaker observed, "is to impose stiff penalties on such behavior and _____ offenders to the full extent of the law."

a. empower . . . accommodate
b. detract . . . chasten
c. exalt . . . puncture
d. deter . . . prosecute

Choosing the Right Meaning

Read each sentence carefully. Then circle the item that best completes the statement below the sentence.

Flashing a sham police shield, the brazen intruder waltzed through the security checkpoint. (2)

1. The word **sham** in line 1 is used to mean
  a. genuine   b. plastic   c. fake   d. expired

When civil war broke out in 1861, tens of thousands were responsive to calls for volunteers that issued from Washington and Richmond. (2)

2. The phrase **were responsive to** in line 1 most nearly means
  a. received   b. understood   c. appreciated   d. answered

An encounter in 1959 between Vice President Nixon and Soviet Premier Nikita Khruschev over the merits of the market economy has come to be known as the "kitchen debate." (2)

3. In line 1 the word **encounter** most nearly means
  a. confrontation   b. agreement   c. chance meeting   d. brawl

When men first walked on the moon on July 20, 1969, the newspapers across the country published supplements devoted to the historic event. (2)

4. In line 2 the word **supplements** is best defined as
  a. extra sections   b. photographs   c. editorials   d. articles

Who would have guessed that the discovery of a minor break-in at the Watergate complex would lead to a scandal of such epic proportions? (2)

5. In line 2 the word **epic** is best defined as
  a. poetic   b. vast   c. fantastic   d. tragic

Antonyms

*In each of the following groups, circle the word or expression that is most nearly the **opposite** of the word in **boldface** type.*

1. submissive
a. foreign
b. defiant
c. trustworthy
d. intelligent

2. detract from
a. change
b. enhance
c. study
d. hurt

3. prosecute
a. defend
b. arrest
c. try
d. jail

4. empower
a. authorize
b. forbid
c. strengthen
d. abandon

5. disquieting
a. disturbing
b. unexpected
c. comforting
d. latest

6. far-fetched
a. lame
b. plausible
c. wordy
d. foolish

7. exalted
a. pleasant
b. new
c. lowly
d. high

8. glum
a. cheerful
b. strange
c. sad
d. typical

9. affirm
a. examine
b. describe
c. defend
d. deny

11. uncouth
a. criminal
b. strange
c. silly
d. genteel

13. amalgamate
a. divide
b. merge
c. devour
d. forbid

15. transformed
a. ruined
b. empty
c. preserved
d. improved

10. atrocities
a. crimes
b. supplies
c. fatalities
d. kindnesses

12. deter
a. finance
b. encourage
c. study
d. stop

14. wholesome
a. harmful
b. recent
c. surprising
d. desirable

16. celestial
a. heavenly
b. beautiful
c. infernal
d. invisible

Word Families

A. On the line provided, write the word you have learned in Units 13–15 that is related to each of the following nouns.
EXAMPLE: glumness—**glum**

1. exaltation _____

2. appendage, appendix _____

3. affirmation, affirmative _____

4. deterrent, deterrence _____

5. prowler _____

6. accommodation, accommodator, accommodativeness _____

7. unscrupulousness _____

8. adherent, adherence, adhesive _____

9. fluency _____

10. abstention, abstainer, abstinence _____

11. confiscation _____

12. supplementation _____

13. disquiet _____

14. commemoration _____

15. stupefaction _____

B. On the line provided, write the word you have learned in Units 13–15 that is related to each of the following verbs.
EXAMPLE: audit—**audition**

16. replicate _____

17. respond _____

18. submit _____

19. misapprehend _____

20. sulk _____

In each of the following groups, circle the word that is best defined or suggested by the given phrase.

1. an exact reproduction of an aircraft carrier
   a. replica   b. trait   c. sanctuary   d. epic

2. joined the competing companies to form one huge business organization
   a. amalgamate   b. affirm   c. exalt   d. accommodate

3. a rush of energy
   a. surge   b. audition   c. epic   d. pantomime

4. "Unless you pay me $500, I'm going to make trouble for you."
   a. adhere   b. extort   c. enumerate   d. underscore

5. a measure taken in advance to prevent an accident
   a. precaution   b. allegiance   c. puncture   d. encounter

6. great disorder and dislocation caused by a revolution
   a. sham   b. upheaval   c. sanctuary   d. beacon

7. The knights swore lifelong loyalty to King Richard the Lion-hearted.
   a. beacon   b. allegiance   c. tally   d. trait

8. My poor bicycle is damaged beyond recognition.
   a. deterred   b. mangled   c. punctured   d. pantomimed

9. Before we make a decision, we must have all the facts.
   a. tally   b. data   c. atrocity   d. misapprehension

10. She speaks French like a native.
   a. celestial   b. responsive   c. fluent   d. uncouth

11. walked the streets of the city searching for helpless victims
   a. surge   b. deter   c. prowl   d. retaliate

12. At 2:30, actors will have a chance to try out for different parts.
   a. audition   b. pantomime   c. supplement   d. mangle

13. wishing for a place of refuge from the crazy world
   a. taskmaster   b. replica   c. atrocity   d. sanctuary

14. That man does not seem to have any morals when it comes to business.
   a. submissive   b. glum   c. unscrupulous   d. wistful

15. "That costly failure taught me that I'm not as smart as I thought I was."
   a. chasten   b. accommodate   c. surge   d. mangle

16. He is only interested in people for what he can get out of them.
   a. sulky   b. berserk   c. disquieting   d. self-seeking

17. How she longed to see her childhood home!
   a. responsive   b. submissive   c. wistful   d. sulky

18. "Things are bad, and all the signs are that they're going to get worse."
   a. pessimist   b. taskmaster   c. beacon   d. optimist

19. what a district attorney does with a legal case
   a. commemorate   b. prosecute   c. confiscate   d. enumerate

20. acted out in silence
   a. atrocity   b. encounter   c. pantomime   d. precaution

Building with Classical Roots

pre—before

This prefix appears in **precaution** (page 165). Some other words in which this prefix appears are listed below.

prearrange	**prefer**	**preliminary**	**preoccupy**
precise	**prehistoric**	**premature**	**preside**

From the list of words above, choose the one that corresponds to each of the brief definitions below. Write the word in the blank space in the illustrative sentence below the definition.

1. to absorb one's attention completely or at the expense of other things

She was so _____ with the novel that she forgot to return my phone call.

2. belonging to the period before written history

The museum has a fascinating new exhibit that explains how scientists identify and classify the bones of _____ animals.

3. very definite or clear, exact; very careful; strict

The doctor left _____ instructions on how to clean, dress, and care for the wound in order to avoid infection.

4. coming before the main business or action; introductory; something that comes before the main event, a curtain-raiser

Although the young boxer lost the _____ bout, knowledgeable fans could readily see that he had promise.

5. to arrange ahead of time

One important task of a travel agent is to _____ transportation and accommodations in order that the client can focus on enjoying the trip.

6. to like better, choose over something else; to put forward, press

Although many customers _____ to order healthy appetizers and main courses, restaurant owners report an increased interest in rich desserts.

7. to have authority over, oversee

Tomorrow is the first opportunity our principal will have to _____ at the community school board meeting.

8. unexpectedly early in development; coming too soon

The expectant mother was alerted to the possibility of a _____ birth, so she took extra good care of herself.

From the list of words on page 178, choose the one that best completes each of the following sentences. Write the word in the blank space provided.

1. The police decided to _____ charges against the driver of one of the vehicles involved in the accident on Highway 11.

2. Cave paintings, deserted dwellings, and artifacts found in the Southwest are the only traces that remain of certain _____ Native American cultures.

3. Article I, Section 3, Clause 4 of the United States Constitution calls for the Vice President to _____ over the Senate but not to vote except to break a tie.

4. They claimed that their meeting was accidental and unplanned, but the investigation later confirmed that they had in fact _____ it.

5. Although polls suggested an upset in the making, analysts cautioned that it would be _____ to declare the underdog the winner.

6. The thieves were so _____ with dividing up the loot that they failed to notice that the police had surrounded their hideout.

7. The directions for assembling the bicycle were so _____ that we had no difficulty at all in putting it together.

8. A _____ hearing was held to determine whether there was sufficient evidence to try the accused.

---

*Circle the **boldface** word that more satisfactorily completes each of the following sentences.*

1. The (**premature, precise**) frost that damaged the citrus trees affected hundreds of groves in the region.

2. Most first-time airline passengers (**preoccupy, prefer**) a window seat to enjoy the view, but frequent flyers report that they find aisle seats to be more comfortable and convenient.

3. To honor the couple on their twentieth wedding anniversary, family members chipped in to (**prearrange, preside**) an elegant night on the town for the happy pair.

4. Musicians do not know for sure how (**prehistoric, premature**) music may have sounded, but archaeologists do have an assortment of ancient instruments that can offer clues.

5. The babysitter was totally (**prearranged, preoccupied**) with chatting on the phone, so we never hired him again.

6. It is the duty of the shop steward to (**preside, prefer**) over informal hearings that address issues of concern to his coworkers in the factory.

7. The (**prehistoric, preliminary**) findings suggest that new treatments may hold promise for the future, but doctors advise patients not to get their hopes up too soon.

8. "Smart" weapons are highly technical devices that allow trained users to plan extremely (**precise, preliminary**) strikes against desired targets.

Review Units 13–15 ■ 179

Analogies *In each of the following, circle the item that best completes the comparison.*

1. surge is to **forward** as
a. billow is to back
b. deter is to forward
c. recede is to back
d. constrain is to forward

2. wistful is to **sadness** as
a. glum is to gloom
b. sheepish is to confidence
c. sluggish is to speed
d. frigid is to warmth

3. stupefy is to **dumbfounded** as
a. infuriate is to jubilant
b. motivate is to chastened
c. delude is to resourceful
d. irk is to irritated

4. berserk is to **control** as
a. logical is to clarity
b. numb is to sensation
c. nimble is to skill
d. dogged is to persistence

5. adapter is to **transform** as
a. hammer is to puncture
b. compactor is to compress
c. foil is to conserve
d. manacle is to topple

6. rigorous is to **stamina** as
a. adverse is to sincerity
b. inevitable is to discretion
c. gross is to initiative
d. intensive is to concentration

7. prowl is to **stealthy** as
a. amble is to hasty
b. saunter is to leisurely
c. maneuver is to inept
d. lag is to strident

8. adhere is to **forsake** as
a. amalgamate is to partition
b. avenge is to retaliate
c. prevaricate is to dissect
d. waylay is to liberate

9. allegiance is to **devoted** as
a. support is to disinterested
b. ingenuity is to arid
c. fidelity is to faithful
d. favor is to submissive

10. sulky is to **resentment** as
a. contrite is to remorse
b. responsive is to boredom
c. jovial is to anger
d. boisterous is to contentment

Choosing the Right Meaning *Read each sentence carefully. Then circle the item that best completes the statement below the sentence.*

I didn't realize that the history text I had purchased was a used one until I opened it and found underscores on every other page. (2)

1. In line 2 the word **underscores** is defined as
a. overrulings   b. mistakes   c. notes   d. underlinings

Can you name the artist who prophesied that in the future everyone would experience a dole of fame—15 minutes' worth, to be exact? (2)

2. The word **dole** in line 2 is used to mean
a. small portion   b. handout   c. allowance   d. staggering amount

Scattered over the Gettysburg battlefield are monuments exalting the men—both Southerner and Yankee—who fought and died there. (2)

3. The word **exalting** in line 1 most nearly means
a. elevating   b. honoring   c. uplifting   d. naming

"The breeze with sea commenced to flirt
And ruffles trimmed the water's skirt." (A. E. Glug, "Flotsam and Jetsam")   (2)

4. The best definition for the word **ruffles** in line 2 is

a. driftwood   b. sand castles   c. ripples   d. seaweed

The opening scene of the play is set in a run-down waterfront saloon frequented
by hoodlums and petty thieves.   (2)

5. In line 2, the word **petty** most nearly means

a. narrow-minded   b. piddling   c. big-time   d. small-time

Two-Word Completions   *Circle the pair of words that best complete the meaning of each of the following sentences.*

1. The district attorney decided not to _____ the case when it
became clear that the evidence against the accused was too slight to win anything
but his _____.
a. prosecute . . . acquittal   c. supplement . . . compliance
b. formulate . . . reimbursement   d. implement . . . ingratitude

2. There were so many _____ on both sides during the battle of
Antietam that it was the _____ conflict of the Civil War.
a. enigmas . . . smuggest   c. fatalities . . . goriest
b. setbacks . . . pettiest   d. assailants . . . eeriest

3. Some modern scientists believe that the _____ with which a gigantic
meteor crashed into the Earth millions of years ago set off the chain of events that led to
the _____ of the dinosaurs and the close of the Age of Reptiles.
a. misgivings . . . diversity   c. leeway . . . duration
b. impact . . . extinction   d. precaution . . . affluence

4. In classical times, the great temple of Apollo at Delphi housed the most famous
_____ in all Greece. Deep within the confines of this ancient
_____, a priestess sitting on a golden tripod revealed the will of
the gods to all who sought her assistance.
a. sage . . . queue   c. beacon . . . fossil
b. panorama . . . terrain   d. oracle . . . sanctuary

5. According to Greek myth, Theseus was able to find his way back out of the
Labyrinth, a(n) _____ of passages and galleries built to house a
fearful monster, by following a(n) _____ of wool that he had slowly
unrolled from a large ball as he penetrated deeper and deeper into the bowels of the
confusing building.
a. rendezvous . . . barrage   c. maze . . . strand
b. format . . . earmark   d. agenda . . . facet

Enriching Your Vocabulary

Read the passage below. Then complete the exercise at the bottom of the page.

Myths Become Facts

The religions of ancient Greece and ancient Rome were crowded with gods and goddesses. The stories of these beings and their deeds are called *myths*, which inspired both awe and fear.

We often unknowingly refer to these mythical beings. For example, *Zeus*, the king of the gods in Greek mythology, was renamed *Jupiter*, or *Jove* by the ancient Roman religion. The word *jovial* (Unit 8) originally meant "to be like Jove" and over time has come to mean good-humored.

The ancient Greeks and ancient Romans were careful observers of the stars and planets. Jupiter, like the planets *Mercury, Venus, Mars, Saturn, Neptune*, and *Pluto* are named for Roman gods.

Centuries later, American scientists set out to reach the *titanic* (Unit 12) goal of landing a person on the moon and returning him safely to Earth. Mercury, the Roman god known for his speed, inspired the name of the first manned space project. The series of flights that actually took us to the moon was named after *Apollo*, the Greek god of prophecy, music, and healing. The Apollo missions proved that space exploration is humanly possible, not just the stuff of myths and legends.

From left: Neptune, Uranus, Saturn, and Jupiter

In Column A are 8 more words and names with roots in Greek and Roman mythology. Match each word with its meaning in Column B.

Column A

_____ **1.** January
_____ **2.** June
_____ **3.** Athens
_____ **4.** lunar
_____ **5.** Europe
_____ **6.** herculean
_____ **7.** tantalize
_____ **8.** museum

Column B

a. month named for Juno, the queen of Roman gods

b. to torment; the word comes from the plight of Tantalus, who was condemned to endure constant hunger and thirst

c. having great size, strength, or courage, such as that of the Greek god Hercules

d. city named for Athena, Greek goddess of wisdom

e. continent named for the princess Europa, whom the Greek god Zeus admired and pursued

f. where objects of art or wisdom are displayed, inspired by the Muses, Greek goddesses of art and science

g. month named for Janus, the Roman god of beginnings

h. having to do with the moon, after Luna, the Roman moon goddess

Selecting Word Meanings

*In each of the following groups, circle the word or expression that is **most nearly the same** in meaning as the word in **boldface** type in the given phrase.*

1. a **deluge** of congratulations
a. shortage   b. trickle   c. flood   d. absence

2. provided the necessary **data**
a. information   b. money   c. assistance   d. equipment

3. showed more **grit** than anyone else
a. judgment   b. fear   c. courage   d. restlessness

4. an **instantaneous** decision
a. immediate   b. poor   c. delayed   d. wise

5. a **gory** movie
a. foreign   b. new   c. bloody   d. funny

6. found him **dawdling**
a. loafing   b. working   c. fighting   d. napping

7. **restricted** his activities
a. limited   b. widened   c. guided   d. ended

8. a **serene** mountain lake
a. peaceful   b. polluted   c. cold   d. large

9. a skilled **mimic**
a. athlete   b. politician   c. speaker   d. imitator

10. met with **scant** success
a. much   b. little   c. popular   d. sudden

11. keep as a **memento**
a. reminder   b. safeguard   c. pet   d. ornament

12. pay the **arrears**
a. overdue debts   b. prices   c. fines   d. taxes

13. a **parody** of justice
a. mockery   b. example   c. cause   d. fear

14. corrected the **misapprehension**
a. plan   b. formula   c. examination   d. misunderstanding

15. **scour** the countryside
a. visit   b. search   c. guard   d. invade

16. had many **misgivings**
a. setbacks   b. doubts   c. victories   d. presents

17. **confronted** my accuser
a. avoided   b. attacked   c. faced   d. ignored

18. an **arid** discussion
a. informative   b. barren   c. heated   d. quiet

19. denounce as a traitor

    a. seize   b. betray   c. sentence   d. condemn

20. the **inevitable** result

    a. sudden   b. unavoidable   c. regrettable   d. unexpected

21. appended her signature

    a. forged   b. added   c. erased   d. examined

22. read the **synopsis**

    a. report   b. summary   c. editorial   d. advertisement

23. played a **sluggish** game

    a. new   b. slow   c. winning   d. brilliant

24. the **onset** of the battle

    a. conclusion   b. scene   c. beginning   d. noise

25. managed to **retrieve** the ball

    a. inflate   b. recover   c. lose   d. buy

Antonyms

*In each of the following groups, circle the **two** words that are **most nearly opposite** in meaning.*

26. a. affluence   b. diversity   c. strife   d. poverty

27. a. clarity   b. trait   c. murkiness   d. sham

28. a. empower   b. conserve   c. squander   d. underscore

29. a. abstain   b. confiscate   c. indulge   d. enumerate

30. a. strident   b. responsive   c. incalculable   d. mellow

31. a. rotund   b. compliant   c. boisterous   d. disobedient

32. a. skillful   b. bumbling   c. optional   d. taut

33. a. inhabitant   b. oaf   c. pacifist   d. warmonger

34. a. expend   b. pacify   c. occupy   d. vacate

35. a. verge   b. deter   c. idolize   d. detest

36. a. clever   b. frigid   c. smug   d. hot

37. a. maximum   b. giddy   c. celestial   d. minimum

38. a. partisan   b. petty   c. sinister   d. impartial

39. a. douse   b. relish   c. adhere   d. loathe

40. a. wither   b. acquit   c. thrive   d. amble

Supplying Words in Context

In each of the following sentences, write on the line provided the most appropriate word chosen from the given list.

Group A

refute	immense	prevail	gainful
delude	vow	maze	debut

41. His arguments were so soundly based and so well presented that no one could _____ them.

42. The _____ distances between stars are measured in light-years.

43. Now that the two candidates have finished their long, hard campaigns, it is up to the voters to say which one will _____.

44. Let us _____ to do the very best we can to carry out our duties honestly, efficiently, and humanely.

45. You are just _____ yourself if you think you can do well in school without regular, systematic study.

Group B

keepsake	pantomime	misrepresent	unerring
sabotage	rendezvous	sleuth	eerie

46. My long-awaited _____ with Eileen turned out to be a terrible flop when she got sick and couldn't make it.

47. In the days of silent movies, actors and actresses had to express ideas and emotions by means of _____.

48. We have learned by experience that she is so shrewd that her judgments of people are almost _____.

49. What a(n) _____ feeling it gave us to listen to ghost stories as we sat around the flickering campfire!

50. I cannot believe that these repeated breakdowns of the machinery are no more than "accidents"; I suspect _____!

Group C

fray	epic	tally	subordinate
taskmaster	puncture	compact	allegiance

51. In big-city apartment houses, where space is very valuable, kitchens are likely to be extremely _____.

52. The story of the men who first climbed to the top of Mount Everest is a(n) _____ of human courage and strength.

53. Coach Robinson is a strict _____, who expects instant obedience and 100% effort from all his players.

54. Only a tiny _____ in the skin showed where the doctor had made the injection.

55. I am grateful to my parents, who have always _____ their own interests and desires to the well-being of their children.

Words That Are Unfavorable

*The words listed below are **unfavorable** or **negative**. Select the one that applies most suitably to each of the following short descriptive sentences or paragraphs. Write the word on the line provided.*

crotchety	bungle	self-seeking	cringe
libel	ingratitude	gloat	bigot
prevaricate	vandalism	hypocrite	uncouth

56. He is only interested in other people for what he can get out of them.
_____

57. In that book, the author made a statement which he knew to be untrue and which was intended to ruin a political career.
_____

58. You can't depend on a word he says. He seems to tell lies for the sheer joy of lying.
_____

59. As my grandmother used to say, "Anyone with manners that bad must have been raised in a stable."
_____

60. The mechanic did such a bad job of repairing our car that he actually caused us additional trouble and expense.
_____

61. She sat there with a big smile on her face, obviously enjoying the fact that I was in the most painful situation of my life.
_____

62. For no good reason, someone had tipped over the statue of Washington in the park and had tried to hammer it into pieces.
_____

63. What do you think of people who have strong prejudices against anyone who differs from them in race, religion, or social background?
_____

64. No one can get along with him. You never know what is going to make him fly off the handle. He can get impossibly cranky fifty times a day.

_____

65. Some children are not thankful for all that their parents have done for them and are always demanding more.

_____

Words That Are Favorable

*The words listed below are **favorable** or **positive**. Select the one that applies most suitably to each of the following short descriptive sentences or paragraphs. Write the word on the line provided.*

sage	persevere	optimist	initiative
wholesome	disinterested	amiable	fidelity
discretion	acute	strapping	fluent

66. He is a naturally friendly young man, who can get along pleasantly with almost anyone.

_____

67. We greatly admire the sharpness of her mind. She sees right through to the heart of a problem without being misled by secondary matters.

_____

68. She takes a positive and upbeat attitude toward life. She believes that most problems can be solved and that things usually work out for the best.

_____

69. We admire her because she can get things started on her own, without being supported or guided by other people.

_____

70. He is faithful to his family and friends, true to his religion, and loyal to his community and his country.

_____

71. Once he starts something, he keeps at it with all his energy. He won't let himself get discouraged, even when things go wrong.

_____

72. When the judge hears a case, she has only one concern— to arrive at a just and fair decision.

_____

73. Professor Hahn has had a wide range of experience and has thought deeply about the problems of life. He has much wisdom to give to his students.

_____

74. He is a big, husky fellow, with the strength and the stamina of a professional athlete.

_____

75. The reason she is so attractive is that she gives the impression of radiant health, not only physically but also mentally and morally.

_____

*In each of the following, circle the word or expression that best completes the meaning of the sentence or answers the question, with particular reference to the meaning of the word in **boldface** type.*

76. A habit that is deeply **ingrained** is
    a. a bad one
    b. hard to change
    c. easy to get rid of
    d. of no great importance

77. Which of the following would be a **chastening** experience?
    a. winning a scholarship
    b. going to a party
    c. spending the day at the beach
    d. doing poorly on this exam

78. a school course dealing with **vocations** will help you
    a. plan for a career
    b. become a good dancer
    c. become a "math shark"
    d. develop your speaking ability

79. For what purpose might you join a **queue**?
    a. to make new friends
    b. to see a hit movie
    c. to speak at a school assembly
    d. to enjoy a beautiful day

80. A person who **reminisces** a great deal might be criticized for
    a. living in the past
    b. insulting other people
    c. using foul language
    d. borrowing money

81. A crisis is said to be **global** if it applies to
    a. only one nation
    b. almost all the nations of the world
    c. big business
    d. transportation

82. A basketball player who lacks **stamina** would be likely to
    a. miss foul shots
    b. tire quickly
    c. argue with the referee
    d. show a lack of team spirit

83. You would seek **sanctuary** if you were
    a. hungry
    b. being pursued
    c. in the dark
    d. rich

84. The word **martial** comes from the name of the Roman god Mars. We can guess from this that Mars was the god of
    a. love
    b. war
    c. good health
    d. farming

85. If you were **ravenous**, you might head for a
    a. hospital
    b. restaurant
    c. library
    d. skating rink

86. A person who has carried out an **abduction** will probably
    a. receive a prize
    b. be arrested for kidnapping
    c. get a ticket for illegal parking
    d. go to the hospital

87. For performing a **valiant** deed, a soldier would probably be
    a. transferred
    b. given a medal
    c. called a coward
    d. given a new uniform

88. A person who is generally considered to be an **oracle** should be
    a. kept in a closed room
    b. put on a diet
    c. listened to carefully
    d. turned over to the police

89. Which of the following would have **facets**?
a. a planet
b. an umbrella
c. a diamond
d. a chair

90. If you are in a debating contest and you want to be **logical**, you should
a. smile a great deal
b. speak in a loud voice
c. make fun of your opponents
d. try to reason accurately

91. Which of the following might be a suitable nickname for a person who is **glum** most of the time?
a. "Deadeye Dick"
b. "Waltzing Matilda"
c. "Dapper Dan"
d. "Weeping Willie"

92. A **pessimist** is a person who
a. is sure everything will turn out for the worst
b. expects the best but is prepared for bad luck
c. refuses to worry about what the future may bring
d. depends on fortune-tellers for guidance

93. a student who is lost in a **reverie**
a. has taken a wrong turn
b. has a toothache
c. is daydreaming
d. is well prepared for final exams

94. If you receive news that is **disquieting** you will probably be
a. delighted
b. serene
c. pleasantly surprised
d. upset

95. Which of the following are typical of **contemporary** life?
a. hoopskirts and sun bonnets
b. TV and computers
c. colonies in outer space
d. log cabins

96. A ballplayer would be most likely to receive an **ovation** for
a. winning a game with a home run
b. losing a game by striking out
c. arguing with the umpire
d. not playing because of an injury

97. Which of the following might best be described by **saunter**?
a. a 50-yard run for a touchdown
b. a stroll in the park
c. a mad dash to catch a bus
d. a forced march

98. A person who is wearing **manacles** is probably a
a. prisoner
b. model
c. judge
d. teacher

99. A study program might properly be called **intensive** if it
a. is a lot of fun
b. is open to everyone
c. calls for hours of hard work
d. will help you get a summer job

100. You will **affirm** your mastery of the words taught in this book if you
a. spell them incorrectly
b. forget what they mean
c. never use them in class
d. score 100% on this Final Test

INDEX

The following tabulation lists all the basic words taught in the various units of this workbook, as well as those introduced in the *Vocabulary of Vocabulary, Working with Analogies, Building with Classical Roots,* and *Enriching Your Vocabulary* sections. Words taught in the units are printed in **boldface** type. The number following each entry indicates the page on which the word is first introduced. Exercises and review materials in which the word also appears are not cited.